Enterprise Information Management

Enterprise Information Management

Edited by **Brian Jackson**

WILLFORD PRESS

New York

Published by Willford Press,
118-35 Queens Blvd., Suite 400,
Forest Hills, NY 11375, USA
www.willfordpress.com

Enterprise Information Management
Edited by Brian Jackson

International Standard Book Number: 978-1-68285-250-7 (Hardback)

Printed in the United States of America.

Contents

Permissions

List of Contributors

Preface

EIM is a specialised branch within the vast discipline of information technology. The main objective of enterprise information management is to use organisation's information and databases effectively, primarily to support various decision making processes and managing different business operations efficiently. This book aims to provide a broad overview of significant topics like implementation of information technology in emerging sectors, evaluation of different techniques and processes currently used in information technology management and knowledge management, etc. It will prove to be a valuable source of reference for all the students and academicians engaged in this field.

Various studies have approached the subject by analyzing it with a single perspective, but the present book provides diverse methodologies and techniques to address this field. This book contains theories and applications needed for understanding the subject from different perspectives. The aim is to keep the readers informed about the progress in the field; therefore, the contributions were carefully examined to compile novel researches by specialists from across the globe.

Indeed, the job of the editor is the most crucial and challenging in compiling all chapters into a single book. In the end, I would extend my sincere thanks to the chapter authors for their profound work. I am also thankful for the support provided by my family and colleagues during the compilation of this book.

Editor

CRITICAL FACTORS IN THE IMPLEMENTATION PROCESS OF INTEGRATED MANAGEMENT SYSTEMS

Ademir Antonio Ferreira
University of São Paulo, São Paulo, SP, Brazil

Márcio Shoiti Kuniyoshi
University of São Paulo, São Paulo, SP, Brazil

ABSTRACT

This study is the result of research whose purpose was to study the implementation process of integrated management systems, called ERP Enterprise Resource Planning in the business environment. This study, more specifically, tried to identify the variables in this process and that, somehow, made it easy or caused some type of difficulty implementing the system. Based on the mixed method approach (Creswell, 2003), the study was performed by means of the content analysis of technical and scientific publications about this theme and by means of a field research for data collection from primary sources. The content analysis was based on the per mile procedure by Bardin (1977), making it possible to identify critical factors that may be found in the implementation of ERP system projects. Primary data was collected from structured interviews with the managers in charge of the implementation of the system, in each of the 12 companies in different sectors of the economy and based in Brazil. Based on this information, it was possible to test the factors extracted from the content analysis and then develop a list of factors that may effectively influence the implementation process of the system. In order to recognize the possible relations between the selected factors, the Spearman (r_{sp}) correlation coefficient was applied and the multiple regression analysis was performed by means of the stepwise procedure. The purpose of the regression analysis was to determine the relation of the "Assessment of the Implementation" dependent variable with other dependent variables in the selected categories. The results of these analyses showed that the support of the top management, the communication process for the clear evidence of this support, the technical support of the ERP program provider together with the project team expertise, training and qualification processes of the team in the system operation are significantly correlated and relevant factors for a successful implementation of the project.

Keywords: integrated management systems; ERP; Implementation; projects.

Address for correspondence / Endereço para correspondência

Ademir Antonio Ferreira, Professor at the Administration Master´s Degree Program of the Vice Dean´s Office of Research and Extension Courses of the University of São Paulo, Senior Professor in the FEA/USP Administration Department, Av. Prof Luciano Gualberto, 908 - Cidade Universitária – 05508-900, São Paulo, SP, Brasil

Márcio Shoiti Kuniyoshi, Professor at the Administration Post-Graduation Program University of São Paulo, Rua Alfeu Tavares, 149 - Campus Rudge Ramos, CEP: 09641-000 Rudge Ramos - São Bernardo do Campo, São Paulo – SP, Brasil

1.   INTRODUCTION

The implementation of the integrated management systems from different origins and based on the ERP (Enterprise Resource Planning) technology have become a reality, increasingly present in the business environment. In addition to the increased competitiveness and recognition of the strategic value of information, many other reasons justify the growth of purchases and implementation of these integrated systems in companies at the end of the last century.   . Some of them mentioned their executives´ fear and the related caution about problems that could have happened to the existing systems upon the arrival of the year 2000 , a phenomenon commonly known as the Y2K bug, incurring costs to redefine or adjust information systems already in use by companies.

In addition to these reasons for the growth of integrated management systems, there are others such as the benefits that a system of this large size may offer regarding the information systems existing at that time, that is, the companies' executives were likely to work with information from integrated management processes and operations, instead of information reports from the various nonintegrated systems existing within the companies. Besides these aspects, the emergence of many providers of integrated management systems based on ERP technology and the consequent promotion and offer of a product that aimed to meet the possible needs of directors, executives and managers of major companies gave rise to a large and potential market and greatly boosted their purchase and implementation within companies.

Finally, it must be highlighted the fact that many subsidiaries of foreign companies operating in Brazil were encouraged by their head offices abroad, which had already implemented this type of system, to purchase and implement an ERP-technology based system, with the purpose of integrating their international operations.

Recent research on the ERP system has aimed to evaluate the influence of the ERP system on organizational strategic activities (Ferreira et al, 2012 and Martins et al, 2013); to identify the contribution from Enterprise Resource Planning systems for the management of information and knowledge (Souza et al, 2013); to identify success factors in the use of ERP systems for the competitiveness of the hotel industry (Azevedo et al, 2014); to evaluate ERP-system user satisfaction at medium-sized clothes manufacturers in the State of Fortaleza (Teles & Silva, 2014); and to understand the implementation and updating of the ERP system through comparison analysis, taking success critical factors described in the pertinent literature into consideration (Valentim et al, 2014), among other studies.

The decision to purchase and implement an integrated management system, based on ERP technology, requires that the executives in charge of this decision making consider a series of variables related to the internal and external environment of the company, where the system will be implemented. It is a fact that the purchased integrated system was, originally, developed from a set of business management processes and operations which are set and incorporated within themselves. Every provider who offers products to the market comes from different business environments.

Therefore, being familiar with the environments of the industries that have given rise to these systems may be of great interest to the system-purchase decision makers. Belloquim (1998, p.39) states that "one of the major problems of the integrated management packages, a general name with which integrated management systems that use the ERP technology are referred to, has always been that fact that the company needs to adapt to the packages and not the packages adapt to the company."

Although the systems enable some adaptations (parameterizations) to be made in order to accommodate business processes which are actually put in practice in the company, such adaptations and adjustments are subject to limitations. The good practice for implementation suggests that the processes in practice in the company be redesigned by means of process engineering so that they fit the format of the ones already incorporated in the acquired system. In this regard, the concept that ERP systems are commercial packages developed from standard models of business processes are highlighted by other authors such as Souza & Zwicker, (1999, p. 3), who state the following:

"...like all other commercial packages, integrated systems based on ERP technology are not developed for a specific client and they aim to meet general requirements of the highest number of companies possible, precisely to explore gain of scale in its development. In order to be developed, it is necessary, however, to use business process models. These business models are sourced from the experience gained by the companies that provide them, in repeated implementation processes in companies, or they are developed by consultancies and by research on best practices regarding the execution of business processes."

Therefore, one of the crucial variables to be considered in the decision to purchase or implementation of an integrated system is the analysis of the adherence of the features of the integrated systems available on the market with business processes. Also, according to Souza & Zwicker, (1999 p. 4), there would be the need of a parameterization process, which consists in the adaptation of the features of the many ERP system modules through the definition of the parameter values already available on the system itself.

The implementation of the integrated management systems implies, necessarily, the allocation of the company´s team of technicians and managers, authorized and licensed by the systems´ provider, who will monitor the whole implementation process.

Significant investments are also involved in relation to resources and hours worked by the team of technicians and managers in the process, parameterizations (or formatting processes) of the program, team training, and purchase of the required equipment, among others, causing significant changes in the management and operations of the companies that adopted the systems. As a matter of fact, the expected final result is an implemented integrated management system operating at full capacity in all its existing modules. This means that the integrated management system must be capable to provide reliable information, available whenever and wherever the company´s managers need it to support their decision-making processes.

Certainly, this is an organizational change program and, therefore, the factors that may be disruptive or resist to this change need to be recognized by the agents of change, and minimized in the negative influence they may result in the process. Every organization may be understood and analyzed from three aspects: structure, technology and behavior.

The structure involves the management hierarchy, internal work systems and processes, communication flows and the establishment of mission, objectives and organizational policies. The technology refers to the operational systems adopted, equipment, process and product engineering, R&D, and work methods, among others. Behavior is related to human resources policies, to knowledge, skills and attitudes of the people who participate in it, to interpersonal relationships and values, individual and collective principles fostered by the organizational culture. These three elements are highly interdependent and in constant interaction under the influence of common forces, thus, any change in any of them may affect the other elements. (Ferreira et al.,1997, p.69)

Therefore, the behavioral change process is at the same level of importance and magnitude as the technological change being implemented and, in order to be effective, it needs to recognize how these three elements relate to one another and try to change the three of them as far as possible (Stoner, 1988, p. 263).

The search to identify these factors, the interrelation or interdependence between them, as well as the attempt to evaluate the level influence and contribution to the implementation process, to be successful, compose the specific problem of this research and the purpose of this study. In order for the readers to follow the steps of the research, this paper describes below a brief introduction to the field of information systems and, in particular, to the origins and purposes of an ERP system.

In chapter 3 conceptual assumptions of the research are presented and chapter 4 shows the methodology used and a chart of the methodological steps, with details about the activities performed by each of them. Chapter 5 describes the analysis techniques used in the research: the content analysis by Bardin (1977) for the identification of critical factors, the Spearman correlation coefficient and the multiple regression analysis performed by means of the stepwise procedure. Chapter 6 contains the results achieved, analysis and interpretation of the indexes calculated by applied technical statistics and a summary of the behavior of the factors identified for each of the 8 selected categories. Chapter 7 shows the authors´ conclusions and recommendations for further studies.

2.   INFORMATION SYSTEMS

Many authors regard trustworthy information owned by companies as a competitive edge between them. Aware of the value of information, companies have long had information systems. Laudon & Laudon (1997, p. 06) regard information systems as:

"a *set of interrelated components working together to collect, retrieve, process, store, and disseminate information for the purpose of facilitating planning, control, coordination, and decision making in businesses and other organizations".*

Based on this initial concept, management information systems have been upgraded and highly improved as information technologies have been developed with the advent of faster computers, more complex programs and languages, faster networks and more suitable databases accessed by multiple users.

The evolution of information systems happened, and has happened, mainly due to the need of companies´ managers who constantly require information that may be accessed in real time from different places whether internal and external to the environment of the companies.   Depending on the nature of the information required by the top and middle management levels of the companies, the IT team in charge of the development of systems has created many types of management information systems with a focus on specific functional areas such: marketing, human resources management, production management, finance and controlling, and costs, among others.   Knowledge development in IT has made it possible for more comprehensive information systems to be expanded to the organizations' strategic level.

According to Bancroft, Seip and Sprengel (1998) apud Valentim et al (2014, p.112), management system program codes used to be developed internally by the IT team and modified depending on the company's needs and, often times, developed upon request from a department. Lack of planning and, in some cases, of technical competences of the team members created systems dedicated to each department and in an isolated manner, which hindered the effective integrated business control.

As a result of this development of system concepts and of the information technology itself, companies started to use, as of the early 90s, the EIS – Executive Information Systems. These systems provided information to the managers, directors and presidents involved in the strategic decision-making process of a company, Information was given by means of texts, charts, tables, and flowcharts, making it possible to evaluate the respective types of performance: operational, economic and financial of the company while competing with their competitors in the marketplace.

A retrospective view of the evolution of these computer systems developed between 1960 and 1990, and still used by many companies, under a critical perspective, was offered by Souza & Zwicker (1999, p.2), stating that:

Many of the computer systems developed in the 70s, 80s and early 90s were built based on rather inflexible technologies and to meet the needs of the different departments in an isolated manner. As a result, it is the impossibility of using them for an integrated and effective business control. Although the idea of integrated information systems had existed since the early 80's, with the emergence of structured analysis and software engineering, the presence of a series of unaddressed operational and technological difficulties did not allow this view to be implemented in most companies."

In the mid 90s, a new concept of integrated management systems emerged in the business environment, based on ERP technology. As they are systems integrated with all the departments of an organization, enabling managers to access consolidated information about the results achieved and about the operational and financial performance of their decision; they were then known as integrated management systems.

According to Stamford (2008) apud Valentim et al (2014), ERP provides a single information flow, which is continuous and consistent across the company under a single database. It is a tool for the improvement of business processes, guided by these processes, with online and real time information and not by the functions and departments of a company. ERP allows all transactions made by the company to be viewed, drawing a big picture of business processes."

2.1.   Emergence and expansion of the integrated systems

Regarding the origin of ERP technology, there is a consensus among integrated management systems scholars, who regard it as a natural evolution of the planning and control systems of production resources and materials: systems known as MRPs and adopted by companies in all regions of the industrialized world over the last decades of the last century. Authors such as Kalakota & Robinson (2002, p. 231) agree that the ERPs represent a natural evolution of the planning and control systems of materials, stating that:

"the historical origin of ERP is in inventory management and control software packages that dictated system design during the 1960s. The 1970s saw the emergence of Material Requirements Planning (MRP)..... During the 1980s, the misnamed MRPII systems emerged to extend MRP's traditional focus on production processes to other business functions, including order processing, manufacturing, and distribution. As the MRPII contributions became visible, executives aimed at similar benefits through the integration of the processes of other functions to cover areas of Finance, Human Resources, and Project Management. MRPII is a misnomer, as it provided automated solutions to a wide range of business processes, not just those found within a company's manufacturing and distribution functions. As a result, MRP II was renamed as ERP."

Integrated management systems must be understood from the concept of systems and ERP - Enterprise Resource Planning- technology, that is, a Company's Resource Planning. By taking the development of computer systems as a basis, authors such as Souza & Zwicker (1999 pp. 2 and 3) explain the function of integrated systems:

"..."ready-to-use" integrated computer systems, developed by specialized companies, are capable of generating information from performed operations through most of or the entirety of business processes. They were initially known as integrated management systems, or simply "integrated packages". They are composed of various modules, they communicate and update the same base or central database. Information input by a module is instantly provided to the other modules on which it depends. Integrated systems based on ERP also enable the use of planning tools that may analyze the impact of decision making in manufacturing, supplies, finance, or human resources, across the company.

There is also the consensus that integrated management systems emerged when companies coexisted in a global business context, where they expanded their activities to many countries and they needed to coordinate their subsidiaries' operations all over the world. Therefore, they needed information that would help them integrate the distinctive contributions of each branch within the scope of their global business strategy.

Many companies became aware of the fact that for them to expand their business to a global level, they needed to implement a system capable to collect, process, generate, store, and disseminate integrated information from the various transactions and multiple business processes which are developed continuously, simultaneously and in parallel in all units of the company, with business units in various states in the same country or, as it is common in transnational companies, in different countries. The system integration by the different ERP modules helps managers understand what is happening in the most remote areas where business is conducted by the head office and by its subsidiaries across the country or across the world.

With access or availability of more qualified information, business managers can define more appropriate corporate strategies in order to compete in the global business environment, a common characteristic since the beginning of the third millennium,

3. CONCEPTUAL ASSUMPTIONS

In theoretical and operation terms, the main relevant aspects and indexed to the study are conceptualized as follows:

• **Implementation of Integrated Management Systems:** it is an act of change that implies the introduction of a new information technology to the business environment, as an integrated management system capable to provide integrated information that serves as a support to managers in management and operational decision-making processes of the company.

• **Critical Factors in the implementation process:** a set of variables clustered in categories that explain motions, forces, actors and existing and active acts in the internal or external environment of the company in which the implementation process of integrated management systems is executed, capable to facilitate, promote, speed up or leverage the process or, on the other hand, hider and make the successful execution of the process impossible.

• **Successful Implementation Process of Integrated Management Systems:** in technical terms, as a successful implementation process is defined as the one in which the integrated management system introduced to the company is capable of operating all its modules, generating and providing reliable and updated information to the company´s managers, also easy to be accessed by the company´s authorized users at management and operational levels.

• **Intensity of individual contribution of each factor in the implementation process:** in technical terms, intensity of individual contribution of each factor (that is, the set of variables clustered in categories) is defined as the force and power that it has to influence (or contribute) so that an ERP project implementation is successful.

At the operational level, critical factors are all the categories of variables that were recognized and selected by means of the results from the application of the content analysis research method. Through face-to-face interviews, the managers in charge of the implementation of the integrated management systems in the researched companies classified the intensity of the contribution of each factor as a facilitator or a hindrance in a successful ERP project implementation.

It is assumed that it is possible to identify factors (that is, the set of variables clustered in categories) that influence the implementation process of integrated management systems in companies, based on the ERP technology, regarded as successful or unsuccessful in the end. It is accepted that the managers in charge of the implementation of the integrated management systems in their companies are the most qualified people to provide an assessment of the process, whether it was successful or not in the end. This assumption is based on the fact that these managers have fully had the experience of conducting the process and are capable to assess whether it was successful or not in the end.

4. METHODOLOGY USED IN THE RESEARCH

The research methodology was based on the mixed method approach: qualitative and quantitative. According to Creswell (2003), the mixed method approach is applicable in order to take advantage of both approaches, qualitative and quantitative.

The research methodology was based on two different methods that combine aspects of exploratory qualitative and qualitative approaches. It was conducted based on primary and secondary data from companies operating in Brazil, which experienced the implementation process of integrated management systems, based on ERP technology. The two research approaches refer to the content analysis of publications about this theme and to the traditional field research based on data collection from primary sources.

- **Content Analysis:** an investigation was performed, based on the publication of scientific papers, dissertations and theses about the implementation of the integrated management system over the last 5 years. The objective of this research method consists of identifying and analyzing the content in scientific publications in order to identify indicators that help to see a reality that is not always clear in the texts (Bardin, 1977). With the use of this content analysis method, it was possible to identify factors (that is, a set of variables clustered in categories) that are capable of facilitating or hindering a successful implementation process of integrated management systems projects.

- **Primary data collection** by means of a structured interview with open and closed questions, in 12 companies willing to be interviewed face-to-face, out of a group of 36 previously contacted companies. The interviews in these companies were conducted with the managers in charge of the system implementation. The purpose of the interviews was to consider the validity of a list of identified factors, as an introductory process, by the content analysis, group them in organizational variables and evaluate, from the interviewees' perceptions, the influence of these factors in the ERP implementation process. With these interviews, it was possible to test factors extracted from publications and make a definitive list of factors that effectively prove to be strong enough to facilitate or hinder the successful implementation process according to the scope of the company. Chart 1 summarizes the tree steps of the methodological development of the research.

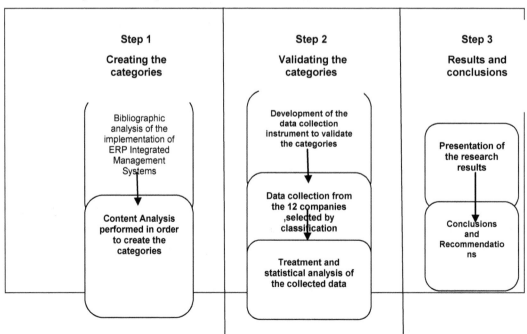

Chart 1 – Diagram of the methodological steps of how the research is conducted

Source: developed by the authors

5. PRESENTATIONS, ANALYSIS AND INTERPRETATION OF RESULTS

The content analysis process is composed of the following steps: pre-analysis, in-depth analysis of the material, treatment and interpretation of the results presented. The pre-analysis organizes the initial ideas in order to conduct the research through an accurate conceptual framework, which makes it possible to explore by means of the content analysis of the available information, relevant factors that will be subject to the validity of research with the companies that have had similar experiences. The analysis units were composed based on real cases from scientific papers, dissertations and theses that addressed the theme related to the implementation of ERP-technology based integrated management systems, published over the last 10 years.

From this material, it was possible to identify external and internal factors to the implementation process that facilitated or hindered the implementation process. These factors were grouped in accordance with their similarity and the categorization used for this purpose was based on the per mile procedure by Bardin (1977, p. 119). The per mile procedure is recommended by experts when the categories are defined afterwards, that is, the categories are not previously established, providing more diversified and abundant themes. The word "mile" means the repetitions of occurrences of a given phenomenon described in the content of a scientific text or a speech. In other words, it means that the phenomenon was very frequently found in a text, resulting in a relevant increased score. From this score, the name of the category is previously defined, which groups a set of variables which describe it.

In the first stage of the categorization, variables related to the implementation process of integrated management systems, based on ERP technology, were grouped by similarity, that is, they were grouped according to their purpose and their relation with internal and external factors. From there, it was possible to identify the main categories that describe the central points addressed by this research. Chart 2 shows the 26 variables identified and the 8 categories that were grouped and that comprised the critical factors, the purpose of this study.

5.1. Statistical Analysis

In addition to the use of descriptive statistics to perform the different analyses, and with the purpose of recognizing possible relations between the selected factors, the non-parametric statistics technique was applied, also known as the Spearman (r_{sp}) correlation coefficient and the multiple regression analysis by means of the stepwise procedure.

VARIABLES IDENTIFIED	CATEGORIES
1. Stated IT Strategy 2. Location and how to implement 3. Clear objectives, focus and scope 4. Implementation Model of the ERP system 5. Understanding of the organization's culture 6. Budget invested in the ERP System	**1) Organizational strategy and culture**
7. Support of the top management 8. Decision-making process structure	**2) Support of the top management**
9. Training and education (internal team and end users) 10. Interdepartmental relations	**3) Qualified users and team involved in the implementation**
11. Hardware infrastructure 12. Software infrastructure	**4)Hardware and software infrastructure**
13. Customer/ Software Provider Relationship 14. Technical support of the provider	**5) Customer – Provider Relationship**
15. Project Management 16. Project Team 17. Performance assesment and monitoring 18. Presence of the "Champion" 19. Project Manager with a suitable profile to the implementation	**6) Management of the project implementation**
20. Experience of external consultants in the implementation process 21. Test and solution of ERP software problems	**7) Presence of the external consultants**
22. Change Management 23. Communication Management 24. Expectations Management 25. Minimum Customization and High Standardization 26. BPR (Business Process Reengineering)	**8) Change Management in the business process**

Chart 2. **Categories identified in the literature about the implementation of ERP**

Source: **developed by the authors**

According to Stevenson (1981, p.382),

"Spearman´ rank correlation coefficient is a non-parametric measure to evaluate the relationship of two monotonically related variables, when data are arranged in ranks. [...] The purpose of the calculation of the correlation coefficient in these cases is to determine up to what extent the two sets of ranks agree or disagree. This technique can also be extended to other types of measurement, as long as they can be converted into ranks."

Spearman´ rank correlation coefficient (r_{sp}) may range from -1.00 to +1.00, such as Pearson´s **r.** When r_{sp} is close to 1.00, this means that two sets of ranks are very similar, and if r_{sp} is close to -1.00, the sets of ranks are very different. If there is agreement in some items and disagreement in others, r_{sp} gets close to 0 (zero), which suggests the absence of a relationship between the two sets.

On the other hand, the multiple regression analysis is a statistical technique that makes it possible to evaluate the functional relationship between two or more variables and to make projections. According to Hair (2005, p.137),

" the goal of regression analysis is to predict a single dependent variable from the knowledge of one or more independent variables."

In this case, the dependent variable corresponds to the final assessment of the implementation process and the independent variables correspond to the categories of selected factors. In order to perform calculations and application of the selected statistical techniques correlation and regression, the Statistical Package for the Social Sciences (SPSS version13) was used.

6. RESEACH RESULTS

The companies that formally conducted the evaluation process showed the following percentage, related to the interviewees´ perception of the level of success of the system implementation:

- 18.02% considered that, after experiencing the whole implementation process of the integrated management system, the evaluation of the results achieved shows that the implementation of the new systems is entirely successful.

- 72.72% considered that, after experiencing the whole implementation process of the integrated management system, the process was very successful due to the results achieved and the manner it was executed.

- 9.1% considered that, after experiencing the whole implementation process of the integrated management system, the change made did not meet expectations and, although they did not take the failure of such a change into consideration, they admitted that the new system did not show any satisfactory results.

6.1. Summary of conclusions of the category analysis

After being classified by the content analysis, the factors listed in chart 2 were submitted to the interviewees' analysis, who should rate them on a scale of 7 levels of agreement, from "very facilitative" to "very hindering" and point 4 on the scale meaning "Indifferent", that is, it did not influence the process.

Through the interviews, it was possible to see that no respondent regarded any of the researched factors as hindering in the implementation process of the system. This means that the assumptions previously presented in the content analysis were confirmed by the interviewees and the positive variables for the execution of the process were present in the researched organizations.

CATEGORIES	SUMMARY OF THE ANALYSES
1) Organizational strategy and culture	-54.5% of the researched companies agreed that the previous analysis to assess them facilitates the implementation process. - 58.4% made a plan to monitor the implementation process. - 54.55% agreed that the allocated budget is a very important factor - 72.8% agreed the decision-making process must be established from the beginning, being a very important factor for the implementation of the project.
2) Support of the top management	- For 88,3% of them, it is an essential factor for the implementation of the ERP project.
3) Qualified users and team involved in the implementation	- 55.55% fully agreed that it is important to engage all the employees in the decision of acquiring the integrated management system. - 66.7% agreed that there is the need to provide training to the employees: project team members and employees.
4) Hardware and software infrastructure	-81.81% of the researched companies agreed that hardware and software structure is important for the implementation of the system.
5) Customer/ Software Provider Relationship	-72.73% of the companies had support of providers and agreed that this is an essential service for a successful implementation of the system.
6) Management of the project implementation	- 66.67% of the executives fully agreed that having an IT team, future users and external consultants leads to the successful implementation of the project -.83.4% believe that an integrated and engaged project team facilitates the implementation process of the system. A cooperative relationship, strong communication and participation of the many departments of the company and, more specifically, the project team serve to complement in the integration of the business processes of the organization. - 41.67% of the respondents that agreed that the internal team´s knowledge (mastery) of ERP features is a factor that facilitates the implementation process. - 66.7% of the executives interviewed fully agreed or strongly agree that a competent project team is a factor that facilitates the successful implementation of the system.

7) Presence of the external consultants	-83.34% of the executives interviewed said that the existence and use of external consultants is very important or highly important in order to ensure the successful implementation of the integrated management system.
8) Change Management in the business process	-70% of the respondents fully and strongly agreed that change management is a factor that facilitates the successful implementation of the ERP system. -72.4% of the executives interviewed fully or strongly agreed that an open and transparent communication policy is a factor that facilitates the successful implementation of the ERP system. - 72.72% of them answered that, after experiencing the implementation process of the system, the respondents regarded the process as successful.

Chart 3 - **Summary of conclusions of the category analysis**

Source: developed by the authors

What is possible to infer from this situation is that the lack of recognition of the importance and influence of any of these factors in a change project of this size may effectively hinder the development of the implementation of the process and curb expectations related to the performance of the system and expected benefits.

The figures presented and commented on so far, based on the statistical tables of frequency distribution of the collected data and generated by the SPSS software, compose the first identification focus and analysis of the influential factors in the implementation process of an integrated management system, according to the interviewees' perception. With the purpose of indentifying which of all the categories of the indentified and analyzed factors are the ones that contribute the most to the successful implementation of an integrated management system, a statistical treatment of the data by means of the application of two more statistical techniques was performed: the Spearman correlation coefficient and the multiple regression analysis.

6.2. Application of a non-parametric statistical treatment technique of the Spearman correlation coefficient

With the purpose of finding possible relations between the factors, that is a set of variables clustered in categories, previously analyzed, the Spearman correlation coefficient was adopted in order to verify how the factors influence and are influenced during the implementation process.

The results from the application of the Spearman correlation coefficient.(where the Spearman correlation coefficient is significant to the $p > 0.01$ level) proved to be highly meaningful and that there is a strong relation between the following factors:

- "Support of the top management" and "communication management in the process of the implementation" are strongly correlated (0.738), that is, they are highly dependent on one another.

- ▪   "Support of the provider" and "knowledge of the program and its features by the project implementation team" showed a correlation level of 0.857.

- ▪   "External consultants" and "support of providers" are correlated at a coefficient of 0.820.

- ▪   "Assessment of the implementation of the ERP project" and "training of users" showed a correlation of 0.885.

These indicators of strong correlations between factors enable the following researcher´s interpretations:

➢   the support of the top management is a critical factor for a successful implementation of the ERP project and the communication process is essential to clearly show this support and also to show the necessary transparency in the decisions made by top managers about the conditions offered and the situations faced in the implementation of the system, as well as to ensure the engagement of all in the development of the change process.

➢   Technical support of the ERP program provider and the expertise of the project team are critical factors to enable the execution of the implementation phases and, as a consequence, as the elements that ensure the higher likelihood of the success in this endeavor. In order to achieve an optimal level, it is essential that the relationship between the implementation team and the software provider be continued, productive and cooperative. This type of relationship is essential for the exchange of knowledge and experiences that will certainly contribute to the successful implementation in a decisive manner.

➢   Training and qualification processes of the team in the system and their features are relevant factors for a successful implementation. Thus, the correlation between the training of the end user and the assessment of the result of the implementation help to interpret the fact that a positive assessment of the implementation process of the system is strongly related to the proper preparation of the people who will participate in their operation or who will use it. The knowledge of the purposes, characteristics and technology being adopted must be shared with all the people who will be integrated into the new system.

As for the planning factor, regarded as highly relevant by the literature for being a facilitator in the implementation processes of ERP projects, the Spearman correlation coefficient test in the field research did not show a high correlation with the other categories, making it possible to consider that, for the interviewees, planning was not made as it should have been made or it may not be fully followed during the execution phase, due to the significant changes in the original plan.

Another possible explanation for the conclusion process may be found in the fact that in complex change projects, typical of the implementation of an ERP integrated management system, it is very difficult to plan in advance all the incidents that may change the course, resources and deadlines previously specified. Therefore, planning, though necessary, is hardly ever executed as planned, due to the countless contingencies and unpredicted situations faced on the daily basis in the course of the project,

On the other hand, through the field research it was clear that no interviewee regarded the presence of any of the selected factors as a hindrance in the development of the implementation process of the system. This means that all the previous assumptions found by the available literature about this theme were taken into consideration by the interviewees and the active variables were present in the researched organizations. It is important to highlight the fact that when analyzing the Spearman correlation coefficient for a small sample (n=12), it seems to be safe to use level 0.001 to accept H_0.

6. 3. Regression Analysis

In this process of analysis of the research results, the purpose of the use of the multiple regression statistical technique was to measure the relationship between a dependent variable – *Assessment of the Implementation* – with the other independent variables (categories and selected factors).

Considering the fact that the number of cases in this quantitative research does fulfill the minimum requirements related to the size of the sample, at least five cases/observations for each variable, in order to apply regression analysis, it is important to highlight that there is no intention to justify or infer the cause and effect relationship in this analysis, but, rather, there is an attempt to understand which variables better explain the dependent variable, according to the interviewed executives from the researched companies.

Through the Stepwise method (default) of sequential search of the linear regression of the SPSS software, version 13, each independent variable, which best contributes to the dependent variable, are analyzed and selected by the program, which also excludes those that are least important

The achieved results from the application of this method and generated by the program showed that *Training of Users* and *Decision-Making Process* variables are the ones that best explain the *Assessment of the Implementation Process* dependent variable, according to the parameters in Table 1 below. Significance tests for regression coefficients provide researchers with an empirical evaluation of their "real" impact. Although this is not a validity test, it determines whether the impacts represented by the coefficients are generalizable to the other samples of these populations.

Model		Method
1	Training of Users	*Stepwise* *Probability-of-F-to-enter <= .050,* *Probability-of-F-to-remove >= .100*
	Decision-making process	*Stepwise* *Probability-of-F-to-enter <= .050,* *Probability-of-F-to-remove >= .100).*

Table 1 – **Independent variables that best explain the dependent variable**

Fonte: **SPSS (Versiom 13)**

6.3.1 Coefficient of Determination (R^2)

Table 2 shows the indicators generated by SPSS software for analysis of the relationship between these two variables. The regression (R^2) coefficient of determination has a coefficient of 0.893. This value indicates that the use of variables, **Training of Users** and **Decision-Making Process**, reduces errors at 89.3%, that is, these variables represent 89.3% of the explanatory power and quality of adjustment.

The Standard Error of Estimate (Table 3) is another precision measure of the analysis and represents a standard deviation estimate of the real dependent values in relation to the regression (022725).

Model	R	R^2	R^2 adjusted	Standard Error
1	.945(a)	.893	.857	.22725

Table 2 - **Summary of the Linear Regression Model**

Source: **SPSS (version 13)**

6.3.2 Variance Analysis

Test F measures the global performance of the regression line, trying to find, in general, whether the regression was relevant or whether the explained variation by the regression method is greater than the variation given by means (that is, that R^2 is greater than zero). In this case, the significance was 0.001 and it shows that the regression is relevant, that is, it confirms that two independent variables explain the dependent variable, according to Table 3.

Model		Sum of the Squares	df	Mean Square	F	Significance
1	Regression	2.579	2	1.290	24.970	.001
	Residue	.310	6	.052		
	Total	2.889	8			

df = number of estimated coefficients (degrees of freedom),

Table 3 – **Variance Analysis** (test F)

Source: SPSS, version 13

The result of F = 24.970 means that it is possible to explain the variation 24.970 times more than we use the means and this is not likely to occur at random (less than 5%).

6.3.3 Test "t"

.*Test t* measures the significance of the partial relation for the variables reflected in the regression coefficient. For this research, it was established a confidence level of 0.05 and the variables, **Training of Users** (0.00171) and **Decision-Making**

Process (0.04504), show lower coefficients than this confidence interval. Therefore, they are significant at this level to justify the regression performed. Table 5 shows the partial *t* value of variables in the equation measures the partial correlation of the variable reflected in the regression coefficient.

Test t helps determine whether any variable should be eliminated from the equation whenever a variable is added. In this case, it is noticed that both variables are relevant to the regression; however, the other independent variables of the research, when compared with these two variables, prove to be not very significant to the regression. Table 4 shows the indexed resulting from the application of test t for these two variables.

Model		Non-standardized coefficients		Standardized Coefficient	T	Significance
		B	Standard Error	Beta		
1	Constant	0.72535	0.48546		1.49417	0.18575
	Training of Users	0.64789	0.12061	0.76237	5.37164	0.00171
	Decision-making process	0.20423	0.08091	0.35823	2.52413	0.04504

Table 4 - **Analysis of the regression variables in the equation** *(test t)*

Source: SPSS, version 13

As for beta (ß) coefficient, it is noticed that *Training of Users* (0.76237) is the variable with the highest level of relative importance in the statistics of the regression and the *Decision-Making Process* (0.35823) is the variable that shows a lower level of relative importance.

Other factors did not show a functional relationship with the dependent variable and were rejected by the program. Nevertheless, in the descriptive part of the research results, all selected factors were regarded as, at a high or low level of importance, facilitator of the implementation process of the system. As noted before, the number of cases studied was not enough to perform a consistent application of this analysis technique and then we can only consider that these two variables are the ones that best explain the success of the implementation process of the system and that other factors analyzed are conditioning to facilitate this change process.

7. CONSIDERATIONS AND RECOMMENDATIONS

From the analysis found in the literature about the implementation of integrated management systems, a list of 8 categories of factors was created, which best explain the successful ERP implementation projects. Factors in each category, which facilitate or hinder the implementation process of integrated management systems based on ERP technology, were identified in the internal and external environment of the company. It was found, through the research, the presence and level of influence of these factors in the implementation process of the system experienced by the companies. No factors researched were regarded as a hindrance to the development of the process.

By considering the fact that the implementation of an ERP project is a costly, slow and complex change process, all the factors identified in this research may be regarded as relevant and critical for the ERP to be successful. However, the existence of a set of factors that per se result in a successful implementation of the ERP project does not represent a consensus among the many scholars and interviewed executives. One of the reasons for this lack of consensus about the set of factors, that is, variables grouped in categories, is explained by the fact that an implementation project, although it has to follow through all the basic and common phases to everyone interested in it, it is also involved by the characteristics and by the culture of the organization, usually reflected in the behavior of the people there working.

Referring to the existing disagreement among this theme's managers, researchers and scholars, Bergamaschi (1999) states that:

"...one of the reasons for the lack of consensus about the set of factors, that is variables grouped by categories, is explained by the fact that an implementation project must be dynamic and, therefore, it has different needs and challenges in the different phases to be addressed during the implementation process."

Based on the descriptive and statistical analyses of the research results and conclusions, some recommendations are made to the organizations that intend to adopt an ERP-technology based integrated management system in order to plan more securely all the phases of the change and implementation process of a new management model, as well as foreseeing potential areas of conflicts and problems that can be minimized by a priori or immediate actions. It is recommended that all business efforts to implement an integrated management system take into consideration the following criteria and arrangements:

▪ the implementation project should comprise and explain the mission, objectives and critical dates, budget and a communication program. Communication is a critical factor and must be composed of a permanent and continuous program during the implementation phase. The communication program, besides containing all the above mentioned elements, it also should inform and show to the people involved in it, in a clear and defined manner, what the focus of the project is and the requirements that must be complied with, regarding deadlines and costs.

▪ the clear support of the top managers during the implementation is necessary, as an effective way to use all resources and show support and a transparent commitment to the project. This encourages other team members to follow the example and feel the support coming from above.

▪ to hire the services of external consultants that, in addition to being recognized for the professional competence and licensed by the provider and experienced in the implementation of the integrated management systems, they also need to devise a planned change management program, or be part of the change management program of the company, evaluate the organizational climate and recognize individual behavioral characteristics and organizational culture.

- to consider, in the definition of the system to be implemented, besides the evaluation of the technical specifications and product offered, the necessary technical support that the system provider is committed to giving during the implementation and then future maintenance, when all the work systems of the company are being processed by this new model.

- to put together and develop a team in charge of the implementation project and change, led by a competent project manager capable of leading and coordinating the activities performed by the multidisciplinary members of the team, by the external consulting and the users involved in the process

- ; to promote qualification and previous training courses to team members in all technical and managerial aspects of the new system, as well as the activities related to change management. Before the effective introduction of the new system, to provide training programs and qualification of final users related to the working and operational features in each specific module,

- to recognize the need to develop and discuss with the project team, the basic rules in order to plan an efficient decision-making process that enables the resolution of problems during the implementation process, mainly when it comes to the aspects related to discrepancies between processes incorporated into the ERP system and processes adopted by the organization.

Though limited by a sample of 12 organizations, within a universe composed of hundreds of organizations, this research´s results may be useful and significant to many companies that plan to adopt or are experiencing the early phases of implementation. In addition to these considerations and recommendations, there is a very delicate and important aspect, which could be addressed by future research: the effective benefits drawn by the organization that adopted ERP.

In practical terms: is it possible to evaluate qualitatively and quantitatively the gains from decision making, in the readiness and reliability of the information generated by the system, in the contribution to business planning, in meeting the needs of stakeholders, in projecting the costs of the processes and other particular issues.?

Although it was not meant to be objective of this research, a short introduction to this field, during the interviews with managers, proved to be innocuous and evasive, suggesting that there was not data or information that could answer these questions. Naturally, the high cost of this system requires, at a certain stage, a cost-benefit evaluation or analysis of the amount spent on this acquisition.

On the other hand, the difficulty obtaining this type of information may exist due to the lack of a formal evaluation by organizations; that is, an analysis of the costs against possible and/or real revenues, or due to the necessary confidentiality of the information that the company wants to keep. However, it is a relevant aspect to further the studies about this theme.

REFERENCES

Azevedo, P. S.; Romão, M., Rebelo, E. (2014) *Success factors for using ERP (Enterprise Resource Planning) systems to improve competitiveness in the hospitality industry.* Tourism & Management Studies, (Special Issue), p. 165-168.

Bardin, L. (1977) *Análise de conteúdo.* Edições 70. Lisboa.

Bergamaschi, S. (1999) *Um estudo sobre projetos de implementação para gestão empresarial.* Dissertação de Mestrado. FEA/USP.

Belloquim, A. (1998) *ERP: a Nova Solução Definitiva Para Todos os Problemas.*

Creswell, J. W. (2003) *Research design: Qualitative, quantitative, and mixed method approaches.* 2 ed. Sage Publications. Thousands Oaks. CA.

Ferreira, G. K. A.; Neves, J. T. R.; Vasconcelos, M. C. R. L.; Carvalho, R. B. (jan./jun. 2012) *Gestão estratégica da informação: influência do sistema ERP (sistema integrado de gestão) nas ações estratégicas organizacionais sob a ótica dos consultores da TOTVS S.A.* Gestão Contemporânea, ano 9, n. 11, p. 61-90. Porto Alegre.

Hair, J. F. Jr., Anderson, R. E.; Tatham, R.L.; Black, W. C. (2005) *Análise Multivariada de Dados.* 5ª ed. Bookman. Porto Alegre.

Kalakota, R. & Robinson, M. (2002) *E-business - Estratégias Para Alcançar o Sucesso No Mundo Global,* 2ª ed. Bookman, Porto Alegre.

Laudon, K. C. & Laudon, J. P. (1999) *Sistemas de Informações,* 4ª ed., LTC – Livros Técnicos e Científicos S.A. Rio de Janeiro.

Martins, H. C.; Martins, M. D.; Muylder, C. F.; Gonçalves, C. A.; Dias, A. T.(Jun. 2013) *Configuração das Imagens Ideativas, Planejamento e Redução de Riscos: a implantação do Sistema ERP em um a Instituição Pública de Ensino.* Rev. Adm. UFSM, v. 6, número 2, p. 353-372. Santa Maria

Souza, C. A. & Zwicker, R. (1999) *Um Modelo de Ciclo de Vida de Sistemas ERP: Aspectos Relacionados à Seleção, Implementação e Utilização. I*n SEMEAD, Seminário de Estudos em Administração, Departamento de Administração da FEA/USP, p.1-13.

Souza, P. M.; Vasconcelos, M. C. L. R.; Tavares, M. C.; Carvalho, R. B. (out. 2013) *Contribuições dos Sistemas Enterprise Resource Planning para a Gestão da Informação e do Conhecimento: Um Estudo em uma Empresa de Pequeno Porte na Área Gráfica.* Perspectivas em Gestão & Conhecimento, v. 3, Número Especial, p. 109-127. João Pessoa.

Stamford, P. P. (2008) *ERP: prepare-se para esta mudança.* KMPress. Disponível em: <http://www.kmpress. com.br>. Acesso em: jul. 2014.

Stevenson, W. J. (1981) *Estatística aplicada à administração.* São Paulo. Harper & Row do Brasil. São Paulo.

Teles, F. & Silva, R. M. (abr./jun. 2014) *Avaliação da Satisfação dos Usuários de Sistemas ERP nas Médias Empresas de Confecção do Vestuário de Fortaleza.* Revista Produção Online, v.14, n. 2, p. 533-559. Florianópolis, SC.

Valentim, O. A.; Politano, P. R.; Pereira, N. A.; Araujo Filho, T. (2014) *Análise comparativa entre a implementação e atualização do sistema ERP R/3 da SAP considerando os fatores críticos de sucesso descritos na literatura: um estudo de caso em uma empresa do segmento de bebidas.* Gestão & Produção, v. 21, n. 1, p. 111-124, São Carlos. SP.

Stoner, J. F., (1988) Administração. Prentice Hall, São Paulo

2

IMPACTS OF A RELATIONSHIP MODEL ON INFORMATIONAL TECHNOLOGY GOVERNANCE: AN ANALYSIS OF MANAGERIAL PERCEPTIONS IN BRAZIL

Adriano Weber Scheeren
Joaquim Rubens Fontes-Filho
Getulio Vargas Foundation, Rio de Janeiro/RJ, Brazil
Elaine Tavares
Coppead, Federal University of Rio de Janeiro, Rio de Janeiro/RJ, Brazil

ABSTRACT

The aim of this article is to analyze the impacts, based on the perceptions of managers, of the deployment of a model to govern the relationship between business areas and IT in a large Brazilian financial organization. To undertake the case study of this deployment, the research firstly performed documental analyses of the process and then sent electronic surveys to a sample of managers in order to evaluate their perceptions of the model's impact in terms of the formalism of the organization's internal processes, strategic alignment between business areas and IT and levels of governance in the organization. The results revealed that managers perceived improvements in the quality of technological solutions, levels of IT governance, the understanding of IT area needs and business area demands, but they also stated that the negotiating process was more complex and there was no increase in their level of satisfaction with IT. These results of the study may contribute to the development of instruments for the evaluation of the impacts of the deployment of relationship models on important organizational aspects.

Keywords: Information Technology; IT Governance; IT Alignment; Relationship Model; IT Strategy

Address for correspondence / Endereço para correspondência

Adriano Weber Scheeren, Getulio Vargas Foundation Brazilian School of Public and Business Administration (FGV/EBAPE) Praia de Botafogo, 190 - room 502 - Rio de Janeiro (RJ) - CEP 22250-900 Tel: 55-21-37995753 Master's Degree in Management from the FGV/EBAPE, with a Bachelor's Degree in
Informatics from the Federal University of Santa Maria (UFSM – RS). Researcher in the Corporate and Organizational Strategy and Governance Studies Group (NEEG) at the FGV/EBAPE. He works in a financial institution controlled by the Federal Government in the technology division that manages its relationship with the organization's business areas.

Joaquim Rubens Fontes-Filho, Getulio Vargas Foundation Brazilian School of Public and Business Administration (FGV/EBAPE) Praia de Botafogo, 190 - room 502 - Rio de Janeiro (RJ) - CEP 22250-900 Tel: 55-21-37995753 Professor at the FGV/EBAPE, Ph.D in Administration from the FGV/EBAPE,
Master's Degree in Public Administration (FGV/EBAPE) and in Production Engineering (UFRJ/COPPE), Bachelor's Degree in Production Engineering (UFRJ), and coordinator of research projects funded by the CNPq and of the Corporate and Organizational Strategy and Governance Group (NEEG) at the FGV/EBAPE.

Elaine Tavares, Coppead Graduate School of Business Federal University of Rio de Janeiro Rua Pascoal Lemme, 355 - Ilha do Fundão 21941-918 - Rio de Janeiro – RJ Tel: 55-21-25989859 Professor at Coppead/UFRJ. Post-Doctoral Degree at CERGAM - Centre d'Etudes et de Recherche en Gestion da Université Aix- Marseille III, France. Ph.D in Administration from the Brazilian School of Public and Business Administration of the Getulio Vargas Foundation (FGV/EBAPE). Master's Degree in Business Administration from the FGV/EBAPE. Bachelor's Degree in Industrial Design from the Pontifical Catholic University of Rio de Janeiro. She has 15 years of professional work experience in large companies, mainly in the financial and educational areas.

1. INTRODUCTION

The Information Technology (IT) area is becoming increasingly important in organizations, whether as a main activity or a facilitator of a firm's business and to make business processes more agile. In the banking sector specifically, the reconfiguring of IT from mere back-office functions to its current position as a fundamental element of electronic banking reflects this growing importance. According to the 2010 figures from the Brazilian Bank Federation (Federação Brasileira de Bancos [Febraban], 2011), the main relationship channel with bank customers was self-service, which accounted for 32% of the 55.7 billion bank transactions performed followed by Internet-based transactions with a 23% share, with 27.8 million mainly individual customers using internet banking. According to this entity the banking sector's TI-related investments and expenditures totaled more than 22 million BRLs in 2010, representing a 15% increase over the previous year, thus revealing a solid growth in total IT and communication expenditure (Febraban, 2011).

This importance, shown by the fact that the banking industry is one of the biggest investors in IT worldwide and Brazil's largest consumer of IT products and services (Faria & Maçada, 2011), makes it crucial to perfect processes in order to align IT efforts with the strategic importance represented by each initiative in business terms, establishing the criteria governing competition between business areas according to the prioritization of IT activities. Determining which demands should take priority constitutes an important challenge for IT and business areas, either because initiatives with a greater potential return may be difficult to implement (Graeml, 2000) or due to the intangible nature of the services or innovations produced.

The findings of an international survey showed that the 548 executives who were consulted considered that there was still a significant gap between corporate IT area expectations and performance, and professionals of this area were recommended to improve their knowledge of business demands (Roberts & Sikes, 2008). In Brazil, Rodrigues, Maccari and Simões (2009) found a similar gap in a survey that focused on IT executives of the country's 100 largest firms.

Thus, IT governance can be used to foster the alignment between Information Systems (ISs) and business strategy, in addition to improving the performance and contribution of these systems to operational performance (Dameri & Perego, 2010). IT governance appeared during the 1990s and rapidly became an important instrument for promoting this alignment and the integration of organizational activities with IT (De Haes & Grembergen, 2004).

Although organizations, when deploying a model to govern the relationship between business areas and IT, focus initially on improving the strategic alignment between these areas, they also aim at achieving improvements in IT area processes. When business areas and the IT area work in a collaborative fashion to improve IT processes, the value added to the business tends to be proportionately greater (Graeml, 2000).

1.1   Research problem and objectives

The aim of this article is to analyze the benefits and limitations resulting from the deployment of a model to govern the relationship between business areas and the IT area, characterized as an IT governance mechanism, based on the perception of holders of management positions.   The term "relationship model" is used in the sense of a systematic approach aimed at developing norms for governing the relationship between the cited internal areas of organizations and this systematic approach can be reproduced as long as certain conditions are present. The methodology was based on a case study of a large Brazilian financial firm which observed and analyzed the perception of managers before and after the introduction of the relationship model, regarding the extent to which its implementation facilitated the alignment between IT project priorities and organizational strategy.

Before 2004, negotiations to prioritize IT initiatives in this firm occurred directly between business area customers and the internal areas of the IT division. No attempt was made to align the priorities to be given to these initiatives with the business strategies and investments as a whole or align them inside each business area. This situation led to constant interruptions in the development of technology demands due to the need to cater urgently to a demand that was considered to have a higher priority.

Seeking to improve its governance structures in this area the organization has developed and deployed, as of 2005, a model to govern the relationship between business areas and the IT area. This model attributes the responsibility for prioritizing demands directed to the IT area to the business area itself which bases its decisions on the corporation's strategy. The model is operationalized through periodic meetings between executive managers of the firm's business and IT areas, in which the prioritization of demands is aligned between areas.

The first section of this article, which consists of a bibliographical review, discusses the need for strategic alignment between business and IT areas, the contribution of IT governance, the relationship between these areas and the degree of formalism involved. The following section presents the method used, the relationship model analysed in the case study and the research hypotheses. The article proceeds with a section analyzing the study's findings followed by the last section containing some final considerations.

2. THEORETICAL REFERENCES

2.1 Relationship between business areas and IT

The significant impact that IT investments and their decision-making processes have on an organization's success (Dean & Sharfman, 1996; Devaraj & Kohli, 2003) and the difficulties encountered in aligning the expectation of business area and IT managers (Roberts & Sikes, 2008),   make it fundamental to understand how organizations govern their investment decisions in this sphere (Xue et al., 2008). Given the strategic importance of this type of decision and the financial resources involved, firms have to refine their IT initiative selection mechanisms and various management tools have been used to involve and create awareness among business executives regarding IT-related decisions (Lunardi & Dolci, 2009).

The IT investment decision process consists of a sequence of actions that begins with the identification of a problem associated with systems, thus opening up an opportunity and culminating with the approval of an IT project (Boonstra, 2003). An IT investment prioritization mechanism should be based on the return of projects and assets for the organization and in their alignment with business objectives (Fernandes & Abreu, 2006).

Given that a variety of organizational actors influences the decision-making process, it is not enough to consider only final deciders, as this could generate a reductionist view of the IT investment decision process (Xue et al., 2008). All the main parties involved should be considered as part of the decision process – all the way from the pre-deciders, who make the IT investment proposals, to final deciders. Prahalad (2006) defends the potential of Chief Information Officers (CIOs) as facilitators of the implementation of business strategies through the use of IT operational excellence processes. Their functions are to assure the transformation of business through IT's aligned strategies.

It is important to highlight that these deciders may face limitations in their choices as in the case of regulated sectors. Facó, Diniz and Csillag (2009) observe that the definition of a firm's competitive priorities is a function of the market and the operational resources available, which include information technology. In the case of banking, which is one of the economy's most regulated sectors, it is also necessary to consider the delimitations imposed by the regulatory framework on activities and strategic choices, with impacts on both decisions regarding operational resources and the actual appointment of deciders given that, as observed by Andrade (2005), in the case of Brazil, Central Bank authorization is necessary for appointments to the bank's statutory bodies.

IT's effectiveness depends on the way it is organized and conducted within the parameters of a business. These are precisely the middle-level functions that link the operational base to the strategic top management. To achieve this, Lutchen (2003) advocates six critical steps: (1) CIOs should understand the firm's business and align IT with the fundamentals of this business; (2) CIOs should administer IT as a distinct business which supports corporate objectives and sustains its profits; (3) CIOs should link IT strategy to the strategy of the business in a pragmatic way, adjusting their processes with quality and efficiency; (4) CIOs should help business units to define their needs (and risks), improving their services through controlled and efficient management; (5) CIOs should consolidate a high quality, result-oriented customer service culture in IT; and (6) CIOs should be compensated based on the contribution of their IT initiatives to the firm's profitability.

Executives should recognize the IT's status as a primary factor of production and make it a top management responsibility, instead of isolating it as a technical segment, distant from leadership (Raghupathi, 2007). There should be an effective exchange of ideas in firms and a clear understanding of the initiatives needed to ensure the success of corporate strategies, with a view to aligning IT investments with these strategies (Lunardi & Dolci, 2009). Fernandes and Abreu (2006) define strategic alignment between businesses and IT as a process that transforms a firm's business strategy into IT strategies and actions that seek to ensure that business objectives will be supported. As IT is able to enhance business strategies that could not be implemented without its help, this strategic alignment is bidirectional, i.e., from business strategy to IT strategy and vice-versa.

Lunardi and Dolci (2009) identified the following advantages of the IT area's involvement with other areas: (i) prioritization of IT projects according to business strategy, (ii) enhanced perception of IT's value, (iii) participation of IT in the formulation of the firm's strategy, (iv) visibility and transparency of the IT area and (v) planning of IT initiatives according to the firm's strategy. The authors affirm that the use of various mechanisms to support the prioritization of IT projects that are most aligned with the firm's strategy increases the other areas of the organization's perception of the IT area's value.

Corroborating this view, Graeml (2000) affirms that IT's alignment with the firm's business is enhanced when IT assumes a strategic support role aimed at achieving organizational objectives. Based on the CMM (Capability Maturity Model), the author describes the partnership between the business and IT areas as being a function of the alignment existing between the former areas and the role of the organization's IT area. This alignment may be in a phase in which it is still conducted by the business area or in the phase in which the IT area initiates the creation of opportunities for these business areas. This alignment can also be well established with strong ties existing between these areas. In terms of the IT area's role in the organization, it may either act as a mere receiver of requests, as an area that provides consultancy services for business areas or as an area that collaborates with other areas of the organization. According to this same author (Graeml, 2000), the degree of partnership that exists between business areas and the IT area can be classified as "non-existent", "increasing" or "established".

In Brazil, there seems to be an alignment between IT and basic business processes, despite the evidence of a lack of synchronization. Rodrigues *et al.* (2009) studied the design of IT management in the largest 100 Brazilian firms and observed that 63% of them have formal IT plans aligned with their business plan, although only 30% update these plans. However, 37% of IT executives did not perform this alignment or did not recognize its importance and only 14% bothered to continuously update alignment indicators.

2.2 Strategic alignment and IT governance

The growing importance of IT for firms makes it essential to perfect control mechanisms (Weill & Ross, 2006). Muhanna and Stoel (2010) observe that, in general, investors attribute a higher market capitalization to firms with a greater IT capacity, based on the view that this area contributes to improving an organization's future prospects in terms of size and risk associated with future returns.

The dynamic synchronization of business strategies and IT is not sufficient to guarantee IT's effective in terms of its contribution to the business (Shpilberg, Berez, Puryear, & Shah, 2007), given the possibility that alignment problems may occur. The authors warn about the possibility of inefficiency associated with the IT group's competencies, in a situation where the IT group understands business objective priorities but is unable to respond effectively with adequate technologies or solutions, thus producing an alignment trap. They suggest that attention should be paid to three determining factors of IT's effectiveness for business: emphasis on simplicity, correct and efficient outsourcing and adequate attribution of responsibilities. Laartz, Monnoyer and Scherdin (2003) sustain that if there is overall inefficiency in project execution (in terms of time and budget), there may be ineffectiveness in IT's alignment with specific and important business objectives. Even so, IT can still be aligned. Thus, competencies may need to be examined and not necessarily the alignment strategy in use (Rodrigues Maccari & Simões, 2009). In addition, one should be aware that various structures, processes and mechanisms related to IT effectiveness may function in a specific organization but not in others (De Haes & Van Grembergen, 2004; Dameri & Perego, 2010).

These alignment problems are taken into account in the sphere of IT governance, a concept that became a widely used yardstick during the 1990s when Henderson, Venkatraman and Loh used the term to describe the complex process of aligning IT with the business (Loh & Venkatraman, 1993; Henderson & Venkatraman, 1993). IT governance contributes to a better alignment between ISs and business strategies in order to improve IS performance and results and reduce IT risk. It thus has a dual objective: to contribute to organizational performance and involve ISs more closely in the future challenges of the business (Dameri & Perego, 2010).

The IT Governance Institute (Information Technology Governance Institute [ITGI], 2009) affirms that IT governance consists of organizational and leadership structures, as well as processes, that ensure that a firm's IT area maintains and extends an organization's objectives and strategies. Weill and Ross (2006) define IT governance as the specification of decision rights and framework of responsibilities in order to encourage desirable behavior in IT use. Fernandes and Abreu (2006) call attention to the fact that IT governance seeks to encourage the sharing of IT decisions with other areas of an organization and is not restricted merely to the implementation of "best practices". Rau (2004), understanding governance to be the way in which an organization defines, monitors and achieves its strategies, considers that its application to the IT area assumes that its effectiveness is associated with the ability of technology investments to ensure that business objectives will be attained in an effective and efficient manner.

It is difficult to find a single definition for IT governance, but it usually encompasses: alignment between information systems and business strategy, strategic decisions regarding investments in IT and IS and the generation of value through the use of IS in business (Dameri & Privitera, 2009; Luftman, 1996; Van Grembergen, De Haes, & Guldentops, 2004; Weill & Ross, 2006).

IT governance depends on multiple contingencies (Sambamurthy & Zmud, 1999): corporate governance model, corporate strategy, organization of the business, distribution of authority, etc. Xue et al. (2008) identified IT governance archetypes which varied according to the characteristics of IT investments in relation to the external and internal environments. Thus, one can perceive that it is important for IT governance mechanisms to be adequate for the firm in which they are being deployed, in order to fit in with the organization's other management mechanisms. Organizations should develop their own IT governance policies and procedures and disseminate them for implementation (Nolan & McFarlan, 2005; Raghupathi, 2007). Moreover, in order to deploy an effective IT governance system it is necessary to harmonize current functionalities with an orientation towards the future in IT investment decisions (Weill, 2004).

IT governance exists in all organizations that use IT given that, conceptually and despite its polysemic nature, governance "is about steering and the rules of the game" (Kjaer, 2004, p. 7), so that, independently of quality and its standards, it can be found in organized systems as the act or way of governing. However, the organizational quality and practices of IT governance varies among firms, depending on aspects such as whether rights and responsibilities are well distributed among appropriate people, whether formalized processes for important tasks are in place or whether there is adequate documentation (Simonsson, Johnson, & Ekstedt, 2010).

Thus, many firms are refining IT governance mechanisms in order to direct their expenditures in this area as a strategic priority. These firms initiated the deployment of IT governance so as to obtain alignment between business areas and the IT area, with the aim of generating value for the business (Fernandes & Abreu, 2006). Alignment is defined here as the degree of commitment of the IT group to the priorities of the business, the allocation of resources and realization of projects and delivery of solutions that are consistent with the objectives of the business (Shpilberg *et al.*, 2007).

This alignment can be achieved by understanding that IT governance is part of corporate governance and by adjusting a model of IT governance according to best practices observed in the market (De Haes & Van Grembergen, 2004). Thus, IT governance is the responsibility of the management team as an integral part of corporate governance. Governance reflects the leadership, organizational structure and the processes that ensure that IT supports and enhances the organization's strategies and objectives (Raghupathi, 2007).

2.3   Advanced relationship: process formalism

The evolution of IT's role in organizations – from providing technology to establishing a strategic partnership with business areas - has led this area to seek fresh ways of fulfilling its new role in organizations. In recent years, the duration of the business cycle and firms' technology cycle have both been reduced. However, this reduction in the time taken by the IT area to cater to business area demands has not been sufficient to correspond to the expectations and needs of other areas of the organization adequately. Thus, the perception is that the IT area is always late in terms of fulfilling business area demands (Graeml, 2000; Tavares & Thiry-Cherques, 2011).

According to Rodrigues *et al.* (2009), IT in Brazilian firms meets basic demands but is not equipped to use the best automated practices, acting much more according to a solution supplier logic than as a promoter of innovation. However, it is possible to observe a quest for new ways of achieving greater maturity in the governance mechanisms of its internal processes (Gartner, 2009). Through these improvements in IT processes, organizations are seeking, in conjunction with the other components of IT governance – organizational mechanisms and structures – to attain higher levels of efficiency in the IT area, achieve its strategic objectives and strengthen its role as strategic partner of business areas.

Organizations have increased the degree of formalism in the relationship between the business and IT areas especially in terms of the presentation of demands. The IT area has also increased its use of frameworks and market models (CMM, CMMI, MPS-Br, PMBoK, CobIT), in order to improve its internal processes and its quality, productivity, efficiency and communication with business areas, as well as also explore possibilities for innovation. Rodrigues *et al.* (2009), when researching Brazilian organizations, found that management is oriented towards systems (ITIL, COBIT) that do not optimize business processes. It is important to emphasize that models such as COBIT (Control Objectives for Information and related Technology): (i) are generic models, designed for a hypothetical firm; (ii) concentrate on SI audits; (iii) are instruments of control and not governance directives; (iv) are not adequate for aligning IS with strategy and to create value for the business based on ISs (Dameri & Perego, 2010).

Research undertaken in various countries by Deloitte Touche Tohmatsu (2009) into the balance between IT and business areas identified that firms are increasingly institutionalizing the relation between these areas and seeking the ideal point in this relationship. According to this study, this kind of formalized and structured management mechanism enables the IT area to listen to the needs of the business areas, thus constituting a good way of starting to align the organizations IT and business areas.

Khatri and Brown (2010) affirm that to design a governance structure it is necessary to identify fundamental decisions that need to be taken and those responsible for them. The authors show how structured and unstructured mechanisms can be used to deploy a governance structure. For example, a committee of business leaders can review and approve IT projects. Web portals can be used to disseminate procedures and policies. Compensation systems can be employed to reinforce the value the firm attaches to information assets.

3. METHODOLOGY

In order to identify benefits and limitations of the deployment of models to govern the relationship between business areas and the IT area, the research performed a case study of a large Brazilian financial firm in order to evaluate its managers' perceptions of the model. Data collection was based on documental analyses of the development and deployment of the model and the results of a questionnaire whose construction was based on hypotheses derived from the theoretical references and distributed electronically to a sample of managers.

3.1. Definition of Research Hypotheses

The possible impacts of the deployment of this model governing the relationship between business areas and the IT area were divided into three categories of analysis, as shown below:

1. *Formalism in the Organization's Internal Processes* – this category evaluated the model's impacts on aspects related to the organization's internal processes. It is supposed that these impacts derive from the need to increase the degree of internal formalism in the execution of the organization's internal processes in order to support negotiations and enable them to be effective.

2. *Strategic Alignment between Business Areas and IT*– in this category the results of the relationship model were evaluated in terms of impacts on the strategic alignment between the firm's business areas and the IT area. One may suppose that by fostering the alignment of IT initiatives with strategic directives, one of the consequences of the relationship model is to increase the perception of strategic alignment between these areas.

3. *Levels of Governance in the Organization* – in this category the research evaluated the perceptions of the relationship model's impacts on the organization's levels of governance. One may suppose that a relationship model that generated perceptions regarding both the formalism of the organization's internal processes and strategic alignment between the firm's business areas and its IT area should also be perceived as having had effects on the organization's levels of governance.

Based on the categories of analysis presented the research defined the following hypotheses:

No.	Hypothesis: *In an organization with a relationship model instituted between business areas and the IT area,*	Reasons/Consequences
1	managers identify improvements in the quality of IT solutions developed.	The need for greater formalization in internal processes resulting from the adoption of a model of this kind should lead to the creation of more detailed and consequently better understood demands (on the part of business areas), as well as generating improvements in these areas' internal processes. One may suppose that some of the consequences of the deployment of a relationship model of this kind would include an increase in the perception of the quality of technological solutions developed an improvement in the organization's internal processes.
1.a	managers of the business areas identify an increase in the level of satisfaction of business area expectations on the part of the IT area.	
1.b	managers of the IT area identify a greater clarity in the demands passed on by the business areas to the IT area.	
2	managers identify an increase in the level of strategic alignment between areas.	As one of the objectives of the deployment of a model for governing the relationship between an organization's business and IT areas is to ensure that prioritized demands are the ones most aligned with the firm's corporate strategies, one may suppose that managers will perceive an increase in the level of this alignment.
2.a	managers of business areas know and understand the strategies and needs of the IT area.	
2.b	managers of the IT area know and understand the strategies and needs of the business areas.	
2.c	managers perceive IT as a strategic partner of the business areas and not as a mere technology provider.	
3	levels of IT governance and corporate governance are perceived by managers as being greater than without the use by the organization of this kind of model.	
3.a	managers of business areas understand that the organization's level of corporate governance are greater and that the risks represented to the organization by the IT area are known.	As a relationship model of this kind can be understood as an instrument of IT governance that can have an effect outside the organization, one may suppose that managerial perceptions in this regard will be enhanced.
3.b	managers of the IT area understand that the organization's levels of IT governance are enhanced and that the risks represented to the organization's business by the IT area are known.	

Table 1 – Research Hypotheses

3.2. Data Collection and Analysis

The research universe was composed of managers of the organization which constituted the object of the case study who worked in the areas that managed its business and technology. The research selected divisions and business units responsible for at least four technology solutions and, in the case of the technology division, all the areas responsible for the construction of technological solutions, both applications and infrastructure. 705 managers were selected from a universe of 1.000. They were each sent a questionnaire and 161 replies were received (22.84% of the total). In addition, documental research was conducted in the organization. The latter's aim was to describe and clarify the model used to govern the relationship between business areas and the IT area. The field research tool – an electronic questionnaire sent – was divided into the following sections:

Section	Objetive	Operationalization
1	To obtain information about the respondent.	Selection of aspects such as number of years at the company and area, position, participation in relationship model meetings and knowledge of results.
2	Perform a general evaluation of the adequateness of the situation prior to the deployment of the model governing the relationship between IT areas and business areas.	Selection of the reasons given for their evaluation of the situation regarding the negotiation of IT demands in the organization before the relationship model.
3	Provide data to evaluate hypotheses related to the analytical category "Formalism in the Organization's Internal Processes".	Each of these sections was composed of 10 items for evaluation. The latter were evaluated once relating to the period before and once after the deployment of the model, with the difference between these periods being a consequence of this deployment. Each of the evaluations was performed using a Likert type scale of 5 items, in which respondents selected total inadequateness at one extreme and total adequateness at the other.
4	Provide data to evaluate hypotheses related to the analytical category "Strategic Alignment between Business Areas and IT".	
5	Provide data to evaluate hypotheses related to the analytical category "Levels of Governance in the Organization"	
6	Perform a general evaluation of the adequateness of the situation after the deployment of the model governing the relationship between IT areas and business areas.	Selection of the reasons given for their evaluation of the situation regarding the negotiation of IT demands in the organization after the relationship model.

Table 2 – Sections of the Research Tool (Questionnaire)

Sections 1, 2 and 6 of the questionnaire received a descriptive statistical treatment, aimed at (i) detailing the sample's profile, (ii) establish the level of adequateness of the demand negotiation process which existed prior to the deployment of the model under evaluation and their main reasons and (iii) establish the level of adequateness of the situation regarding the negotiation of demands after the deployment of the relationship model and their main reasons. In the case of the remaining sections (3, 4 and 5), the research used two forms of evaluation for the research hypotheses: (i) a factorial analysis followed by an analysis of the difference between the averages of the groups formed by the situation before and the situation after the deployment of the model, and (ii) selection of significant variables undertaken by the authors according to face validity followed by an analysis of the difference between the averages of these groups.

4. PRESENTATION AND ANALYSIS OF THE RESULTS

5. 4.1 Relationship Model

The creation of a model to govern the relationship between business areas and the IT area sought to organize the requests and prioritization of IT demands in the firm. Before 2004 both the negotiation and prioritization of IT initiatives were based on direct negotiations between business areas customers and the internal areas of the technology division that were responsible for the application that automated the solution. This form of negotiation and prioritization hindered the alignment of the priorities of these initiatives with the organization's corporate and investment strategies and even alignment with the internal priorities of each business area. The effect of this situation on the IT area could be seen in the constant interruptions in the development of a specific technology demand owing to the need to urgently prioritize a demand that had been identified as having a higher priority than those currently being catered to.

As a result of this direct negotiation between business areas and the area responsible for the solution in the IT area, there was little formalism in the definition of demands, which would involve the simplification of specifications for the implementation of requests, given that those in charge of both the business area and the IT area had a thorough knowledge of the technological solution.

In order to organize the negotiation of IT-related demands between its internal areas, the firm developed a model to govern the relationships between the organization's business management areas and the IT area, which was deployed in 2005.

The first step in the creation of this new model as to assign a business manager to each of the organization's ISs. Thus, all new needs or those that represent changes in systems are analyzed by the area that is responsible for specific business in the firm. The needs are then evaluated according to their degree of alignment with the organization's strategies and listed in order of priority. This list of demands is then forwarded to the IT area which assesses how each need can be met and the number of hours necessary to fulfill the demand.

After the IT area has performed its evaluation a final, monthly, prioritization meeting is organized joining all executive managers of the business area and the technology division. With the information regarding how each demand will be met and respective schedules now at hand, the business area maintains or alters the order of priority of its demands. The demand priorities negotiated during previous meetings can be changed due to the appearance of more urgent demands or the need to comply with a new law or norm. At these meetings participants also report the progress of demands prioritized in previous prioritization meetings.

4.2   Sample profile and descriptive analysis

The distribution of managers who replied to the 161 questionnaires according to their position in the organization is presented in Table 3. 24 managers of the business areas and one from the IT area stated that they did not have the knowledge or information necessary to evaluate the model and were removed from the sample, thus leaving only 136 valid questionnaires. In proportional terms, more IT area employees participated than those from the organization's business areas, or 33.17% and 13.72% respectively.

Area	Position	Quest. Sent	Quest. Replied		Valid Quest.	
			No.	%	No.	%
Business Area	General Manager	5	1	20.00%	0	0.00%
	Executive Manager	105	16	15.24%	8	7.62%
	Division Manager	392	76	19.39%	61	15.56%
	Team Manager	1	0	0.00%	0	0.00%
	Area Total	**503**	**93**	**18.49%**	**69**	**13.72%**
IT Area	General Manager	2	0	0.00%	0	0.00%
	Executive Manager	10	3	30.00%	3	30.00%
	Division Manager	48	18	37.50%	18	37.50%
	Team Manager	142	47	33.10%	46	32.39%
	Area Total	**202**	**68**	**33.66%**	**67**	**33.17%**
Area Total	*General Manager*	*7*	*1*	*14.29%*	*0*	*0.00%*
	Executive Manager	*115*	*19*	*16.52%*	*11*	*9.57%*
	Division Manager	*440*	*94*	*21.36%*	*79*	*17.95% %%%% %*
	Team Manager	*143*	*47*	*32.87%*	*46*	*3.17%*
	Overall Total	*705*	*161*	*22.84%*	*136*	*19.29%*

Table 3 – Questionnaire Respondents

The descriptive data revealed the seniority of respondents: 94% of managers had worked at the company for more than 15 years and 40% for more than 25 years. It could be supposed that these executives' level of knowledge of the organization was correspondingly high. More than 70% of respondents affirmed that they took part or had already taken part in the relationship model's negotiation meetings, showing that they were familiar with the negotiation process. As regards respondents' level of knowledge of the results of the meetings, the research found that that slightly less than 70% of survey respondents knew about what was negotiated in the negotiation meetings. This percentage is more than 10 percentage points greater in the group of IT area managers (74.63%) than in the group of business area managers (63.77%). This difference is possibly due to the fact that for the IT area the demands negotiated at these meetings constitute direct inputs for the planning of activities, whereas in the business areas monitoring is attributed to only some of the managers.

Table 4 presents the distribution of replies according to company area to the question that sought to evaluate the perception of respondents regarding the adequateness of the process involving the negotiation of demands between the business areas and the IT area, according to pre-defined reasons, before the implementation of the new relationship model, thus prior to 2004. Most managers considered that the previous situation was inadequate, mainly because strategic aspects of the requests were not considered and due to the lack of process formalism.

Reply	No.	%	Reason	No.[*]	Perc. of/ No.Repl
No reply	5	3.68%			
Inadequate	106	77.94%	Because direct negotiation between parties perhaps would not consider aspects such as the strategic importance of requests.	87	82.08%
			Because agility in the implementation of requests may cause system unavailability.	14	13.21%
			Because the lack of formalism may hamper the understanding of the request, which could cause problems in systems.	74	69.81%
Adequate	25	18.38%	Because the negotiation occurred directly between the business area and the person responsible for the application in the IT area without intermediations.	19	76.00%
			Because the agility one had to implement requests in the systems offset the problems resulting from lack of formalism.	17	68.00%
			Because the specifications for implementation of requests were simpler, given that responsible parties in both the business and IT areas had a deep understanding of the matter.	17	68.00%
Total	136	100.00%			

Table 4 – Evaluation of the Situation Before the Relationship Model

*Obs.: * More than one reply was permitted*

After the deployment of the model the research found a significant difference regarding the perception of the model's adequateness, with the managers of the IT area recording the perception of a higher level of adequateness. Table 5 presents the reasons selected by respondents to evaluate the model's adequateness or inadequateness. The main reason given for justifying the inadequateness of the new model, given by 45 of the 71 managers who considered the model to be inadequate, or 63.38% of this group, related to the fact that demands were prioritized by the business area responsible for managing the IT solution, thus enabling their interests to take precedence over the need for alignment with the organization's strategy. On the other hand, among the reasons given for justifying the perception of adequateness, one should highlight the attribution to business areas of the responsibility for prioritizing demands for applications under their responsibility.

Reply	No.	%	Reason	No*	Perc. of/ No.Repl
No Reply	3	2.21%			
Inadequate	71	52.21%	Because it added complexity to the process by obliging business areas to first of all negotiate with the solution management area.	28	39.44%
			Because it permitted new prioritizations on very short notice, perhaps causing the suspension of activities.	20	28.17%
			Because it did not permit the prioritization of demands that were more aligned with the organization's strategy, privileging instead the demands of the business area that manages the solution.	45	63.38%
			Because it permits prioritizations outside the negotiating process, then reducing the transparency of the process.	31	43.66%
Adequate	62	45.59%	Because it stipulates business areas that are responsible for the prioritization of demands for applications under their responsibility.	51	82.26%
			Because it permits the reformulation of prioritizations at relatively brief intervals, which is fundamental for the dynamism of a firm in the financial area.	36	58.06%
			Because it permits the prioritization of demands that are more aligned with the company's strategy, which can be demonstrated by the good results obtained by the organization.	39	62.90%
			Because, in exceptional cases, it allows the negotiation to take place outside the negotiating agenda in order to make the process more agile.	34	54.84%
Total	136	100.00%			

Table 5 – Evaluation of the Situation After the Relationship Model

*Obs.: * More than one reply was permitted*

Table 6 shows a comparative evaluation of the adequateness of the negotiation process before and after the deployment of the relationship model, revealing a significant improvement in perceptions of adequateness on the part of IT area managers. However, this was not observed in the case of business area managers:

Area	Reply	Before the Model		After the Model	
		No.	Perc. of/Area	No.	Perc. of/Area
Business Area	No reply	5	7.25%	2	2.90%
	Inadequate	40	57.97%	41	59.42%
	Adequate	24	34.78%	26	37.68%
	Total Business Area	**69**	**100.00%**	**69**	**100.00%**
IT Area	No reply	0	0.00%	1	1.49%
	Inadequate	66	98.51%	30	44.78%
	Adequate	1	1.49%	36	53.73%
	Total IT Area	**67**	**100.00%**	**67**	**100.00%**
Area Total	*No reply*	*5*	*3.68%*	*3*	*2.20%*
	Inadequate	*106*	*77.94%*	*71*	*52.21%*
	Adequate	*25*	*18.38%*	*62*	*45.59%*
	Overall Area Total	*136*	*100.00%*	*136*	*100.00%*

Table 6 – Comparative Evaluation of Situations Before and After the Model

4.3 Verfication of the research hypotheses

The evaluation of the research hypotheses was performed using distinct methods. In the case of hypotheses 1, 2 and 3, the variables linked respectively to sections 3, 4 and 5 of the research tool, presented in Table 2, were grouped using factorial analysis - the aim of this procedure was to identify factors or dimensions underlying the data that summed up the evaluations (Hair, Anderson, Tatham, & Black, 1998) – and the research performed a difference of means test. For the other hypotheses, derived from the previous three, the variables were grouped, based on documental analysis, according to their face and construct validity (Babbie, 1995) in order to identify the variables that best summed up what the research was trying to measure with each of these hypotheses. The research thus used two forms of evaluation for the research hypotheses: (i) a factorial analysis followed by an analysis of the difference of means between the groups formed by the situation before and the situation after the deployment of the model and (ii) selection and grouping of significant variables – undertaken by the researchers - followed by an analysis of the difference of means between these groups.

The data grouped around factors, whether supported by the factorial or qualitative analysis, were substituted by the arithmetic average of the components of the new factors/groups, and some missing values were replaced by averages, thus computing compound averages. (Hair *et al.*, 1998).

As a result of the factorial analysis process, the following factors – two for each of the main hypotheses (1,2 and 3) – were extracted to evaluate these research hypotheses: (i) "Internal Processes" and "Perception of Quality" factors related to hypothesis 1, (ii) "Strategic Prioritization of Demands" and "IT Area – Business Area Relationship" factors related to hypothesis 2, and (iii) "IT Governance" and "Perceptions Outside the Organization" factors related to hypothesis 3. The reliability of factors and groups of variables verified by Cronbach's Alpha attained values of over 0.7 in all cases, thus above the acceptable limit (Hair *et al.*, 1998).

The evaluation of the differences between the averages of the factors and the groups of variables in the situations before and after the deployment of the relationship model used the non-parametric statistical test - Wilcoxon signed-rank test for matched pairs - in order to analyze differences between paired observations and which take into account the magnitude of differences (Malhotra, 2006). Thus, the test exhibits the number of negative differences, positive differences and equalities between the paired evaluations and also presents the probability associated with the Z statistic which, when lower than the level indicating the probability of occurring unwarranted rejection of the null hypothesis – significance level defined in this case as 0.05 – indicates a statistically significant difference.

Evaluating the significance level of the Z statistic, associated with the Wilcoxon tests, applied to the factors and groups of variable cited, it was possible to verify that, with the exception of the "IT Area- Business Area Relationship" factor and the group of variables related to hypothesis 1.a, the significance levels were lower than 5%, indicating significant differences between the averages. In the case of the factors/groups of variables that showed a significant difference, the research also verified that, in most cases, the evaluations relating to the situation after the deployment of the relationship model were considerably more favorable than in the case of the previous situation, thus evidencing perceptions of the model's adequateness. Table 7 presents, for each hypothesis, the averages of the evaluations before and after the model. The averages of each of the factors related to the main research hypotheses and the groups of variables related to the additional assumptions are shown in the following table.

Hypothesis/Factor	Before / After theModel do Modelo	Qty.	Average	Sig. Dif.
Hypothesis 1 – Factor "Internal Processes"	Before	130	2,495	
	After	130	3,251	*
Hypothesis 1 – Factor "Perception of Quality"	Before	130	3,208	
	After	130	3,447	*
Hypothesis 2 – Factor "Strategic Prioritization of Demands"	After	128	2,396	
	After	128	3,162	*
Hypothesis 2 – Factor "IT Area- Business Area Relationship"	Before	128	3,040	
	After	128	3,099	

Hypotheis 3 – Factor "IT Governance"	Before	128	2,129	
	After	128	3,110	*
Hypothesis 3 – Factor "Perceptions Outside the Organization"	Before	115	2,304	
	After	115	3,276	*
Hypothesis 1.a	Before	63	3,107	
	After	63	3,223	
Hypothesis 1.b	Before	67	2,186	
	After	67	3,283	*
Hypothesis 2.a	Before	62	2,782	
	After	62	3,137	*
Hypothesis 2.b	Before	65	1,961	
	After	65	3,100	*
Hypothesis 2.c	Before	128	2,896	
	After	128	3,172	*
Hypothesis 3.a	Before	60	2,539	
	After	60	3,282	*
Hypothesis 3.b	Before	67	1,798	
	After	67	3,115	*

Table 7 – Averages of the Evaluations of the Situations Before and After the Model

* $P < 0,05$

Thus, based on the tests performed, one can affirm that at a significance level of 5%, the averages between the groups are different for all factors, with the exception of the "IT Area – Business Area Relationship", for which the null hypothesis of equality of means was not rejected, and for the group of variables related to hypothesis 1.a. Thus hypotheses 2 and 1.a. were rejected. In the analysis of hypothesis 2.a. owing to the large number of equalities, it was possible to conclude that the relationship model had only a moderate effect on this group of variables, although the hypothesis was confirmed.

Analyzing the overall results, one can see that, in all cases, the averages of the evaluations of the situation before the deployment of the model, performed by the business areas for all factors used to evaluate the main hypotheses, were greater than the averages of the evaluations of this same period performed by IT area managers. In other words, the perception of business area managers in relation to the situation before the model was more favorable than that of IT area managers.

While in the case of IT area managers the comparison of the situations before and after the deployment of the relationship model, measured by the averages of factors, shows an increase in the perception of adequateness in the case of all factors, business area managers only perceived this in the case of four factors ("Internal Processes", Strategic Prioritization of Demands", "IT Governance" and "Perceptions Outside the

Organization"). Table 8 summarizes the results of the evaluations of the research hypotheses, indicating which were confirmed or rejected:

No.	Hypothesis: *In an organization with a relationship model instituted between business areas and the IT area...*	Evaluation
1	managers identify improvements in the quality of IT solutions developed.	Confirmed
1.a	managers of business areas identify an increase in the level of satisfaction of business area expectations on the part of the IT area.	Rejected
1.b	managers of the IT area identify a greater clarity in the demands passed on by business areas to the IT area.	Confirmed
2	managers identify an increase in the level of strategic alignment between areas.	Rejected
2.a	managers of business areas know and understand the needs of the IT area.	Confirmed
2.b	managers of the IT area know and understand the strategies and needs of business areas.	Confirmed
2.c	managers perceive IT as a strategic partner of the business areas and not as a mere technology provider.	Confirmed
3	levels of IT governance and corporate governance are perceived by managers to be greater than without the use by the organization of this kind of model.	Confirmed
3.a	managers of business areas understand that the organization's levels of corporate governance are increased and that the risks to the organization represented by the IT area are known.	Confirmed
3.b	managers of the IT area understand that the levels of IT governance are enhanced and that the risks to the organization's business represented by the IT area are known.	Confirmed

Table 8 – Results of the Evaluations of the Research Hypotheses

5. CONCLUSION

One of the aims of IT governance, considered in conjunction with its associated mechanisms, is to facilitate alignment between ISs and business strategies. The case study presented in this paper, considering a relationship model designed to facilitate the selection and prioritization of IT projects, made it possible to demonstrate the validity of the hypotheses formulated - based on a review of the literature - regarding the model's positive impacts. The managers of the organization, as a result of the deployment of this relationship model, were able to perceive improvements in the quality of the technological solutions developed, an increase in the levels of IT and organizational governance and the value of the IT area as a business partner. The managers of the IT area recorded a greater clarity in the demands made by the business areas, an increase in the levels of knowledge and understanding of the strategies and needs of the organization's business areas and an increase in the levels of governance and risks involved in IT.

However, the managers in the sample did not observe an increase in the level of strategic alignment between the areas of the organization with the introduction of the model which could be attributed to the greater complexity resulting from the greater number of stages and actors involved. It is significant to also observe that managers did not identify an increase in the business areas' level of satisfaction regarding their expectations relating to the IT area. The results showed that for these managers the benefits expected from the deployment of the model were not perceived by the business areas to the same extent as by the IT area.

It is possible that the organization's business areas lacked adequate resources to cope with the greater complexity resulting from the new relationship model and which would have reduced the costs of adaptation and given the managers of these areas a clearer perception of the gains obtained from the implementation of this process. But it is also possible to suppose that other variables influenced managers' perceptions, such as the power relations between areas, past conflicts or even the actual training of managers related to the development of competencies in aspects necessary for the definition of models and the negotiation of prioritization agreements. Future studies could monitor other variables and contingent factors that could influence managers' perceptions.

The main contribution of this study lies in the evaluation of the way a relationship model of this kind affects some organizational aspects, such as (i) the quality of the organization's technological solutions, (ii) strategic alignment between the business areas and the IT area – contributing to the development of a closer degree of partnership between these areas –, (iii) management of the risks of technological solutions in the firm and (iv) the organization's levels of governance. The results described can be applied to various types of large organizations that also have a great number of business areas which demand technological solutions and need to develop their IT governance processes. These organizations can understand the impacts of this type of relationship model, obtaining information that could be useful for drawing up their own IT governance strategies.

However, one should consider the fact that the efficient functioning of these kinds of models depends on various contingent factors (Sambamurthy & Zmud, 1999; De Haes & Van Grembergen, 2004; Xue et al., 2008, Dameri & Perego, 2010) and this imposes limitations on the results of this research that are inherent to the case study method, given that it records only the contingencies of the firm and sector chosen. Moreover, the choice of an organization in the banking sector means that one should also consider the limitations imposed by the sector's high degree of regulation on the firm's strategic choices and decisions regarding operational resources.

REFERENCES

Andrade, L. P. (2005). *Governança corporativa dos bancos no Brasil.* (Masters dissertation). Pontifícia Universidade Católica. Rio de Janeiro, Rio de Janeiro, RJ, Brasil. Retrieved from <www.maxwell. lambda.ele.puc-rio.br/cgi-bin/PRG_0599.EXE/6673_1.PDF?NrOcoSis=1 8862&CdLinPrg=pt>.

Babbie, E. (1995). *The practice of social research* (7th ed.). Belmont: Wadsworth Publishing.

Boonstra, A. (2003). Structure and analysis of IS decision-making process. *European Journal of Information Systems, 12*(3), 195–209.

Dameri, R. & Perego, A. (2010). Translate IS Governance framework into practice: the role of IT Service Management and IS performance evaluation. *Proceedings of the European Conference on Information Management and Evaluation*, Lisboa, Portugal, 4.

Dameri, R. P., & Privitera, S. (2009). *IT governance*, FrancoAngeli: Milano.

De Haes, S., & Van Grembergen, W. (2004). IT governance and its mechanisms. *Information System Control Journal, 1*.

Dean, J., & Sharfman, M. (1996). Does decision process matter? A study of strategic decision-making effectiveness. *Academy of Management Journal, 39*(2), 368–396.

Deloitte Touche Tohmatsu (2009). *2009 Survey on IT-business balance: Shaping the relationship between business and IT for the future*. Retrieved from http://www.deloitte.com/assets/Dcom-Belgium/Local%20Assets/Documents/EN/be_ITBusinessBalance-2009.pdf.

Devaraj, S., & Kohli, R. (2003). Performance impacts of information technology: Is actual usage the missing link? *Management Science, 49*(3), 273–289.

Facó, J. F. B., Diniz, E. H., & Csillag, J. M. (2009). O processo de difusão de inovações em produtos bancários. *Revista de Ciências da Administração, 11*(25), 151–176.

Faria, F. A., & Maçada, A. C. G. (2011). Impacto dos investimentos em TI no resultado operacional dos bancos brasileiros. *Revista de Administração de Empresas, 51*(5), 440–457.

Federação Brasileira de Bancos. (2011). *O setor bancário em números 2011.*

Fernandes, A. A., & Abreu, V. F. (2006). *Implantando a governança de TI: da estratégia à gestão dos processos e serviços*. Rio de Janeiro: Brasport.

Gartner. (2009). *Gartner 2009 CIO Survey*. Retrieved from http:// www. Oracle.com/global/kr/download/seminar/2009/fmw/090825_architect_day_session_05.pdf.

Graeml, A. R. (2000). *Sistemas de informação: o alinhamento da estratégia de TI com a estratégia corporativa*. São Paulo: Atlas.

Hair, J. F., Anderson, R. E., Tatham, R. L., & Black, W. C. (1998). *Multivariate data analysis*. Upper Saddle River: Prentice-Hall.

Henderson, J. C., & Venkatraman, N. (1993). Strategic alignment: Leveraging information technology for transforming organizations. *IBM Systems Journal, 32*(1), 472–485.

Information Technology Governance Institute (2009). *About IT governance*. Retrieved from http://www.itgi.org/template_ITGI.cfm?Section=About_IT_Governance1&Template=/ContentManagement/HTMLDisplay.cfm&ContentID=19657

Khatri, V., & Brown, C. (2010). Designing data governance. *Communications of the ACM, 53* (1), 148-153.

Kjaer, A. M. *Governance.* (2004). Cambridge: Polity Press.

Laartz, J., Monnoyer, E., & Scherdin, A. (2003). Designing IT for business. *McKinsey Quarterly, 3,* 77–84.

Loh, L., & Venkatraman, N. (1993). Diffusion of information technology outsourcing: Influence sources and the Kodak effect. *Information Systems Research, 3*(4), 334–359.

Luftman, J. N. (1996). *Competing in the information age.* Oxford: Oxford University Press.

Lunardi, G. L., & Dolci, P. C. (2009). Governança de TI e seus mecanismos: uma análise da sua disseminação entre as empresas brasileiras. *Anais do Encontro de Administração da Informação,* Recife, Brasil, 2.

Lutchen, M. (2003*). Managing IT as a business: a survival guide.* Hoboken: John Wiley & Sons.

Malhotra, N. K. (2006). *Pesquisa de Marketing: uma orientação aplicada* (4a ed.). Porto Alegre: Bookman.

Muhanna, W. A., & Stoel, M. D. (2010). How do investors value IT? An empirical investigation of the value relevance of IT capability and IT spending across industries. *Journal of Information Systems, 24*(1), 43–66.

Nolan, R., & McFarlan, F. (2005). Information technology and the board of directors. *Harvard Business Review, 83*(10), 96–106.

Prahalad, C. K. (2006). CIOs Hold key to operational excellence. *Optimize, 5*(5), 66.

Raghupathi, W. (2007). Corporate governance of IT: A framework for development. *Communications of the ACM, 50*(8), 94–99.

Rau, K. (2004, Fall). Effective governance of IT: design, objectives, roles, and relationships. *Information Systems Management, 21*(4,) 35–42.

Roberts, R., & Sikes, J. (2008, November). McKinsey global survey results: IT's Unmet Potential. *McKinsey Quarterly.* Retrieved from https://www.mckinseyquarterly.com/PDFDownload.aspx?ar=2277.

Rodrigues, L. C., Maccari, E. A., & Simões, S. A. (2009). O desenho da gestão da tecnologia da informação nas 100 maiores empresas na visão dos executivos de TI. *Journal of Information Systems and Technology Management, 6*(3), 483–506.

Sambamurthy, V., & Zmud, R. (1999). Arrangements for information technology governance: A theory of multiple contingencies. *MIS Quarterly, 23*(2), 261–290.

Shpilberg, D. Berez, S., Puryear, R. & Shah, S. (2007). Avoiding the alignment trap in information technology. *MIT Sloan Management Review, 49*(1), 51–58.

Simonsson, M., Johnson, P., & Ekstedt, M. (2010). The effect of IT governance maturity on IT governance performance. *Information Systems Management, 27*(1), 10–24.

Tavares, E., & Thiry-Cherque, H. (2011). Interaction between information systems and work in the Brazilian banking sector. *Revista de Administração de Empresas, 51*(1), 84–97.

Van Grembergen, W., De Haes, S., & Guldentops, E. (2004). Structures, Processes and Relational Mechanisms for IT Governance. In W. Van Grembergen (Ed.). *Strategies for Information Technology Governance* (pp.1–36). Hershey: Idea Group Publishing.

Weill, P. (2004). Don't just lead govern how top-performing firms govern IT. *MIS Quarterly Executive, 3*(1), 1–17.

Weill, P., & Ross, J. W. (2006). *Governança de TI: tecnologia da informação*. São Paulo: M. Books.

Xue, Y., Liang, H., & Boulton, W.R. (2008). Information Technology Governance in Information Technology Investment Decision Processes: The Impact of Investment Characteristics, External Environment, and Internal Context. *MIS Quarterly, 32*(1), 67-96.

3

ACHIEVING MATURITY (AND MEASURING PERFORMANCE) THROUGH MODEL-BASED PROCESS IMPROVEMENT

Jose Marcelo Almeida Prado Cestari
Arthur Maria do Valle
Edson Pinheiro de Lima
Eduardo Alves Portela Santos
Pontifical Catholic University of Parana, Curitiba, Parana, Brazil

ABSTRACT

This paper presents the approach adopted by a software development unit in order to achieve the maturity level 3 of CMMI-DEV and therefore obtaining better performance. Through historical research and secondary data analysis of the organization, the paper intends to answer the following research question: "Could the adoption of maturity/best practices models bring better performance results to small and medium organizations?" Data and analysis conducted show that, besides the creation of indicator's based management, there are some quantitative performance improvements in indicators such as: Schedule Deviation Rate, Effort Deviation Rate, Percent Late Delivery, Productivity Deviation and Internal Rework Rate

Keywords: performance management, CMMI, process improvement, quantitative benefits, performance indicators.

Address for correspondence / Endereço para correspondência

Jose Marcelo Almeida Prado Cestari, Programa de Pós-graduação em Engenharia de Produção e Sistemas, PUCPR. Rua Imaculada Conceição, 1155. CEP: 80215901 - Curitiba, PR – Brasil. Doutorando em Engenharia de Produção e Sistemas (PUC-PR), mestre e bacharel em informática pela UFPR. Possui certificações PMP, Lead Auditor ISO-9001:2000, ITIL, COBIT, IBM, MCTS e ISF (ISO 27002).

Arthur Maria do Valle, Programa de Pós-graduação em Engenharia de Produção e Sistemas, PUCPR. ISD Brasil – Av. Cidade Jardim, 400 – 7º andar – Edifício Dacon – CEP 01454-902 – São Paulo, SP. Brasil. Doutorando em Engenharia da Produção e Sistemas, PUCPR. Mestre em Informática Aplicada (PUCPR-2002) na área de Engenharia de Software. Formado em Ciência da Computação (PUCPR-1997) e Administração de Empresas (UFPR-2000)

Edson Pinheiro de Lima, Professor do Programa de Pós-graduação em Engenharia de Produção e Sistemas, PUCPR. Graduado em Engenharia Elétrica pela Universidade Tecnológica Federal do Paraná, Mestre também em Engenharia Elétrica na Universidade Estadual de Campinas, Doutor em 2001 pela Universidade Federal de Santa Catarina, na Área de Engenharia de Produção.

Eduardo Alves Portela Santos, Professor do Programa de Pós-graduação em Engenharia de Produção e Sistemas, PUCPR. Graduado em Engenharia Mecânica pela Universidade Federal da Bahia, Mestre em Engenharia Mecânica e Doutor em 2003 pela Universidade Federal de Santa Catarina.

1. INTRODUCTION

There is a lot of doubt regarding the benefits of adopting a formal approach (model based) for software development projects. Researchers and academia, which defend the use of a software engineering approach, methodology, best practices, maturity models and so on, are usually criticized by companies and professionals because of the excess of work, process bureaucracy, lack of dedication (no time) of the employees for these kinds of activities (Rocha, 2005), resistance to changes (Fetzner, 2010) and lack of evidenced measures correlating a maturity process and the achievement of performance. In that way, this is a problem that deserves to be studied and verified, since companies are always looking for better productivity, quality, efficiency, etc.

People who are studying and contributing to this question are usually related to research institutes and/or practitioners around the world. Among then, it is possible to cite the Carnegie Mellon University (through one of its branches called SEI – Software Engineering Institute), the Project Management Institute (PMI), the ITSqc (IT Services Qualification Center) and others. They are releasing new models, courses, papers and best practices that help projects to achieve better results around the world, and consolidating the idea that it is a good thing to have an organized and formal process, managed in order to obtain performance (Goldenson and Gibson, 2003)(Gibson, Goldenson and Kost, 2006).

The main purpose of this paper is to investigate whether process maturity brings better operations performance results. In this sense, there is a brief history of the effort to implement the CMMI Level 3 maturity level and the results (in terms of performance measurement) founded in an organization that was formally assessed as CMMI Maturity Level 3. Note that a CMMI appraisal is performed by an authorized company and auditor, which can officially assess maturity levels, according to the rules and procedures created by SEI, and registered in the SCAMPI-Standard CMMI® Appraisal Method for Process Improvement (2011).

The remainder of this paper is as follows: section 2 presents the theoretical background regarding the main theme of our study. Section 3 presents the method and research protocol. Section 4 describes the organization and the organizational unit. Section 5 contains the process improvement history and approach, respectively. In section 6 the results are described and, in section 7, conclusion and future works are presented.

2. THEORETICAL BACKGROUND

In general ways, performance measurement can be basically divided into two periods (Gomes, Yasin, and Lisboa, 2004): the first period (known as the "traditional measurement systems") began around 1880, and the measures were pretty much related to accounting (e. g., operations costs) and financial control. This approach suffered criticisms because the focus was given only in the financial aspects of a company. After 1980, the second period began. The researchers realized the importance of measuring other areas (besides financial), such as quality, customer satisfaction, process and intellectual capital. A large number of performance measurement systems (PMSs) have been proposed. Among the most widely cited of these PMSs are: the SMART (Cross and Lynch, 1988-1989; Lynch and Cross, 1991), the performance measurement matrix (Keegan et al., 1989), the Balanced Scorecard (Kaplan and Norton, 1992), and the integrated dynamic PMS (Ghalayini et al., 1997).

In order to create measurements to other than financial areas, especially because of the increasing IT aspects, some IT frameworks and models were created in the beginning of the 1990's, and among them, there is the CMM (Capability Maturity Model) and its successor, the CMMI-DEV (Capability Maturity Model Integration for Development), focused on software/systems development. According to CMMI Product Team (2010), CMMI is a maturity model for process improvement and it is a composition of best practices that address development and maintenance activities for the product lifecycle, since its inception until its deployment and maintenance. The model was created basically because of a need from the DoD (Department of Defense – USA). The DoD was dealing with suppliers that were not providing quality (on time, and on budget) software projects and the DoD began a partnership and sponsorship with Carnegie Mellon University, located in Pittsburg. As a result of this collaboration, the Software Engineering Institute (SEI) was created in order to research and develop frameworks, models and good practices, based on the concepts of Crosby (1979), Juran (1988), Deming (1986) and Humphrey (1989). The idea was that the DoD suppliers could follow these practices and be adherent to the model, reducing the risks of poor quality of software development supplied to DoD. The following figure (Fig.1), extracted from CMMI Product Team (2010), illustrates the history of CMMI models:

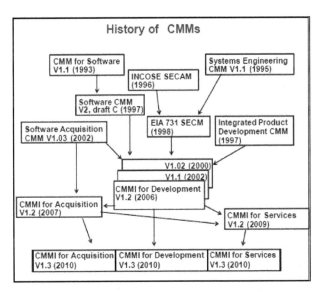

Fig. 1 – History of CMMI models

The SEI identified three critical dimensions that organizations typically focus on, represented by the following figure (Fig. 2) extract from CMMI Product Team (2010):

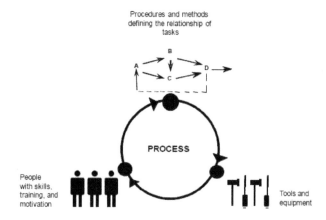

Fig. 2 – Dimensions of a process

The CMMI-DEV model is not a process, but it has a focus on the importance of having a structured process, once that the process is the item that holds everything together. "Processes allow you to align the way you do business. They allow you to address scalability and provide a way to incorporate knowledge of how to do things better. Processes allow you to leverage your resources and to achieve process maturity and analyze business trends", (CMMI Product Team, 2010).

In one of its representations (called *staged*), the CMMI-DEV model defines five maturity levels, as it follows:

- Level 1: Initial. *Ad hoc* and chaotic process. Usually the organization does not have a stable environment and the success of the projects depends on the "heroism" and competence of the employees. The organizations are hardly able to repeat the past success of projects.

- Level 2: Managed. Requirements and the projects are managed. There are measurement analysis, control and planning of the activities. There is a process for managing projects, including the organization of the work products and its control. The management team has visibility about the status, and the stakeholders involved are also managed and there is a commitment established with them.

- Level 3: Defined. Well understood, defined and formalized process for the organization. They are formally described and the use of patterns, procedures, tools and methods are institutionalized. Engineering processes are also enforced in this level.

- Level 4: Quantitatively Managed. Some processes are chosen so they can be statistically and quantitatively controlled and managed. Special causes of variation in the process are identified and analyzed.

- Level 5: Optimizing. The processes are continually improved through incremental actions and innovations. Quantitative objectives are established and reviewed for the process improvement. Focus on analysis of common causes of variation.

Each of the maturity levels above cited contains process areas (PAs) describing practices, activities and artifacts that should be addressed in order to achieve that specific maturity level. The levels are cumulative, i. e., to achieve Level 3, an organization must be compliant with the PAs of Level 2 and Level 3. There are a total of 22 PAs (considering all maturity levels), distributed as following:

- Level 2:

  Requirements Management (REQM)

  Project Planning (PP)

  Project Monitoring and Control (PMC)

  Supplier Agreement Management (SAM)

  Measurement and Analysis (MA)

  Process and Product Quality Assurance (PPQA)

  Configuration Management (CM)

- Level 3:

  Decision Analysis and Resolution (DAR)

  Integrated Project Management (IPM)

  Organizational Process Definition (OPD)

  Organizational Process Focus (OPF)

  Organizational Training (OT)

  Product Integration (PI)

  Requirements Development (RD)

  Risk Management (RSKM)

  Technical Solution (TS)

  Validation (VAL)

  Verification (VER)

- Level 4:

  Organizational Process Performance (OPP)

  Quantitative Project Management (QPM)

- Level 5:

  Organizational Performance Management (OPM)

  Causal Analysis and Resolution (CAR)

3. METHODOLOGY AND RESEARCH PROTOCOL

The following research question was defined: "Do the adoption of maturity/best practices models bring better performance results to small and medium-sized organizations?"

In order to quantitatively evaluate this question, relevant data was obtained, which allows the analysis of performance results before and after the adoption of CMMI-based best practices. For this reason a field study using secondary data was conducted. As a field study, this research has two phases, a) historical data collection and b) data analysis and report, and four activities, as can be seen in figure 3:

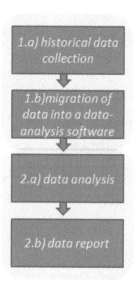

Fig. 3 – Research Methodology

Since the organization had a performance measurement repository, data collection was merely the gathering of historical data and migration of it into a data-analysis software tool. In terms of the analysis, as part of the organization's performance measurement repository, there are measures that can also be used to measure the progress and benefits of the process improvement program. These measures were applied to legacy software development projects as well as to new projects that used the organization's CMMI-based processes and assets. In this sense, some project-based indicators were selected and analyzed via control charts – in terms of mean and variation improvement rates: Schedule Deviation Rate (%); Effort Deviation Rate (%); Productivity Deviation (%); %Late Delivery (%); and Internal Rework Rate (%).

4. CASE DESCRIPTION: ORGANIZATION (COMPANY) AND ORGANIZATIONAL UNIT

Sofhar Gestão & Tecnologia S.A. is a Brazilian company located in Curitiba (capital city of Paraná state). Sofhar was founded in 1986 and since then it has helped its clients to achieve success in national and international markets. Sofhar is specialized in diagnosing and solving problems, seeking solutions through the application of best practices in technology and business management.

Sofhar has a complete structure to meet market needs and these demands are met by providing the following offers (through services and products): Consultancy, Software Development, Infrastructure, Training and Product Sales and Licensing.

An organization, for our purposes, is "an administrative structure in which people collectively manage one or more projects or work groups as a whole, share a senior manager, and operate under the same policies"(CMMI Product Team, 2010). In this sense, the organization is the Software Development Area, not the entire company.

Software Development Area is composed by 15 people, including the area manager and those individuals directly working with software development. Together they implement the roles and processes such as EPG-Engineering Process Group, CCB-Control Change Board, QA-Quality Assurance, organizational training, process improvement, and so on, according to the needs and requirement of each CMMI maturity level.

The organization unit implemented a balanced PMS (as shown in Fig. 4) in order to measure its processes and results during (and after) a software development project. The measures - for projects and for the organization - were created basically according to the structure, recommendations and relevance proposed in Neely at al. (1997), and also according to the (best) practices specified in the Measurement and Analysis PA of the Level 2:

- Establish and maintain measurement objectives derived from identified information needs and objectives

- Specify measures to address measurement objectives

- Specify how measurement data are obtained and stored.

- Specify how measurement data are analyzed and communicated.

- Obtain specified measurement data.

- Analyze and interpret measurement data.

- Manage and store measurement data, measurement specification, and analysis results.

- Communicate results of measurement and analysis activities to all relevant stakeholders.

Some of the performance measures created are represented in the following dashboard figure (Fig. 4):

Project Measures Dashboard

Indicador	Organizational Goals	Measure Status	Risk Category
Project Performance - Cost (CPI - Cost Performance Index)	Improve estimations and performance	OK	Cost
Project Performance - Schedule (SPI - Schedule Performance Index)		Alert	Deadline
Internal Rework	Reduce rework	Alert	Cost
Internal Defects Density	Reduce defects	Critical	Quality
Change Impacts	Reduce change requests	Alert	Scope
Warranty Period Rework	Reduce rework and improve quality	OK	Cost
Adherence to the defined processes	Improve quality, maintain adherence to the model	OK	Quality

Project Risks

	Risk Category	Risk Measures	Quality Assurance Risks
	Deadline	Low	Average
	Cost	Low	Average
	Quality	Low	Average
	Scope	Low	High

Fig. 4 – Project Measures Dashboard

In that dashboard it is possible to see, for each indicator, the related organizational goal, the measure status and associated risk category. The status is usually represented in colors, where green stands for "ok", yellow for "alert" and red for "critical". In case of a "red light", some corrective actions are expected in the project. All measures were defined and are managed according to a "measure framework", containing, among other items: name of the measure, goal, unity (e. g., days, hours), formula, procedures for analysis, those who measure, those who collect, frequency of measurement, frequency of analyses and so on.

All of these project measures are associated with a risk category (cost, deadline, quality, scope) in order to the management be able to have a general view regarding organizational risks and performance.

5. PROCESS IMPROVEMENT HISTORY AND PROGRAM APPROACH

In September 2008 the software development area began a CMMI-based process improvement program in order to enhance the quality of its software projects (and products), especially to achieve more predictability and improve indicators such as SPI (Schedule Performance Index) and CPI (Cost Performance Index). The SEI partner called ISD Brasil helped Sofhar to achieve its goals, as a consultancy company in the program.

As part of the program approach, the partnership with ISD brought agility to Sofhar, especially because it was agreed between both companies that effort and schedule dedicated to process definition phase (writing processes, creating templates and putting all together) should be minimized. One of Sofhar's business goals was to achieve CMMI level 3 in about one year after the beginning of the process improvement project. In fact, the SCAMPI Class A CMMI ML3 was conducted in November, 2009 (about thirteen months after the beginning of the process improvement program).

In order to help Sofhar with this goal, ISD proposed a new approach called "ISD CMMI PME", where PME stands for small and medium-sized business, in Portuguese.

After a (initial) SCAMPI C event (where a gap analysis was made and data about the Organizational Unit was raised) ISD took its historical information about processes (common indicators, common workflows and so on) and tailored (together with Sofhar) its set of organizational process assets considering Sofhar´s context and needs.

These assets are based on ISD´s processes descriptions and templates that cover all CMMI level 3 process areas and were specially designed for micro and small organizations. After few interactions between the companies, the process definition phase was declared finished and Sofhar was ready to use its new organizational processes and assets for software development projects. Some pilot projects were conducted and, in the sequence, another number of projects were conducted using the processes. Meanwhile, ISD provided consultancy in order to verify Sofhar's progress towards CMMI ML 3 compliance. In this sense, some events, including a preparatory SCAMPI class B, were conducted.

Concerning to continuous improvement activities and culture, Sofhar´s assets have naturally evolved (organizational unit is using the sixteenth baseline of its process). In fact, Sofhar had an enormous gain of time, effort and knowledge using the processes and templates delivered by ISD.

6. RESULTS AND BENEFITS

As stated before, in order to address our research question, comparisons of mean (green line in graphics from Fig. 5 to 14) and variation (distance between red lines in each segment in graphics from Fig. 5 to 14) improvement rates in the following two scenarios were performed:

- Scenario a) all completed development projects before (09 projects) and after (21 projects) CMMI-based process institutionalization and

- Scenario b) .Net completed development projects before (3 projects) and after (5 projects) institutionalization of CMMI-based process in the organization, including also projects conducted after being formally assessed as CMMI Level 3.

Although the "before/after" effects are not statistically proven yet, due to small sampling, there are some measurable benefits related to these indicators. Note that each dot represents a project and projects were plotted in chronological order.

In the first scenario (scenario a), there are relevant improvements of mean and variation reduction for Schedule Deviation Rate (see Fig. 5), Effort Deviation Rate (see Fig. 6); %Late Delivery (see Fig. 7); Productivity Deviation (see Fig. 8); Internal Rework Rate (see Fig 9).

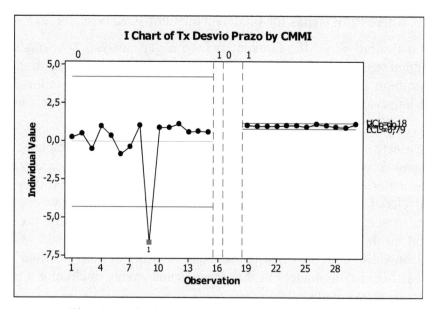

Fig. 5 – Schedule Deviation Rate for scenario a)

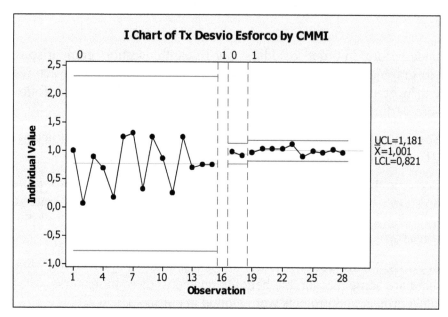

Fig. 6 – Effort Deviation Rate for scenario a)

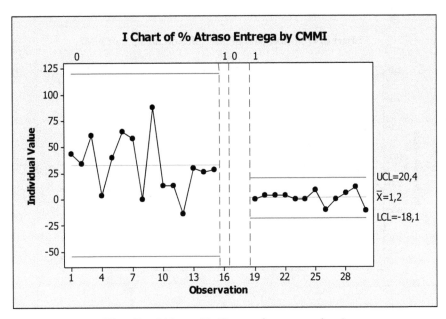

Fig. 7 – %Late Delivery for scenario a)

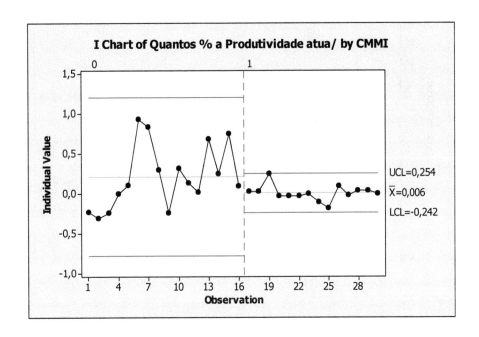

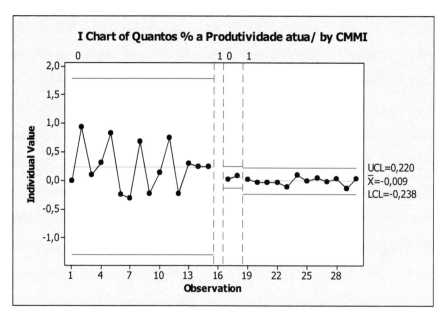

Fig. 8 – Productivity Deviation for scenario a)

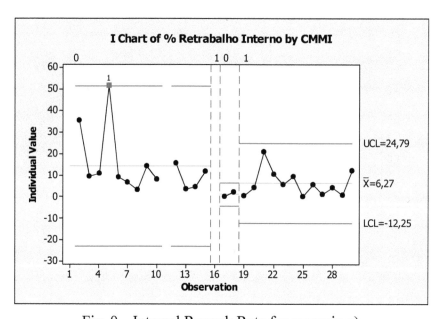

Fig. 9 – Internal Rework Rate for scenario a)

In scenario b), where only projects that used the same technology (i.e. .Net) were analyzed, and relevant mean and variation improvement were noticed for Internal Rework Rate (see Fig. 10) and Effort Deviation Rate (see Fig. 11), Schedule Deviation Rate (see Fig. 12); %Late Delivery (see Fig. 13) and Productivity Deviation (see Fig. 14).

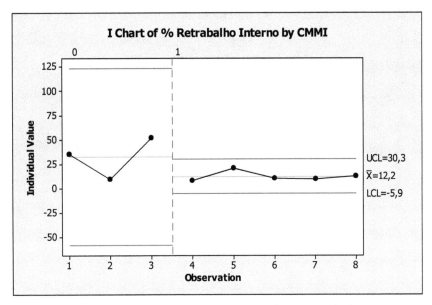

Fig. 10 – Internal Rework Rate for scenario b)

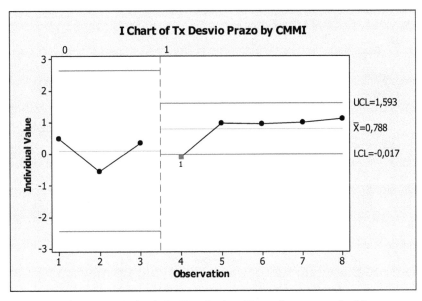

Fig. 11 – Schedule Deviation Rate for scenario b)

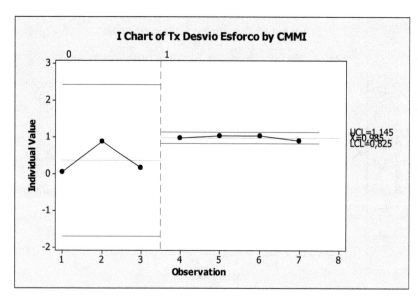

Fig. 12 – Effort Deviation Rate for scenario b)

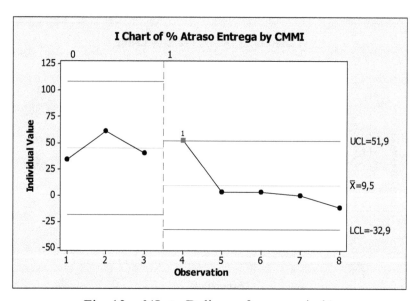

Fig. 13 – %Late Delivery for scenario b)

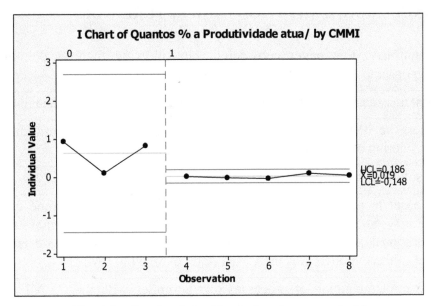

Fig. 14 – Productivity Deviation for scenario b)

In addition to the analysis above, it was also investigated some correlation between performance measures and the process adherence indicator, which measures the percentage of process items that were followed by the project. In this analysis, the following correlation was obtained (Fig. 15):

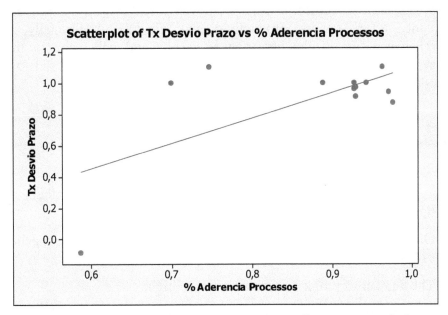

Fig. 15 – Effort Deviation Rate x Process Adherence correlation

Figure 15 above shows a positive correlation of 0,641 (p-value = 0,018) that means that the more adherent to the process the less projects deviate from a planned schedule.

7. CONCLUSION, LIMITATIONS AND FUTURE WORK

In summary, this paper considered the following theoretical elements and guidelines in order to achieve the research project purposes:

• First measurement systems were focused basically on costs management.
• After the 1980's, measurement systems became more multidisciplinary, considering other issues in addition to financial aspects.
• IT solutions became more available.
• In order to address other areas besides the financial one, some quality and maturity models were created and became a reference for measuring other operational areas such as software development and software engineering. One of these models was the CMM (later evolved to CMMI).
• The implementation of processes that complies with the CMMI model can give a certain level of maturity to an organization.
• Maturity levels can bring better performance results to an organization.

Based on the improvement rates of mean and variation of each selected measure in table 1 – where for the majority of indicators an improvement rate range of 20 to 100% was achieved – it is possible to conclude that, at least for Sofhar, a more mature process, with disciplined and managed activities, and compliant with CMMI-DEV Level 3, reveals an improvement of software development project performance results, such as quality, effort, rework, productivity and schedule. Additionally, a relevant correlation between one of the performance results and adherence to the defined processes was also obtained, which corroborates the idea of having (and following) a good process which drives you to a good performance.

	% Internal Rework	% Productivity Deviation	% Effort deviation	% Schedule Deviation	% Late Delivery
variation_improvement (%)	35.3	75.1	75.0	89.5	62.0
mean_improvement (%)	52.7	97.1	26.3	3679.1	78.1

Tab. 01 – improvement rates of mean and variation

Apart from the quantitative benefits obtained, there are, among others, at least the following limitations in this research:

- Only one organization was studied, so it is not possible to do a generalization of benefits and results.

- The number of projects assessed is not so high.

- No cost measures were available.

- The company didn't measure (at that time) human factor variables.

Regarding the last issue above, although the technical aspects are necessary in order to achieve good performance, they are not sufficient to guarantee the success of some tasks (Robbins, 2005). People working with software development must receive a special attention, once behavior and human aspects affect the success of their activities

(Hazzan and Tomayko, 2004). So, it is also important to mention that there are other variables (especially regarding to human factors) that can influence performance, and these variables must be (when possible) analyzed together with more technical issues. Unfortunately, as mentioned before, the organization didn't have measurements or indicators regarding human factors, so it was not possible to check this kind of influence in the correlation analysis.

For future work, a deeper analysis on the performance measure database (also including human factors variables) could be conducted in order to discover, quantify and prove cause-effect relationships that will be a basis to create and use process performance models to better estimate and quantitatively manage development projects as well as organizational performance.

REFERENCES

CMMI Product Team. (2010), "CMMI® for Development, Version 1.3". *Technical Report – Software Engineering Institute (SEI)*. Retrieved from http://www.sei.cmu.edu/library/abstracts/reports/10tr033.cfm

Crosby, Philip B. (1979), "Quality Is Free: The Art of Making Quality Certain". New York: McGraw-Hill.

Cross, K.F. and Lynch, R.L. (1988-1989), "The SMART way to define and sustain success", *National Productivity Review*, Vol. 9 No. 1, pp. 23-33.

Deming, W. Edwards. (1986), "Out of the Crisis". Cambridge, MA: MIT Center for Advanced Engineering.

Fetzner, M. A. M. (2010), "Mudança, Afetividade e Resistência: uma perspectiva no âmbito individual para compreender a implementação de Sistemas de Informação nas organizações". PhD thesis. UFRGS.

Ghalayini, A.M., Noble, J.S. and Crowe, T.J. (1997), "An integrated dynamic performance measurement system for improving manufacturing competitiveness", International Journal of Production Economics, Vol. 48 No. 3, pp. 207-25.

Gibson, D. L., Goldenson , D. R., Kost, K., (2006), "Performance Results of CMMI® - Based Process Improvement", *Carnegie Mellon University: Software Engineering Institute*.

Goldenson , D. R., Gibson, D. L. (2003), "Demonstrating the Impact and Benefits of CMMI®: An Update and Preliminary Results", *Carnegie Mellon University: Software Engineering Institute*.

Gomes, C. F., Yasin, M. M., and Lisboa, J. V. (2004), "A literature review of manufacturing performance measures and measurement in an organizational context: a framework and direction for future research", *Journal of Manufacturing Technology Management*, Vol. 15, No. 6, pp. 511-530.

Hazzan, O., Tomayko, J. (2004), "Human Aspects of Software Engineering: The Case of Extreme Programming". LNCS, 2004, Volume 3092/2004, pp. 303-311.

Humphrey, Watts S. (1989), "Managing the Software Process". Reading, MA: Addison-Wesley.

Juran, Joseph M. (1988), "Juran on Planning for Quality". New York: Macmillan.

Kaplan, R.S. and Norton, D.P. (1992), "The balanced scorecard: measures that drive performance", *Harvard Business Review*, Vol. 70 No. 1, pp. 71-9.

Keegan, D.P., Eiler, R.G. and Jones, C.R. (1989), "Are your performance measures obsolete?", *Management Accounting*, Vol. 71, pp. 45-50.

Lynch, R.L. and Cross, K.F. (1991), *Measure up: The Essential Guide to Measuring Business Performance,* Mandarin, London.

Neely, A., Richards, H., Mills, J., Platts, K. and Bourne, M. (1997), "Designing performance measures: a structured approach", *International Journal of Operations & Production Management*, Vol. 17 No. 11, pp. 1131-1152.

Robbins, S. P. (2005), "Comportamento Organizacional". São Paulo: Prentice Hall.

Rocha, A. R. et al. (2005), "Fatores de Sucesso e Dificuldades na Implementação de Processos de Software Utilizando o MR-MPS e o CMMI", Pro Quality. Retrieved from http://www.cos.ufrj.br/~savio/Arquivos/W2MPSBR/rocha_et_al_2005.pdf.

Standard CMMI Appraisal Method for Process Improvement (SCAMPI) A, Version 1.3 (2011): Method Definition Document. Retrieved from http://www.sei.cmu.edu/library/abstracts/reports/11hb001.cfm

4

INFORMATION TECHNOLOGY MANAGEMENT SYSTEM: AN ANALYSIS ON COMPUTATIONAL MODEL FAILURES FOR FLEET MANAGEMENT

Jayr Figueiredo de Oliveira
Getúlio Vargas Foundation, São Paulo, São Paulo, Brazil
Marcelo Eloy Fernandes
Nove de Julho University, São Paulo, São Paulo, Brazil
Carlos Roberto Camello Lima
Methodist University of Piracicaba, Santa Bárbara d'Oeste, São Paulo, Brazil

ABSTRACT

This article proposes an information technology model to evaluate fleet management failure. Qualitative research done by a case study within an Interstate Transport company in a São Paulo State proposed to establish a relationship between computer tools and valid trustworthy information needs, and within an acceptable timeframe, for decision making, reliability, availability and system management. Additionally, the study aimed to provide relevant and precise information, in order to minimize and mitigate failure actions that may occur, compromising all operational organization base functioning.

Keywords: Computer System, Control System, Information Management, Information Technology, Maintenance Management.

RESUMO

Este artigo propõe um modelo de tecnologia de informação para avaliação de falhas na gestão de frotas. A pesquisa qualitativa realizada por um estudo de

Address for correspondence / Endereço para correspondência

Jayr Figueiredo de Oliveira, Pesquisador da EAESP-FGV. Pós-Doutorado em Administração – Administração de Tecnologias da Informação (EAESP-FGV); Doutorado em Educação (PUC-SP); Mestrado em Administração e Planejamento (PUC-SP) e Bacharelado em Administração de Empresas (UNILUS), MBAs em Gestão de Tecnologias da Informação (UNI-FMU) e em Inovação, Tecnologia e Conhecimento (FEA-USP).

Marcelo Eloy Fernandes, Professor e coordenador do Curso de Superior de Tecnologia em Gestão da Qualidade da Universidade Nove de Julho. Doutorado em Engenharia de Produção (UNIMEP), Mestre em Administração de Empresas (FECAP), Bacharelado em Análise de Sistemas (UNIP).

Carlos Roberto Camello Lima, Doutorado e Mestrado em Engenharia Mecânica (UNICAMP). Professor Titular da UNIMEP, Pós-doutorado em Engenharia e Ciência dos Materiais (SUNY - State University of New York) e Ciência dos Materiais e Engenharia Metalúrgica (UB – Univ. de Barcelona). Graduado em Mecânica (UNESP) e Ciências Econômicas (UFS - Universidade Federal de Sergipe).

caso numa empresa de Transporte Rodoviário Interestadual no Estado de São Paulo, propôs estabelecer relações entre as ferramentas computacionais e a necessidade de informações, fidedignas e em intervalos de tempo aceitáveis como válidas, para as tomadas de decisão, confiabilidade, disponibilidade e gestão de sistemas. Adicionalmente, o estudo visou fornecer informações relevantes e precisas, de forma a minimizar e mitigar ações de falhas que possam ocorrer, comprometendo o funcionamento de toda a base operacional da organização.

Palavras-chave: Sistema Computacional, Sistema de Controle, Gerenciamento de Informação, Tecnologias da Informação, Sistemas de Informação.

1. INTRODUCTION

The hereby article presents a computational model for evaluating failures within the Interstate Road Transport System management, typified as a critical operational process.

This computational model is being idealized according to the latest transformations going on in the organizational scenario, where companies need to keep their competitive edge. Customers are their main target, thereforeimplementing strategic actions becomes an essential step towards contributing to an optimized Maintenance Management with a highly reliable processes expectation, preventing impacts and further charges with products and/or provided services.

Souza and Lima (2003) agree with this guideline which, among other proceedings, was adopted by world-class companies as a manner to ensure their survival and competitiveness along with the consequent market growth – the RCM (Reliability Centered Maintenance methodology) process remains.

On JQME's (2010) concept, the continuous search of companies for cost reductions has required the adoption of severe measures regarding their industrial maintenance plans, mainly by retrenchment of excessive inventory replacement parts and upgrading productivity levels along with company's quality.

In this context, maintainability needs to be examined as an important function amid strategic politics towards extracting results from organizations, thus enabling companies to reach competitive market levels alluding to quality and productivity.

Objective

The general goal of this article is to propose a computational model, working as a support and assistance for previewing and anticipating the decision-making moment in transactional processes, with a focal point on a service provider organization of the Interstate Road System for Public Transport.

Arguments

This survey was based on the bellow enumerated aspects:

1) Reduced number of research dealing with the herewith proposed problem;

2) Priority resulting from aspects that could bring about damages to human life and consequently, financial and economic loss to organizations;

3) And finally, on the hampering of integration regarding scattered information amid multiple computational systems, resulting on delays and problematic decision-making.

Thus, this survey's distinctive proposal, while facing analysis that deals with Reliability Centered Maintenance, relies on the fact that they generally have no consideration towards developing an integrated computational model, whose proposal would be to investigate methods with a focal point on Maintenance Management, strictly speaking, maintenance throughout an operational cycle with broader efficiency and competence.

Service providers for the Road Transport System in general and also for those covering longer distances, like the Interstate Road Transport System, demonstrate operations that need, as for performance dominant factors, high availability and reliability. The final consumer for this type of business is inclined to give negative evaluations to variables derived from mechanic failures, lack of maintenance or the unavailability of an appropriate maintenance program.

For the above reasons and because of the gaps left in previous surveys made in this field, the herewith research is developed in order to classify the actual occurring variables, the scenario within and which the recommendations to minimize occurrences linked to procedure failures are.

Therefore, the first argument towards this research shows that after an extensive revision of the literature on Reliability Centered Maintenance and employment of Business Intelligence Technology, it was observed that until then, some issues had not been duly emphasized while indicating specific utilization of resources for Information Systems and computational models, supporting decision-making for projects of maintenance systems targeted towards the Road Transport System segment.

Some surveys and surveyors stand out when the matter deals with understanding the relation between maintenance and the adoption of Information Technology. In order to exemplify this, we have Campos' (1999) proposal, which deals with the employment and support of Information Technology, aiming for problem solutions to fleet vehicle maintenance management based on a knowledge management system.

Furthermore, there is research supporting the first argument, such as research by Almeida Junior (2003), Oliveira (2010) and Santos (2001), who respectively depict comparisons between maintenance variables in information security systems, the correlation between resource dynamics and information system tools for subway transportation systems. Also through considerations on maintenance processes for bus operating companies, it was perceived that this survey highlights differing perspectives from those originally aimed for this research.

On the other hand, the second argument for this study is produced through the awareness that human life is the most important heritage at all times; therefore, assuring integrity, security and reliability for maintenance systems that concern human life ends up being a fundamental consequence.

Lastly, the third argument is based on the privation of integration between maintenance systems and decision-making support systems. Whereas, when information is found scattered throughout diverse computational systems, it becomes an obstacle for distinguishing the level of importance that an injury/accident indicator supervisor has.

Facing the context of the above exposed matter, the argument of this study relies on the interdisciplinary contribution of showing a proposal to disseminate theoretical fundamentals and good managerial practices while using system tools that support decision-making in organizations, as a basis for their day-to-day business and operations.

Thus, what remains is a search to legitimize an efficient adoption of information systems supporting decision-making and expressively helping to upgrade actions, on the matter of maintenance systems for the Road Transport System segment.

2.   RESEARCH PROBLEM

According to Nunes and Valladares (2002, p.19), "RCM is configured as a strategic and organizational tool of the maintenance field that adds value to the productive process".

This means that the triple combination generated by a technical equipment performance,   allied to professional knowledge of those in charge, handling with decision-making tools aligned to organizations' strategy, brings forth confidence and reliability to the operation, improves operational cost management, allowing to reduce failures and occurrences with maintenance.

Facing this line of thought, this research addresses this issue with the following question: "What would be the feasibility of implementing a computational model that generates performance and unforeseen indicators for Road Transport System, characterized as an essential process for your operation?"

3.   BIBLIOGRAPHIC REVIEW

Centering the hereby paper, we will hither initiate a brief review of the applied concepts of maintenance, whose activities have been increasingly prized within organizations. The review focuses on the importance of the maintenance function to prevent or to avoid failures and damages, consequently resulting in quality improvement, while reaching productivity gains for companies.

Maintenance Overview

Maintenance activities have the purpose of keeping equipment in suitable conditions for operating. These activities may be classified as: planned and not planned corrective maintenance; preventive maintenance; predictive maintenance; detective maintenance and maintenance engineering (Pinto and Xavier, 2001).

Thus, understanding that Planned Corrective Maintenance is a correction carried out from a predictive monitoring through managerial decision making, that is to say, performance on the basis of predictive monitoring or the choice to operate until damaged. Moreover, unplanned corrective maintenance happens when it is noticed that the equipment is not producing as expected, owing to its characteristics relying mainly on the maintenance performance of an event that has already occurred, generally resulting in high costs for the company (Pinto and Xavier, 2001).

According to Siqueira (2009), preventive maintenance enables support in conformance with a pre-established schedule presented by the company, aiming to lessen errors and costs, including performance decline. Its execution is focused on minimizing probabilities for equipment failures.

Predictive maintenance aims for the performance of maintenance, only when equipment needs so (Slack, Chambers and Johnston, *et al.,* 2007). Hence, predictive or supervised maintenance identifies incipient failures before they may even become critic; thus, permitting a most precise planning.

Detection maintenance, in general, searches for hidden irregularities that were undetected by equipment or the system operator, usually related to command or to a protection system (Pinto and Xavier, 2001).

Maintenance Engineering incorporates criteria that increase guaranteed availability and reliability amid maintenance activities, where planning and control are developed with the intention of predicting or previewing failures and further optimizing performance of the maintenance production teams. Concluding, they are assignments that develop, implement and analyze results through computerized maintenance management systems (Pinto and Xavier, 2001).

Reliability

Based on constant incidents, around the year of 1950, with failures and diminishment of availability for the electronic systems of the military field, reliability emerges as a topic of interest in the United States of America. This situation has inclusively driven the United States Department of Defense and the electronic industries to create a survey group to research on the subject of reliability (Villemeur, 1992).

Reliability is understood as something that causes a system to work accordingly to what they were designed for, under particular conditions and during a specific period of time (Son, *et. all*, 2009).

Also, the purpose of Reliability Engineering is to identify failures in system modules that are considered critical, aiding further so that these failures do not happen at an operational level (Rausand and Hoyland, 2004).

Conversely, we have the safety that corresponds to the probability of an operating system complying correctly with its duty. Amid extremely risky systems, both functional and informational security is present, being the latter a protection against failures affecting the entire system safeguarding data integrity.

As far as this is concerned, the Road Transport System may use automatic controls to help activate system security mechanisms, keeping in mind the probability of human failure incidences; thus, preventing accidents.

Security terms for high risk systems are commonly used, as follows: exposure; vulnerability; attack; threats; control (Sommerville, 2007).

But when dealing with risk control management, the term ALARP - *As Low As Reasonably Practicable* (see Figure 1), though seldomly used, is of great utility and may be observed as a guideline for adopting control strategies for risk reduction.

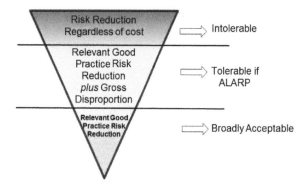

Figure 1 - ALARP Principle.

Source: (IEC, 1997)

It is understood, that the Interstate Road System is a freeway network classified by a high level of accidents and it needs to count on an essentially reliable service in order to transport human lives.

Reliability Centered Maintenance

Failure mode effects that may incidentally occur during a productive process, together with equipment, functions and inter-relations belonging to this field, deserve special attention from the maintenance area.

According to Marçal and Susin (2005), "an effective maintenance process includes all the technical and organizational activities that may guarantee the expected reliability for operating machinery and equipment in general." Maintenance and repairing works that follow particular basic guidelines reduce the chance of having unexpected failures and, as consequence, loss of production, time and unnecessary expenses.

On the other side of the fence, equipment must receive a different treatment, based on their needs and specific importance, thus generating distinctive maintenance policies for different groups of equipment.

According to Siqueira (2009), "one of the characteristics of the Reliability Centered Maintenance (RCM) is to provide a structured method to select maintenance activities for any productive process."

With RCM, working groups can dedicate themselves to upgrading levels of equipment reliability, while concentrating efforts on machinery considered as priority inside the factory structure.

One of the RCM application potentials is by obtaining a maintenance plan with an efficient cost. This method recovers and systematizes knowledge from those involved in its process, thus generating a greater commitment over the performed work.

Data Management and Information Technology

This topic provides information of systems supporting managerial decision-making, along with company's data which are integrated to operational systems, with the aim of improving its performance and reliability.

Data Warehouse

In order to obtain competitiveness and profitability, companies need to control their decision-making process through a faster pace; thus, they need to react with increasing agility while changing their environment, which usually happens through analysis, scheduling and performing tactical actions or suitable strategies.

O' Brien (2008) has reported that a *Data Warehouse* stores information from current and later years, drawn from various operational data banks of an organization. It is basically an already classified, edited, standardized and integrated central data source, that may be used by managers and other final pro users, for a wide range of arrangements and business analysis, market research, and decision-making support.

This resource integrates and consolidates information for various collections; it also dimensions and consolidates data, organizing it with the aim of improving consultation performance. Namely, the Data Warehouse may be considered as a factory of enterprise information .

Kimball (1998) specifies some goals for a Data Warehouse; the main ones are:

a) Provide organizational or corporate data access;

b) Keep reliable and consistent data, in accordance with the company's criteria;

c) Separate, combine and catalogue data so to facilitate and be available for any possible visions of business;

d) Supply means for consulting, analyzing and presenting information;

e) Guarantee reliable data publishing; to assure data quality in order to support business re-engineering.

Data Mart

Data Mart makes part of a *Data Warehouse*. Even though it has a small capacity, its employment attends a department of the company with the same characteristics of the Data Warehouse (Singh, 2001).

Data Mart is denominated this way because it was created from a Data Warehouse with an enterprising scope, where a central data warehouse serves the whole organization or where it creates smaller decentralized warehouses which are the so called Data Marts.

Data Mart usually focuses on a single area of interest or a specific business line, thus permitting it to be set up at a faster pace and at smaller costs, compared to setting up a Data Warehouse with an enterprising scope.

Data Mining

Data Mining storage capacity goes through an everyday challenge, because there is a major growth of data available. So that Data Mining along with all its tools enables a data "mining", in order to generate a solid value of facts, transforming them into knowledge and information. As far as this is concerned, Data Mining may be looked at as a method that searches and detects logic or mathematical descriptions, which are often of complex nature, with sequences and orderliness in a set of data search detecting patterns, associations, adjustments, anomalies, statistic structures and data events.

Data Mining has the following purposes (Elmasri and Navathe, 2002):

a) forecasting – demonstrating how certain attributes will be behave in the future;

b) identifying – the data pattern is used to identify the existence of an element, situation or activity;

c) classifying – data is categorized into different classes and identified based on a combination of parameters;

d) optimizing resources.

BSC (Balanced Score Card)

In order to measure a company's performance, a financial report is usually employed based on assets that enable showing profits or losses; however, the intangible assets have nowadays also become a source of competitive advantage.

So the *Balanced Scorecard (BSC)* emerges, a strategic tool that employs elements capable of supplying such demands. Kaplan and Norton (1997, p. 08), exemplify that:

> "Financial measures reveal the history of past events, an adequate account from companies of the industrial era, when long-term investment capacities and customer relationships were not fundamental for success."

According to Kaplan and Norton (1997, p. 08), "A *Balanced Scorecard* structure is formed through four perspectives: financial, clients, internal processes, and strategic training and growth."

BSC is focused on a search for financial objectives, and also on attributes embedded in the company's mission, and they are a reflection of the vision and strategy of the organization for all the four dimensions of this appliance and thus, for each perspective, besides objectives, goals must be established, and procedures and performance indicators implemented.

Hence, the system enables administrators with a financial performance follow-up of the company, auditing alongside the growth process for capacity construction. In other words, aligning the current performance and focusing on future performances of the company, thus encouraging managers to direct their attention to factors that conceive economic value.

Operationally speaking, these indicators distributed amongst four managerial processes, which contribute to long-term strategic goals bound to short-term actions, precisely, it explains and interprets strategy and vision; communicates and associates objectives and strategic measures; plans and establishes goals aligning strategic enterprises; improves feedback and strategic apprenticeship.

Computational Environment Proposal

This item demonstrates the development of an itinerary for the computational model of maintenance focused on reliability, correlating them to Kimball's (1998) nine steps. It performs the display of a pattern and describes the proposal for generating probability indicators for Road Transport System. Further still, it provides support and outlines the initial feats of the Brazilian Interstate Road Transport System.

General Script Elaboration

While elaborating a script for a computational model for maintenance management focused on reliability, Kimball's (1998) nine steps may be useful; considerations are described o=un the stages below:

1st) Choosing process – process is selected (or functions) on a Data Mart subject in particular;

2nd) Choosing granularity – based on the former chosen stage, granularity of elements to be stocked is chosen and a fact table is developed;

3rd) Identifying dimensions – constructing a list of dimensions so to determine the context of questions about facts at the fact table;

4th) Choosing facts – granularity of the fact table determines facts that may be used at Data Mart. All facts should be expressed at the suggested level by granularity;

5th) Stocking preliminary calculations in the fact table – once facts are selected, they should be reexamined in order to determine whether there is a chance of using preliminary calculation;

6th) Dimension table rounding off – return to dimension tables and add the highest possible text descriptions to dimensions;

7th) Choosing data bank duration – decisions on data records life cycle. The duration refers to the length of action of the fact tables;

8th) Determining dimensional changes – stocking old dimension descriptions should be used as a record of former transactions;

9th) Deciding on consultation priority – subjects that are considered as critical should be studied and treated while assembling Data Mart, pursuing utmost security on transactions.

General Itinerary for Development and Performance Indicators

It is within this topic that we will locate the description of a proposal on contingence indicators planning for Road Transport System. In its core, the proposal gathers a set of information that represents in a detailed manner, operational processes, implicated computational resources, a main source of information assortments, as well as an analysis of the main points of failure for the surveyed model.

In order to be able to analyze questions on the technical and functional feasibility of this paper , we have managed to develop a diagram, shown in Figure 2, in such a manner as to represent the hierarchy of logic steps towards the stages of each assignment, as follows:

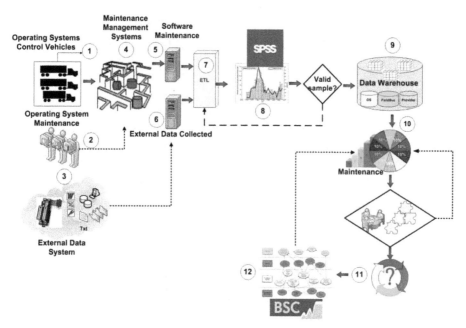

Figure 2 – Computational Model for analyzing Maintenance Indicators

Source: (Authors, 2010)

- Failures and information supply sources: starting from the sketching and auditing of procedures done in the company, aligned to people concerned with maintenance management and operations, it was possible to detect that the main failure sources were among operational systems for vehicle control (1), maintenance operational systems (2), and the external data system (3), that contain data on the electronic reading system installed inside the company's vehicles. Incidences generated from the external data system did not gain a direct access, bearing in mind that this system does not make part of the company's conventional net, since it is a highly available system. However, all the failures detected by the operational control system were registered at the external data providers and maintenance (5 and 6), as well as registered data into work order for a future historic evaluation.

- Collection process, handling and data transference: all collection processes, handling and data transference from system data (4, 5 and 6) are done twice a day by the ETL tool (7) (Extracting, Transforming and Loading), thus ensuring, that the character of the imported information is consistent, upstanding, correct, complete, not redundant and adherent to decision-making through the company's needs.

- Data storing: after the ETL process (7), data is stored on the server (8). The collected data from maintenance transactional systems is stored in the form of selected dimensions, each one set in their own dimensional model inside the *Data Warehouse (8)*.

- OLAP (*On Line Analytical Processing*): along with data already available in the *Data Warehouse (9)*, the organization's managers (10) may begin strategic modeling for decision-making through graphic consultation and/or personalized reports, molded through the organization's needs.

- Feedback process: after an analytical search through the OLAP (On-line Analytical Processing) layer (9), expectations towards secure strategic decision-making, guarantee actions directed to system quality upgrading.

It may be observed that the above described environment has made the information cycle generated by the company most likely to be understood, as well as facilitating visualization and accomplishment of possible testing on analytical and decision-making processes, made necessary in this paper. It is expected, in this particular case, a half day break for updating information on the analytical environment, thus meeting the expectations of participating managers for the company decision-making process.

The concept of Reliability Strategic Indicators (Indicadores Estratégicos de Confiança (IEC)) is originated from the survey and definition of the following authors: Kaplan and Norton (2000), who utilized the *BSC* (*Balanced Scorecard*) method, as a main factor for the Key Performance Indicators (KPI) search. We must hereby highlight that the hereby handled Strategic Indicators were evaluated and adjusted in accordance with the reality of this case survey. As represented in Figure 3, the indicators of this survey have established technological parameters for factors related to acquisition, implantation, expansion and the pursuit of modernizing the current equipped systems of the company. Still on the maintenance point of view, strategies related to maintainability and reliability of equipment operating in corporations were duly defined.

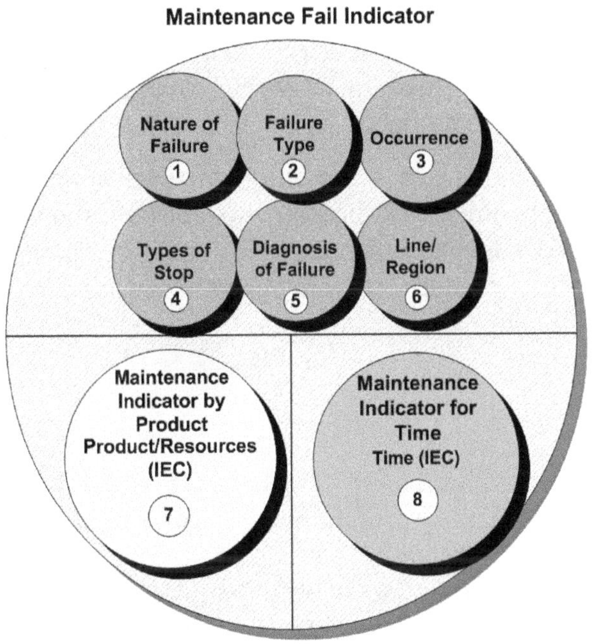

Figure 3 – Strategic Indicators Applied to Maintenance.

Source: (Authors, 2010)

Proceeding, Strategic Indicators will be described, suggested and extracted from this case survey, as follows:

1º) **Failure Aspect Indicator** (1): this indicator is related to the intersection of occurrences with Aspects and equipment Failures;

2°) **Failure Type Indicator** (2): this indicator is related to the type of failure occurring with equipment, measured by the mode (mechanic, electric, structural and human failure,) by type of failure (ductile, fragile, fatigue, thermic fatigue, mechanic fatigue, electric fatigue, corrosion, abrasive, pressure, torsion, magnetic, overcharge, over-tension, knowledge, attention   and deterioration);

3°) **Occurrence Indicators** (3): this indicator deals with items like work order   numbers, type of service, among other;

4°) **Halt Indicators** (4): this indicator deals with halt cases checking for errors   (repair, test, alignment, calibration, lubrication, revision, caster, adjustment,   replacement, cleaning, etc.);

5°) **Failure Diagnosis Indicator** (5): this indicator identifies failure diagnosis symptoms that are related to: overheating, electric crash, high-voltage, motor   abnormal noise, viscosity, wheel abnormal noise, smoke, pigmentation,   coloring, improper signaling, fairing abnormal noise, electric charge evasion,   abnormal trepidation, loss of pressure, oil odor, etc.;

6°) **Line/Region Indicator** (6): this item highlights granularity of data related to   line number, origin, destiny, region and distance between origin and destiny;

7°) **Product x Resource Indicators** (7): this indicator rescues groups of products: air-conditioning, cooling device, gearbox, chassis, differential, steering wheel, electric components, brake, metal repair, cleaning, motor, rolling and   suspension; related to products;

8°) **Time Indicator** (8): this indicator is valid through time variable, according to   established: year, semester, trimester, two months, month, fortnight, week,   days, hours and minutes; other variables are - still hours, hours of service   attendance, standby hours, preventive hours, availability, occurrence hour, etc..

4.   METHODOLOGY

According to Godoy (2007), there are three possible methods to carry out a qualitative research: documental research, case study and ethnography. The hereby adopted qualitative method will use a case study from a company located in the whereabouts of São Paulo, whose operational process meets with the proposal of this project, in other words, it includes critical and complex operations for the Interstate Road Transport System mode.

As reported by Miguel *et.al.* (2010), "amid the qualitative viewpoint, the subjective reality of individuals involved in the survey is considered relevant and contributes to the development of the survey."

The survey is made with a big sized organization, whose segment is the Interstate Road Transport System. The hereby sample is according to the required profile for this study, since it works inside an environment where total reliability is a must for management and application of their operational processes.

Nowadays, the company has significant expenditures with maintenance due to its inherent critical condition, a justification towards which implementing a system that integrates their equipment to a RCM management with a more precise communication net would definitely enable a substantial expense decrease.

Motivated by this case study and with the implementation of a computational model, it is estimated that this company will be able to save expenses with maintenance, which will possibly be progressively reduced and shown during the course of this survey.

According to Miguel *et.al.* (2010) "among the main benefits of leading a case study is the possibility of developing new theories and increasing understanding towards genuine and contemporary events."

Originally, data collection happens by attaining information from the maintenance staff, by means of a previously obtained historical record. Equipment has failure records sourced from their last three years of operation. However, we will only take in consideration components with higher levels of failure propensity and consequent influence on the operational cycle halt, generating high maintenance costs and production loss for this company.

This information will be stored into the RCM programs and integrated to Communication Nets, thus, enabling in advance the delivery of information to the Maintenance Engineering, reporting any situation involving excessive usage or an 80% useful life cycle, proceeding without ceasing the operational cycle.

Equipment records should also be obtained from suppliers in a detailed manner, so to include every single part of the equipment and accessories considered as most urgently important in terms of maintenance when submitted under stressing conditions, as critical process cases may be.

Under Gil's (2002) opinion, "researches may be classified following the proposed objectives and/or with the employed techniques and procedures. Regarding objectives, researches may be exploratory, descriptive or explanatory."

Further in this paper, we further adopt "Theoretical Reference" for the Bibliographic Research, which is a work development whose research problem requires a mere theoretical approach. Although, with almost all research works it becomes necessary some type of labor of this nature, as bibliographic research in this undertaking is exclusively developed from bibliographic sources or papers.

In turn, the researched company's profile in this paper belongs to the Interstate Road Public Transport, which already has fifty years of activity in the Brazilian market.

The company headquarters is located in the Northern region of São Paulo city, near the great Highway Service Centre of the city, which remains as a competitive determinant and distinctintive center, because of the easy availability of vehicles. The service is offered to most of the interior cities and Capital of São Paulo State, owning a fleet of approximately 1,235 buses.

One of the characteristics of this bus fleet is providing comfort to the customer; by aiming at this; the fleet is equipped with modern video and music center equipment, air-conditioning and constant investments with the acquisition of new vehicles.

Regarding considerations with security and bus maintenance, the company usually renews its fleet every two years and executes maintenance after 15,000 km of road running for new vehicles; for those vehicles which have already ran a bit more, maintenance is done after 8,000 km, according to indications of the Instruction Manual.

Being the company's maintenance area the most important and best equipped section, investments are very elevated, roughly R$15 million with components, replacement parts, automation and maintenance fleet management.

The corporate philosophy is that all buses should be submitted to a general revision after ending the day's route; further still, there is a training-bus project that runs throughout the country (Brazil) retraining mechanics and drivers.

The company currently employs more than ninety employees to manage the organization's maintenance; these employees include from mechanical engineers to mechanics trained at the bus supplier's factory, both with lots of operational and business experience.

Buses run up to 900 km of daily journeys, serving millions of people traveling from their homes to other states and municipalities that are very distant from the State of São Paulo. Although the company worries mostly about their service quality, many of the maintenance services are still done through manual work orders, which are transcribed to spreadsheets, generating error probabilities and delays for the decision-making processes.

Another important aspect to be highlighted, for the *in loco* visit done biweekly at the organization since 2009, is the fact that fleet vehicles, manufactured between the years of 2008 and 2010, already have a Fault Detection technology installed within them (*Fieldbus*). Consequently, it has been possible to collect incidents and failure statistics data directly from the source, through reading the application software embedded in the Fieldbus Pattern and language based on an eXtensible Markup Language (XML) Technology.

Subsequently, this information could be transferred to the database of a maintenance control system, where they could be evaluated through a distribution and correlation analysis with their own software. Hence enabling scores and creating a suitable environment for analyzing reliability, thus identifying existing mechanism failures within the installations and probable statistic tendencies.

5.   OUTCOME

This Balanced Scorecard was highlighted from results obtained throughout various tools used during the development of this paper, with which the company's board of directors, management and technical staff carried out many meetings during December 2009, to score through future workable goals to be practiced from January 2010. Figure 4 represents the hereby mentioned strategic map:

Vision	"Being		considered the company in 2011 Interstate transportation model"			
Strategic Themes	Focuson SegmentB	Competing with Environmental Responsibility	Consolidate Operations	Based management information	Expandingthe network	Operate in the segment of Transportation
Finance	Pursue goals of Results	Regulate financial situation and generate cash flow		Generate net income of 6% per month	Eliminate Waste with Corrective Maintenance.	Search Sources of Funding to Grow.
Market	Develop Model to Prevent Failure	Develop Service Model	New Partnes	Consolidationof CorporateImage	Expansion and Fleet Management and Routes	Working in New Business / Study Related Markets
Internal Processes	Mitigate Corrective Maintenance	Informatics Tool	Organize Financial Administrative Area	Organize KPI s	Management Information System	Implement SAD / Maintenance Workshop
People	Empowering Employees	Developing People			Incentives and Participation	
Mission	"Providing the best quality in road transport systems, leading reliability for consumers."					

30/06/07 30/06/08 30/06/09 30/06/10 30/06/11

Figure 4: *Balanced Scorecard.*

Source: (Authors, 2010)

This scoreboard, originated from various debates, illustrates the main points to be worked on, so that the company may be definitely considered a model for the Interstate Transportat System segment, thus providing better quality services to consumers.

Amid this scenario, the managers have structured the above mentioned scoreboard within four perspectives: Financial; Market; Internal Processes and People.

As for Financial perspectives, there are five aspects to be taken in consideration: aiming effective outcomes (sales increase, growth and profits); regulating the financial situation and generating cash flow; producing a 6% liquid profit per month and saving a part of it for expansion; eliminating squandering with corrective maintenance actions; and searching for financing sources in order to grow and expand into new markets.

Within this context, when the subject is maintenance, enterprise managers have perceived that many problems related to this subject are due to a lack of systems with the ability of signalizing the company's actual situation and with the capacity to also integrate all types of information.

Regarding to Market perspectives, managers have delineated seven important parameters, as follows: developing a preventive model for failures; developing service models; new partners working towards the construction of a consolidate enterprise image; expansion planning and fleet and route management; new businesses scheming; and analyzing correlative markets.

These guidelines are intrinsically linked, since all problems that the company had been facing in a recent past and which had been provoking negative consequences, were directly linked to its maintenance; from then on and in order to improve their market image, they begun to develop a new failure prevention model, with a R$7 million investment on Technical Support Systems and Information. Thus new failure prevention models were designed, causing faults to be examined and noticed beforehand, together with service models developed and performed to work efficiently faster.

It has become evident that regarding Internal Processes, managers have started to worry about: Corrective Maintenance; consolidating Informatics application and tools; organizing the financial managerial field; structuring performance indicators; implementing information management; implementing SAD; and organizing mechanical workshops and maintenance so to minimize costs and maximize processes; thus; searching for a better appreciation of human management in their processes.

Another important point to be highlighted in this article is that before implementing the computational model, data remained totally disperse, that is to say, no information integration was available. Resulting in an excessive time demand for managers while analyzing a problem, consequently, delaying decision-making, as shown in a diagram form by Figure 5 below:

Scenario A: The process prior to implementation of the computational model

DT (Decision Making) = $\Delta T1$ $\Delta T2$ + + + $\Delta T3$ $\Delta T4$ + $\Delta t5$

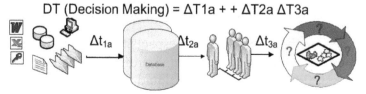

Scenario B: After the implementation of the computational model

DT (Decision Making) = $\Delta T1a$ + + $\Delta T2a$ $\Delta T3a$

Figure 5 – Scenario for Before and After Implementing Computational Model.

Source: Authors, 2010

It became clear that many of the gathered variables by the new system were minimized and surveyed, as for instance, the feature "decision-making duration" which in the past, because of information dispersion, was most tardy. With the new computational model we have regained around a 40% "speed of response to failure".

With this new computational model, information is upgraded with speed since, while dealing with it, those professionals involved have become alert and aware of how to interpret what is going on, thus the employee knows how to proceed and monitor every happening.

6. FINAL CONSIDERATIONS

Results in this paper have presented meaningful gains for operational issues, as well as for features related to fleet vehicle business procedures and management, mainly for the organization linked to the Interstate Road Transport System.

Another important aspect that deserves to be highlighted is the significant time decrease for decision-making. Time slackening for information withdrawal, data unification into a single and reliable repository, paper flux reduction for decision-making process and information dissemination to other fields of the organization have led to the strengthening of operational systems, maintenance and strategy itself.

Pertinent to the strategic question, it has become evident that the proposed computational model integrated to the Balanced Scorecard method was very useful, while implementing the Balanced Scorecard, where we have the possibility to diagnose failures and anomalies.

Related to strategy amid the surveyed company, what mostly called the managers' attention was the wastefulness resulting from a corrective maintenance. With the approach of maintenance centralized on reliability, conceived from the researcher's interface with the company, proposing statistically demonstrated indicators, all the wastefulness of the company became evident.

Within this context, the company has also started to search for new partners, that like them, work on a philosophy based on reliability, in such a manner that their corporate image may consolidate not only in their clients but also in their suppliers, in employees, and in all those participating in the productive chain. Then, it will be possible to work with new businesses and service goods aimed at farthest places, for instance, offering trips to Brazil's neighbor countries, while collecting and distributing goods fortransportat services scheduled in the same trip, thus benefiting from the same vehicle for the service. This was due to a decrease of vehicle breakdowns and guaranteed fleet availability, enabling a wide and new range of business offers.

Regarding internal processes, this survey has been of determinant impact on the managerial decision-making process of the company, while verifying the possibility of consolidating proper tools for decision-making support, as well as the implementation of Managerial Information Systems together with management Indicators.

While analyzing "People's" perspective, managers realized the urgency to entitle employees; develop citizens; provide stimulus and participation. This is a natural process, since when various tools are proposed where information is supplied, there still remains the need to delegate to employees, so that they may interpret data and information and also be able to execute.

The oldest employees should be properly trained, since most of them still bring with themselves the mentality that all this progress going on is only a trend and/or that everything has always worked that way and will continue the same.

Yet amid this strategic scenario, a new computational model has given strategic mobility to the company in order to simulate results, preview failure tendencies and model new environments.

Another significant outcome for this survey, deals with accessibility simulation and analysis for synthetic data as well as for data analytical sampling. Computational tools carry deep insight on business intelligence, thus aiding with simulations and queries generated through an OLAP search and favoring access to key performance indicators of the company.

Perhaps, it may be affirmed that the initially proposed objectives for this paper have been attained and that adopting the hereby dealt with computational resources, supported by the case study, have brought competitive advantages to business and to the environment among which this survey was carried out.

7.   LIMITATIONS AND SUGGESTIONS

Amid continuity possibilities for the same research line, surveys that enable a deep analysis on reliable strategic indicators in different surroundings may be enhanced as appropriate.

Another continuity possibility for this survey is related to knowledge management application for RCM systems through software and modeling supported by decision-making as its primary tool.

Increasing the number of evaluated variables for the Data Warehouse model, or else trying to understand a new model of Information Load that enables diminishing data loading duration and quality of generated data are all also possibilities for enlarging this research.

Still further in this aspect, it is recommended that the proposed model may be compared to other computational tools focused on business management linked to maintenance, as for instance; Reliability Engineering (*Weibull distribution*), RCM, MCC, XFMEA.

Lastly, trying to implement an RCM process with knowledge systems like *Common*KADS, which stimulates integration between software engineering and knowledge engineering, suggests other research lines.

REFERENCES

Almeida Junior., J. R. (2003). *Segurança em Sistemas Críticos e em Sistemas de Informação:* Um Estudo Comparativo, São Paulo, 191 p. Tese – Escola Politécnica da Universidade de São Paulo.

Campos, F. C., (1999). *Proposta de interface para apoio à gestão da manutenção de frotas de Veículos.* São Carlos, 247 p. Teses (Doutorado) – Escola de Engenharia de São Carlos, Universidade de São Paulo.

Elmasri, R.; Navathe, S. B. (2002). *Sistemas de banco de dados: fundamentos e aplicações.* Rio de Janeiro: LTC.

Gil, A. C. (2002). *Como elaborar projetos de pesquisa.* São Paulo: Atlas.

Godoy, E. P. (2007). Desenvolvimento de uma ferramenta de análise de desempenho de redes CAN (Controller Area Network) para aplicações em sistemas agrícolas. *Dissertação (Mestrado em Engenharia) - Escola de Engenharia de São Carlos, Universidade de São Paulo.* São Carlos.

IEC – Functional Safety Electrical/Electronic/Programmable – IEC 61508-1 STD 4-1997 . (1997). *Electronic Safely Related Systems.* International Electrotechnical Comission.

Inmon, W. H.; Hackarthorn, R. D. (1997). *Como usar o Data Warehouse.* Rio de Janeiro: IBPI Press.

JQME, Journal Of Quality In Maintenance Engineering. (2010). *Maintenance Information Systems,* in Emeral, ISSN 1355-2511, January.

Kaplan, R. S.; Norton, D. P. (1997). *A estratégia em ação: balanced scorecard.* Rio de Janeiro: Elsevier.

_____. (2000). *A organização orientada para a estratégia: como as empresas que adotam o balanced scorecard prosperam no novo ambiente de negócios.* Rio de Janeiro: Campus.

Kimball, R. (1998). *Data Warehouse.* São Paulo: Makron Books.

Marçal, R. F. M.; Susin, A. A. (2005). *Detectando falhas incipientes em máquinas rotativas. Revista Gestão Industrial.* 1(21), p. 87.

Miguel, P. A.C. (org.) (2010). *Metodologia de pesquisa em engenharia de produção e gestão de operações.* Rio de Janeiro: Elsevier.

Nunes, E. L.; Valladares, A. (2002). Potencialidades da MCC para a gestão integrada da manutenção e da mudança de organizações. *XXII Encontro Nacional de Engenharia de Produção Curitiba* – PR, 23 a 25 de outubro de 2002.

O'brien, J. A. (2008). *Sistemas de informação e as decisões gerenciais na era da internet.* São Paulo: Saraiva.

Oliveira, A., (2010). *Análise inteligente de falhas para apoiar decisões estratégicas em projetos críticos,* Tese apresentada na Universidade de São Paulo.

Pinto, A. K.; Xavier, J. N. (2001). *Manutenção: função estratégica.* Rio de Janeiro: Qualitymark.

Rausand, M.; Hoyland, A. (2004). *System reliability theory: models, statistical methods and applications.* N. York: Wiley.

Santos, J. E., (2001). *Considerações sobre o processo de manutenção para empresas operadoras de ônibus urbanos de porte médio.* Brasília, 177 p. Dissertação de Mestrado – Universidade de Brasília.

Singh, H. S. (2001). *Data Warehouse: conceitos, tecnologias, implementação e gerenciamento.* São Paulo: Makron Books.

Siqueira, I. P. (2009). *Manutenção centrada na confiabilidade: manual de implementação.* Rio de Janeiro: Qualitymark.

Slack, N.; Chambers, S.; Johnston, R. (2007). *Administração de Produção.* São Paulo: Atlas.

Sommerville, I. (2007). *Engenharia de Software.* São Paulo: Addison Wesley.

Son, Y. T.; Kim, B. Y.; Park, K. J.; Lee, H. Y.; Kim, H. J.; Suh, M. W. (2009). *Study of RCM-based maintenance planning for complex structures using soft computing technique. International Journal of Automotive Technology.*10(5), p.635-644.

Souza, S. S.; Lima, C. R. C. (2003). Manutenção Centrada em Confiabilidade como ferramenta estratégica. *XXIII Encontro Nac. de Eng. de Produção* - Ouro Preto, MG, Brasil.

Villemeur, A. (1992). *Reliability, Availability, Maintainability and Safety Assessment.* Assessment, Hardware, Software and Human Factors. John Wiley & Sons.

5

INFORMATION TECHNOLOGY GOVERNANCE IN PUBLIC ORGANIZATIONS: HOW PERCEIVED EFFECTIVENESS RELATES TO THREE CLASSICAL MECHANISMS

GOVERNANÇA DE TI EM ORGANIZAÇÕES PÚBLICAS: COMO A EFETIVIDADE PERCEBIDA SE RELACIONA COM TRÊS MECANISMOS CLÁSSICOS

Gelson Heindrickson
Tribunal de Contas da União, Brasilia, DF, Brazil
Carlos D. Santos Jr.
University of Brasilia, Brasilia, DF, Brazil

ABSTRACT

Information technology (IT) governance has received a lot of attention lately, with a growing strategic importance currently being given to IT by both public and private organizations. This justifies the existence of a body of scientific literature on IT governance, to which this paper belongs and makes an attempt to contribute to. Towards that end, an empirical study was performed involving 57 public organizations of the Brazilian federal administration, examining the relationship between three governance mechanisms – IT steering committee, IT solution manager, and IT investment portfolio management process and IT governance effectiveness. Based on the literature review, a conceptual model was developed to express the causal relations that these constructs were expected to hold with one another. Through a custom-designed questionnaire submitted to over 180 federal public employees, the causal model was tested using mediation analysis and mostly confirmed. Results indicate that Portfolio Management should always be taken into account for analyses that aim to evaluate the effects of IT steering committees and solution managers on IT governance effectiveness. This means that a nonexistent or an underperforming Portfolio Management Process can lead to a reduction or cancellation of the potential positive

Address for correspondence / Endereço para correspondência

Gelson Heindrickson, Tribunal de Contas da União, Assessoria de Segurança da Informação e Governança de TI

Carlos D Santos Jr., PhD, Laboratório de Estudos Avançados sobre Dados Abertos e Software Livre,Programa de Pós-graduação em Administração (PPGA) Dep. de Administração (ADM)

Universidade de Brasilia (UnB)

contributions of the other two mechanisms to IT governance. By informing decision makers and public managers at some of the main federal public organizations in the country on how to plan and deploy IT to promote a more effective governance, the conclusions presented herein fill a previous knowledge gap in the complementarity and the joint effectiveness of three IT governance mechanisms on the IT dynamics of key public organizations.

Keywords: IT governance; Public organizations; Public administration; Effectiveness; Governance mechanisms; Information Technology; Mediation analysis; Governance.

RESUMO

A Governança de TI é uma área de estudos recente que tem despertado muito interesse devido à importância cada vez maior da Tecnologia da Informação (TI) para as organizações, sejam elas públicas ou privadas. Isso justifica a existência de uma literatura científica sobre o tema governança de TI na qual este estudo se enquadra e para cujo desenvolvimento busca contribuir. Para tanto, realizou-se pesquisa empírica envolvendo 57 organizações públicas integrantes do governo federal brasileiro na qual foram examinadas as relações entre três mecanismos de governança – Comitê de TI, Gestores da Solução de TI e Processo de Portfólio de Investimento em TI – e a Efetividade da Governança de TI. Com base na literatura revisada, um modelo conceitual foi proposto para expressar as relações que esses construtos deveriam ter uns com os outros. Um questionário foi desenvolvido com base nesse modelo e aplicado a mais de 180 servidores públicos federais. As relações Causais foram testadas com análise de mediação e detectadas, em sua maioria, de acordo com o modelo. Os resultados indicam que o desempenho do Processo de Portfólio deveria sempre ser considerado em análises que tenham por objetivo avaliar os efeitos de Comitê de TI e de Gestores da Solução na efetividade da governança de TI. Isso significa que a não existência ou o baixo desempenho do Processo de Portfólio pode reduzir ou anular a contribuição positiva dos outros dois mecanismos para a efetividade da governança de TI. Por informar tomadores de decisão e gestores dos resultados em algumas das principais organizações da administração federal brasileira no planejamento e utilização TI em busca de efetividade da governança, as conclusões apresentadas neste artigo preenchem um vazio de conhecimento sobre as complementaridades e os efeitos de três mecanismos de governança na dinâmica dessas organizações.

Palavras-chave: Governança de TI; Organizações públicas; Administração pública; Efetividade; Mecanismos de governança; Tecnologia da Informação; Análise de mediação; Governança.

1. INTRODUCTION

Information Technology (IT) is currently considered a critical and strategic asset for organizations, both public and private (Affeldt & Vanti, 2009; Albertin & Albertin, 2008a; Albertin & Albertin, 2008b; Assis, 2011; ISACA, 2012).

In order for an institution to obtain the benefits expected from IT use, at acceptable levels of risk and cost, IT governance must be established and maintained (ABNT, 2009; Assis, 2011; Machado, 2007; Ramos, 2009). IT governance can be understood as a set of policies, organizational structures, work processes, roles and responsibilities that are established by the top management in order to steer IT actions and exert control over the use and management of IT throughout the institution (Mello, 2006; Mendonça, 2013; ISACA, 2012).

Studies carried out at the international level by Weill & Ross (2006) and at the national level by Lunardi, Becker & Maçada (2012) reveal that companies that had implemented IT governance performed better in comparison to those that did not or those with a deficient implementation.

An IT governance mechanism that is often mentioned in literature and recommended by audit entities such as TCU – the Brazilian SAI (Supreme Audit Institution) – is the IT Steering Committee or IT Executive Committee (BRASIL, 2008). Surprisingly, a study carried out by Ali & Green (2012) has not identified statistically significant relationships between the action of the IT steering committee and the effectiveness of IT governance, reaching a paradoxical conclusion. That study, though gave priority to private companies and the sample was intentionally filtered in order to include only institutions with a certain level of indirect execution (outsourcing) of IT activities. Therefore, it would not be appropriate to generalize the conclusions of that study to all situations. Further investigations are required. Additionally, it must be taken into account that the respondents to the Ali & Green (2012) survey were representatives of only one group of stakeholders of enterprise IT: IT auditors.

This apparent contradiction provided the initial motivation for the present study as it pointed out the need for investigation that would take into account the specificities of public institutions and engage other stakeholders. Another motivation was the opportunity to include the observation of two IT governance mechanisms in the analysis, which, according to the theoretical framework surveyed, would be closely related to the actions of the IT Executive Committee, namely: the IT Investment Portfolio Management Process and the IT Solution Manager.

Another aspect that has raised our interest in carrying out the present research was the lack of materials available in terms of best practice models, scientific papers and publications in general specifically addressing IT governance in public institutions.

Hence, based on widely disseminated assumptions regarding good practices in IT governance, the aim of the present study is to empirically investigate the relationships that exist between the following IT governance mechanisms at federal public institutions: IT Investment Portfolio Management Process, IT Steering Committee and IT Solution Manager.

Accordingly, our research question is: "How does the action of the IT Committee and of IT Solution Managers relate to the performance of the IT Investment Portfolio Management Process and how do these three mechanisms interact with the effectiveness of IT Governance?". It should be highlighted that only federal public institutions have been included in this research and that we did not aim for an institutional perspective, but for the personal perception of public employees representing the multiple stakeholders of the IT organization.

This paper provides empirical evidence that sheds new light on the relationships that exist between the IT governance mechanisms investigated. It can support public institutions in their implementation of IT governance, as well as provide input for recommendations issued by auditing authorities to the entities under their jurisdiction.

Below, is a brief theoretical framework on the effectiveness of IT governance and the governance mechanisms that have been evaluated and presented, followed by a description of the methods used in the research. Later, we present the results obtained and discuss our conclusions and final remarks.

2. THEORETICAL FRAMEWORK

2.1 IT governance effectiveness

Effective IT governance contributes to improved IT performance, which, on its turn, contributes to improved organizational performance (Assis, 2011; Machado, 2007; Mendonca et al., 2013; Weill & Ross, 2006). But, one might ask, what is an improved organizational performance? A quite objective answer is provided in Cobit 5, an important IT governance framework, that associates IT performance and organizational performance via the creation of value for the business and clarifies that "creating value is to realize benefits at optimal resource cost whilst optimizing risk" (ISACA, 2012, p. 17).

Value creation can also be described as the achievement of certain IT objectives related to certain generic corporate goals, applicable to all organizations (ISACA, 2012, p. 18, Figure 4). These objectives aim to ensure the following aspects, among others: that planned actions and those under way in the IT departments be aligned with the organization's business strategy, so as to give priority to the most important requests of the business to the IT department; that meeting these requests should be in compliance with the requirements, deadlines, quality and the costs agreed; that costs and risks of IT initiatives should be managed and that the expected benefits of the IT actions carried out should be achieved (ISACA, 2012b).

Along the same lines, Dolci & Maçada (2011) have identified a comprehensive set of benefits targeted by organizations regarding different dimensions of IT investments.

As a higher degree of fulfillment of objectives leads to the creation of greater value – which implies in a greater effectiveness of IT governance – this causal relationship justifies the use of the aspects addressed by the objectives mentioned in the questions of the survey form that evaluated the effectiveness of IT governance (Appendix A, item 4).

2.2 IT investment portfolio management

Portfolio management has become a popular topic following the publication of Markowitz (1952), aimed at financial markets. McFarlan (1981) and Ward (1990) have pioneered the use of the portfolio approach in selecting IT investments.

Studies carried out by Weill, Woerner & Rubin (2008) have followed up on the evolution of the use of the IT governance concepts and practices by large private international corporations. In the national scenario, Moraes & Laurindo (2003) have shown positive results obtained from the implementation of the IT project portfolio management process. Dolci & Maçada (2011), was based on case studies carried out with national companies with high investments in information technology, have identified the most important aspects to be considered by the four dimensions usually taken into account regarding IT investment portfolios.

Cobit 5 (ISACA, 2012b) includes IT investment portfolio management among decision-making tools and for supporting the monitoring of actions associated to IT management and use. In this model, the topic is addressed by the following processes and practices:

a)   In the domain of IT governance: EDM02.01 *Evaluate value optimisation*, EDM02.02 *Direct value optimization* and EDM02.03 *Monitor value optimisation*;

b)   In the domain of IT management: APO05.01 *Establish the target investment mix*, APO05.02 *Determine the availability and sources of funds*, APO05.03 *Evaluate and select programmes to fund*, APO05.04 *Monitor, optimise and report on investment portfolio performance*, APO05.05 *Maintain portfolios* and APO05.06 *Manage benefits achievement*.

In the ValIT framework (ITGI, 2008), IT investment portfolio management is addressed under the Portfolio Management (PM) domain. Its objective is to guarantee that organizations may obtain optimal value for its IT investments. Practices associated with portfolio evaluation and balancing fall within this domain, as well as the definition of criteria for these activities. ValIT also addresses the follow up of the portfolios overall performance.

Valuable information sources on how to establish or improve the IT investment portfolio process are: the ITIM framework, designed and published by the United States General Accounting Office (GAO, 2004) and the study carried out by Weill, Woerner & Mcdonald (2009). The standard defined under The Standard for Portfolio Management (PMI, 2008) and the model proposed by Archer & Ghasemzadeh (1999) differentiate themselves in one aspect: they are not limited to the management of IT portfolios, but are also applicable to the management of institutional program and project portfolios in general.

As described by the above-mentioned sources, the objective of the IT investment portfolio management process is to optimize the use of institutional resources, so as to select a set of projects and programs capable of providing the greatest possible returns to the organization. Selected projects and programs must be aligned with corporate strategies and, according to the methodology, their risks, costs, quality, deadlines and levels of service must be properly managed. It has been said that, in order to meet its objectives, a portfolio management process requires the definition of decision-making structures and the fulfillment of some common stages or phases. Despite the fact that each model uses slightly different names, the main ones are: identification and analysis of components/projects, selection and prioritization of components, authorization, monitoring, reviews and risk management. Requirements for portfolio management are project management and program management, but are not limited to them.

This set of characteristics described in literature has provided input for the phrasing of the survey questions that evaluated the performance of the governance mechanism of the IT Investment Portfolio Process (Appendix A, item 1).

The objective and the characteristics of the portfolio management process are clearly congruent with the objectives of the so-called focus areas of IT Governance: strategic alignment, value delivery, resource management, risk management and performance measurement (ITGI, 2007). Hence, it is reasonable to consider the following hypothesis: improvements in the performance of the IT investment portfolio process have a positive influence on the effectiveness of IT governance (hypotheses H3 in Figure 1).

2.3 IT solution manager

There are several different names for the "IT Solution Manager" governance mechanism: business executive, business area, project or investment sponsor or business process owner. In the present article we have chosen to use "IT Solution Manager", as it can be applied to the whole life cycle of an IT solution; it also is less restrictive, as IT may support not only business processes in the strict sense of the word, but also administrative processes, support processes and even processes of the IT department itself.

The role of the TCU IT Solution Manager is internally regulated by TCU Administrative Order no. 156 of 2012 (BRASIL, 2012), whereas other public entities have their own norms on that issue.

It should be noticed that, even though restricted to situations involving the provision of contract-based IT solutions, Normative Instruction no. 4/2010 of the Secretariat for Logistics and Information Technology of the Ministry of Planning, Budgeting and Management (SLTI), the central authority of the System for the Administration of Information Resources and Information Technology of the Federal Executive Power (SISP), defines some attributions of the IT Solution Manager role in the items that address the responsibilities of the contracting planning team (BRASIL, 2010).

Within the ValIT framework (ITGI, 2008), the relevance of the IT solution manager role is expressed in the *Investment Management* (IM) domain of that model. Its objective is to guarantee that individual portfolio components may contribute to generating value for the organization. This domain includes practices related to the identification of business requirements, expected benefits, as well as the preparation of the *Business Case*, a document that issues a formal request and registers essential information about the initiative. It also addresses the follow up of individual performance, i.e., monitors the fulfillment of the benefits of the program or project throughout their life cycle.

In Cobit 5 (ISACA, 2012b), the responsibilities of the IT Solution Manager are presented under different items of the framework. The "RACI" tables show the responsibilities attributed to the Business Executive or the Business Process Owner, i.e., to the unit or sector benefitting from the investments in the IT solution. That can be noticed, especially, in the description of the following processes, key practices and activities of Cobit 5: BAI01 *Manage Programmes and Projects* (several key practices), BAI02 *Manage Requirements Definition* (several key practices), APO12 *Manage Risk,* APO05.06 *Manage benefits achievement,* APO09.03 *Define and prepare service agreements* and PO09.04 *Monitor and report service levels.*

According to the IT Governance Institute, an IT Solution Manager is responsible for: acting as the sponsor of the IT solution, defining business requirements for the IT solution; defining and controlling levels of service for the IT solution; continuously evaluating the benefits of the IT solution; evaluating the risks to the business that are associated with the IT solution; providing resources and establishing priorities for the IT solution, among other responsibilities (ITGI, 2003, p. 51).

Peppard, Ward & Daniel (2007) have revealed that the value of IT investments can only be obtained by means of an ongoing identification and management of the benefits achieved throughout the whole life cycle of the IT solution. And this is the responsibility of business managers, i.e., this responsibility lies with those who we have called "IT Solution Manager".

For the purposes of this study we have considered that the IT Solution Manager is the organizational unit with the greatest interest in the investment, development or hiring of an IT solution (be it a system, software, app or service provided by the IT department). It should be noted that, even though the operational activities of the IT Solution Manager can be delegated to sub-units, departments or specialists, this is not relevant to the analysis proposed in this study.

The questions of the survey that evaluated the performance of the IT Solution Manager governance mechanism were based on the set of characteristics described in literature (see Appendix A, item 3).

The responsibilities of the IT Solution Manager described herein can be easily related to the common roles found in portfolio process models, such as the sponsor and program manager roles (PMI, 2008), including activities that are considered necessary at certain stages or phases of a portfolio management process, especially during the *identification, authorization, review and report,* and *risk management* stages (PMI, 2008), as well as during the *individual project analysis, project development* and *phase-gate evaluation* phases (Archer & Ghasemzadeh, 1999). Therefore, the following hypothesis is to be considered: improvements in the actions of IT solution managers have a direct and positive influence on the performance of the IT investment portfolio process (hypothesis H2 in Figure 1). Likewise, this simple logical and causal relationship seems to indicate that several attributions of the IT Solution Manager can contribute to the fulfillment of the following objectives of IT Governance focus areas: value delivery, resource management, risk management and performance measurement (ITGI, 2007). Therefore, it is reasonable to consider the following hypothesis as well: improvements in the performance of IT solution managers have a direct and positive influence on the effectiveness of IT governance (hypothesis H5 in Figure 1).

2.4 IT Steering Committee

Weill & Ross (2006) have evaluated large numbers of large international corporations over several years and report that IT Steering Committees are important governance mechanisms used by top performing companies. Castro & Carvalho (2010) also have identified the need for a committee composed by representatives of several different areas of the organization to take decisions regarding the selection and prioritization of projects. Likewise, a case study that has been evaluated by Moraes & Laurindo (2003) shows positive results deriving from the joint participation of managers from IT and business areas in the decision-making associated to the selection and prioritization of projects.

The organization is responsible for establishing an IT Steering Committee, composed of directors and managers from the IT and business areas. Among other responsibilities, as established in Cobit 5 under APO01.01 *Define the organizational structure* key practice, that the committee should: "determine prioritisation of IT-enabled investment programmes in line with the enterprises business strategy and priorities; track status of projects and resolve resource conflicts; and monitor service levels and service improvements" (ISACA, 2012b).

Cobit 5 (ISACA, 2012b) also presents other attributions of the IT Steering Committee in its "RACI" tables. That can be especially noticed in the descriptions of the following processes, key practices and activities: BAI01 *Manage Programmes and Projects* (several key practices), APO12 *Manage Risk*, and APO05.06 *Manage benefits achievement.*

According to the IT Governance Institute, it is the responsibility of the IT Steering Committee to: participate in the approval of new IT solutions; evaluate the alignment of proposals for new IT solutions with the organizational strategies; define priorities for projects; ensure that all costs and benefits of the proposals for new IT solutions have been identified; guarantee that projects are being risk-managed; follow up the progress of relevant IT projects, among other responsibilities (ITGI, 2003, p. 52).

According to TCU, all public organizations, in addition to other actions, must establish an IT steering committee, "in order to provide for the allocation of public resources in accordance with the organization's needs and priorities" (BRASIL, 2008). In compliance with its own recommendations, the TCU has implemented a governance mechanism, as part of the Court's internal processes, for that end, called IT Management Committee. The responsibilities of the Committee are established under TCU Resolution no. 247/2011 (BRASIL, 2011) and TCU Administrative Order no. 156/2012 (BRASIL, 2012).

In line with the best IT governance practices and the recommendations of the audit entities, the SISP Information Technology General Strategy (*Estratégia Geral de Tecnologia da Informação* – EGTI) for the 2011-2012 period also foresees the establishment of IT Committees by the organizations that are part of the system (BRASIL, 2011b).

The IT Committee that was evaluated by this study holds the characteristics and attributions of the IT steering committee described in the sources mentioned above, having thus set the basis for the drafting of questions for the survey questionnaire which have evaluated the governance mechanism (Appendix A, item 2).

It can be easily noticed that the attributions of the IT steering committee described herein are related to the usual roles found in portfolio process models, such as the Portfolio Review Board and the Portfolio Manager roles (PMI, 2008). Their activities are considered necessary during the stages or phases of a portfolio management process, especially during the prioritize, balance, authorize, review and report and risk management stages (PMI, 2008), or during the *optimal portfolio selection* and *phase-gate evaluation* (Archer and Ghasemzadeh, 1999) phases. Hence, the evaluation of the following hypothesis is applicable: improvements in the action of the IT committee have a direct and positive influence on the performance of the IT investment portfolio (hypothesis H1 in Figure 1).

Additionally, it can be noticed that there are intersections between the attributions of the IT Steering Committee and the following objectives of the IT Governance focus areas: strategic alignment, value delivery and risk management (ITGI, 2007). Therefore, it is reasonable to consider the following hypothesis as well: improvements in the performance of the IT Steering Committee have a direct and positive influence on the effectiveness of IT governance (hypothesis H4 in Figure 1).

2.5 Conceptual model

This study intends to investigate the conceptual model presented in Figure 1. The variables analyzed – which are often mentioned in several parts of this document – match the identifiers shown in brackets in each rectangle of the figure: COMITE, GESTSOL, PROCPORTF and EFETGOVTI.

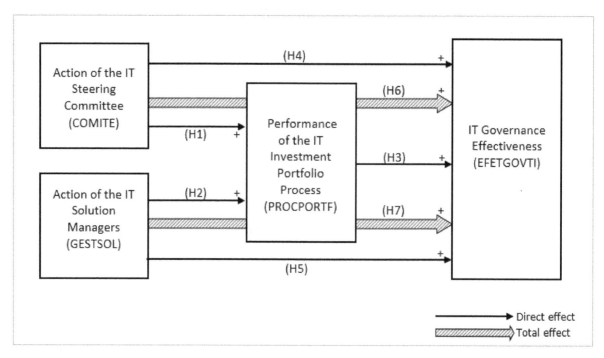

Figure 1 – Conceptual model and hypotheses

The hypotheses that will be evaluated in this study, concerning the relationships between governance mechanisms and between these and IT governance effectiveness, are represented by arrows and identifiers in Figure 1, namely:

a) H1: Improved action by the IT steering committee has a direct and positive influence on the performance of the IT investment portfolio process.

b) H2: Improved action by IT solution managers has a direct and positive influence on the performance of the IT investment portfolio process.

c) H3: Improved performance of the IT investment portfolio process has a direct and positive influence on IT governance effectiveness.

d) H4: Improved action by the IT steering committee has a direct and positive influence on IT governance effectiveness.

e) H5: Improved action by the IT solution managers has a direct and positive influence on IT governance effectiveness.

f) H6: The overall effect of improvements in IT steering committee action is positive on IT governance effectiveness, i.e., the balance between the direct and indirect effects, via portfolio process, of IT committee action on IT governance effectiveness is a positive one.

g) H7: The overall effect of improvements in IT solution manager action is positive on IT governance effectiveness, i.e., the balance between the direct and indirect effects, via portfolio process, of IT solution manager action on IT governance effectiveness is a positive one.

3. METHODS

The survey was done through a questionnaire made available over the Internet between October 10th, 2012 and October 15th, 2012. Federal public servants made up the target audience, encompassing the following IT stakeholders in the participating organizations: internal IT clients, IT servants, internal auditors and IT consultants, encompassing managers and non-managers.

The survey was distributed via email to the representatives of the *TI Controle* community, which gathers several IT managers from federal public institutions. SLTI sent the same survey to public servants that had subscribed to the entity's portal as well. Additionally, the survey organizer spread it to its contacts and provided a website to facilitate the collection of information and access to the form by interested respondents.

The four questions of the questionnaire that evaluated IT Steering Committee action (COMITE), the five questions that evaluated the IT Solution Manager action (GESTSOL) and the five questions that evaluated the IT investment portfolio process (PROCPORTF) had been drafted based on the main characteristics of these governance mechanisms, as described in academic studies, best practice models and other literature sources reviewed. All questions related to independent variables and mediator (COMITE, GESTSOL and PROCPORTF) had been measured according a 5-point Likert scale, which evaluated two dimensions for each question: i) the relevance of the question for IT governance effectiveness, as perceived by the respondent; ii) the degree to which the action or activity proposed by the question had been fulfilled by the institution, according to the respondent's perception. Figure 2 is an example of how these two dimensions evaluated for one of the questions addressing the COMITE variable.

2.4 The IT committee follows up/monitors the realisation of benefits, costs and risks of the most important IT solutions, during the project phase and the operations and maintenance phase.

	1	2	3	4	5
What is said is FULFILLED by the institution	⌒	⌒	⌒	⌒	⌒
It is IMPORTANT to fulfill what is said	⌒	⌒	⌒	⌒	⌒

Figure 2 – Sample question for the evaluation of the "relevance" and "fulfillment" dimensions

The dependent variable – IT governance effectiveness (EFETGOVTI) – was evaluated through a proxy: the respondents' satisfaction regarding the achievement of objectives and the realization of the benefits that are expected from good IT governance and management, aiming at the creation of value for the organization, as stated in the literature review section. The six questions regarding this variable were also evaluated based on a 5-point Likert scale.

For each variable analyzed in the survey, Chart 1 summarizes the main reference sources on the topic and the questionnaire items (Appendix A) that represent the questions used for measuring these variables.

Variable	Main Bibliographic References	Questionnaire Questions (Appendix A)	Cronbach's Alpha Coefficient
PROCPORTF	MCFARLAN, 1981; WARD, 1990; ARCHER & GHASEMZADEH, 1999; GAO, 2004; ITGI, 2008; PMI, 2008; WEILL, WOERNER & MCDONALD, 2009; ISACA, 2012b.	Items 1.1 to 1.5	0.7938
COMITE	ITGI, 2003, p. 52; MORAES & LAURINDO, 2003; WEILL & ROSS, 2006; BRASIL, 2008; CASTRO & CARVALHO, 2010; BRASIL, 2011; BRASIL, 2011b; BRASIL, 2012; ISACA, 2012b; ALI & GREEN, 2012.	Items 2.1 to 2.4	0.8523
GESTSOL	ITGI, 2003, p. 51; ITGI, 2007; ITGI, 2008; PEPPARD, WARD & DANIEL, 2007; BRASIL, 2010; ISACA, 2012b; BRASIL, 2012.	Items 3.1 to 3.5	0.7841
EFETGOVTI	WEILL & ROSS, 2006; DOLCI & MAÇADA, 2011, Figure 2, p. 363; ISACA, 2012, p. 18, Figure 4; ISACA, 2012b, p. 226, Figure 17.	Items 4.1 to 4.6	0.8273

Chart 1 – Variables, bibliographic references and questionnaire questions

For the independent variables and the mediator variable (COMITE, GESTSOL and PROCPORTF), their measurement in each answer was calculated as follows: for each question that is part of the variable, the average value obtained from the answers of all respondents to the "question relevance" dimension was used as a weight that was applied to each answer to the "degree of fulfillment" of the question. The weighted average of the set of questions of a variable times its weights, converted into a 10-point scale, generated a final average of this variable in each answer. The strategy for calculating the measure of a variable based on its components is based on the stated preference weights approach (Decancq & Lugo, 2010, p. 17), according to which the relevance/weight is defined by the respondents themselves.

For the dependent variable (EFETGOVTI), the average measure for each answer was calculated based on the simple average of values to the answers to their questions, converted into a 10-point scale. This strategy for calculating the measure of a variable based on its components was based on the expert opinion weights approach

(Decancq & Lugo, 2010, P. 16); all sources mentioned in the theoretical framework were considered experts – with an equivalent relevance – which provided the basis for the selection of questions.

The selection of items used for measuring the variables is fully justified as it is based on the opinions of respondents and of experts on the topic, according to the previously mentioned approaches. Nevertheless, we also carried out a statistical analysis of the internal consistence or reliability of the questionnaire items that make up each variable of the study. Chart 1 shows that the values of Cronbach's Alpha coefficient obtained for each variable fall within the acceptable range, that is, between 0.70 and 0.95 (Tavakol & Dennick, 2011). It also has been found that the eventual exclusion of items would not improve the Alpha coefficient value in none of the variables, which reinforces the relevance that is given to the items by literature.

The model presented in Figure 1 shows that the IT Steering Committee and the IT Solution Manager can have a direct effect on IT governance effectiveness, as well as indirect and total effects through the Portfolio Process. To evaluate the direct effects shown in this figure, we used the multiple regression analysis technique. In order to take into account the indirect and total effects, the mediation analysis statistics method was used in the study. Its aim is to test the relationships observed between a set of independent variables and a dependent variable upon the inclusion of an additional variable, known as mediator. In the mediated model, the hypothesis is that the independent variable influences the mediator variable, which, on its turn, influences the dependent variable. To be highlighted is that the models that can be analyzed with the method are not limited to three variables and can be applied to several models, with any number of dependent variables and mediator variables. The importance of this type of analysis has achieved notoriety following the studies by Baron and Kenny (1986), and very effective modern techniques are currently available, such as those mentioned by MacKinnon (2008) and Hayes (2009).

We used the "R" statistical software to calculate Cronbach's Alpha coefficient and carry out the multiple regression analysis, as well as the auxiliary correlation tests used in this study. For the mediation analysis we have used the SPSS® Statistics software and the "MEDIATE" (Hayes, 2012a) and "PROCESS" (Hayes, 2012b) macros, which are support tools available on the internet that can be accessed and used by the general public.

4. RESULTS

Below we present the characteristics of the sample and the results of the tests described in the previous section. To test the hypotheses shown in Figure 1, we initially explore the existing correlations between the variables and evaluated the direct effects by means of a multiple regression test. Next, in order to obtain the final results, we used the mediation test.

4.1 Sample characteristics

Sample characteristics (N=189)

Characteristic	Qtty.	Perc.	Characteristic	Qtty.	Perc.
Institution (*)			*Gender*		
ANATEL	5	2,6%	Male	155	82,0%
BACEN	3	1,6%	Female	34	18,0%
CÂMARA DEP.	4	2,1%			
CAPES	4	2,1%	*Has taken some course on*		
CGU	3	1,6%	*IT governance*		
DATAPREV	3	1,6%	Yes	131	69,3%
MDIC	3	1,6%	No	58	30,7%
MIN. PLANEJ.	6	3,2%			
MIN. FAZENDA	3	1,6%	*Works in the IT department*		
SENADO FED.	19	10,1%	*of the institution*		
STN	3	1,6%	Yes	151	79,9%
TST	3	1,6%	No	38	20,1%
SERPRO	3	1,6%			
TCU	72	38,1%	*Type of job/position*		
Others	55	29,0%	Management	92	48,7%
			Non-management	97	51,3%
Working years at the					
institution			*Works as IT auditor, IT*		
Less than 3 years	43	22,8%	*consultant or IT advisor*		
3 to 6 years	41	21,7%	Yes	84	44,4%
6 to 12 years	41	21,7%	No	105	55,6%
12 to 20 years	30	15,8%			
More than 20 years	34	18,0%			

(*) only institutions with at least 3 respondents are mentioned

Table 1 – Sample characteristics

Table 1 presents the distribution of respondents with regards to important grouping characteristics. Other peculiarities of the sample can be found in Appendix B. We had a total of 189 respondents, associated to 57 different institutions, and about one third of all respondents were TCU employees. The large number of TCU respondents can be explained by the fact that the research organizer works at TCU, which has facilitated communication and access to people. An analysis of the rate of respondents in relation to the requests made is not applicable as the main means of divulgation outside TCU were not under the control of the research organizer (indirect means: divulgation made by the IT Control Community and by SISP to its members).

4.2 Preliminary Analysis

The correlation test calculated the Pearson product-moment for each pair of variables and the multiple regression test allowed to estimate coefficients for the calculation of PROCPORTF based on COMITE and GESTSOL and for the calculation of EFETGOVTI based on these three variables. The results are summarized in Table 2 and Table 3, respectively.

Variable	Average	Standard Deviation	Correlations			
			COMITE	GESTSOL	PROCPORTF	EFETGOVTI
COMITE	6.33	2.08	1	-	-	-
GESTSOL	6.11	1.58	0.38***	1	-	-
PROCPORTF	6.03	1.59	0.41***	0.48***	1	-
EFETGOVTI	5.64	1.35	0.35***	0.40***	0.58***	1

Obs.: N=189; ***$p < 0.001$; ** $p<0.010$; * $p<0.050$; ^$p<0.100$

Table 2 – Averages, standard deviations and correlations between variables

As shown in Table 2, initial results indicate there is a statistically significant correlation between all variables of the model, which could support the validity of some of the hypotheses presented in Figure 1.

	D i r e c t e f f e c t s	
Variable	**Coefficients to calculate PROCPORTF**	**Coefficients to calculate EFETGOVTI**
COMITE	0.21*** (H1)	0.07 (H4)
GESTSOL	0.37*** (H2)	0.11^ (H5)
PROCPORTF	-	0.41*** (H3)

Obs.: N=189; ***$p < 0.001$; ** $p<0.010$; * $p<0.050$; ^$p<0.100$

Table 3 – Results of the regression tests, with estimates for the direct effects of COMITE and GESTSOL over PROCPORTF and of these three variables over EFETGOVTI

Additionally, the results of the regression test, shown in Table 3, indicate that the direct effects of GESTSOL and COMITE over PROCPORTF are substantial and statistically significant, which allows us to accept hypothesis H1 and H2 of Figure 1. The direct effects of PROCPORTF over EFETGOVTI also have a high value and are statistically significant, which confirms hypothesis H3 of Figure 1.

The direct effects of GESTSOL and COMITE over EFETGOVTI evaluated by the regression test, though, demonstrated to be small and are not statistically significant, with confidence levels lower than 95% and 90%, respectively, which leads us to reject hypotheses H4 and H5 of Figure 1.

4.3 Mediation analysis

According to the mediation analysis theoretical framework, the direct effect is calculated the same way as in the regression analysis, whereas the coefficient that measures the value of an indirect effect is given by the product of the coefficients of the mediated direct effects. The total effect, though, is calculated as the sum of the direct and indirect effects that have been measured between the same variables. Additionally, data must be submitted to hypothesis tests that allow the validation of the estimated values for such effects, that is, if they can be considered statistically significant (Baron & Kenny, 1986; Mackinnon, 2008; Hayes, 2009).

As seen, the preliminary regression analysis has rejected the direct effects of COMITE (H4) and GESTSOL (H5) on EFETGOVTI, which could discourage the performance of tests regarding the proof of total effects (H6 and H7). Nevertheless, it is known that a variable can have a positive total effect on another variable even though a direct effect is not identified (HAYES, 2012b). This is because its effect may occur through a third variable, a mediator.

In fact, the mediation analysis performed afterwards with the support of the "MEDIATE" macro (Hayes, 2012a) revealed statistically significant indirect effects and total effects, at a confidence level higher than 95% of the GESTSOL and COMITE variables on EFETGOVTI variables when considering the PROCPORTF variable as a mediator. In view of the results of the mediation analysis shown in Table 4, hypothesis H6 and H7 of Figure 1 can be accepted regarding the total effects of COMITE and GESTSOL over EFETGOVTI, respectively.

Variable	Direct effects Over EFETGOVTI	Indirect effects via PROCPORTF	Total effects over EFETGOVTI
COMITE	0.07	0.08~	0.15** (H6)
GESTSOL	0.11^	0.15~	0.26*** (H7)

Obs.: N=189; ***p< 0.001; ** p<0.010; * p<0.050; ^p<0.100; ~ i interval LLCI-ULCI does not contain 0

Table 4 – Mediation test results, with estimates of the direct, indirect and total effects of COMITE and GESTSOL over EFETGOVTI

The mediation test was configured to simulate 10,000 samples or bootstrap samples, while the recommendation by Hayes (2009) is to use at least 5,000. It should be underscored that, in mediation tests using the bootstrap technique, the interpretation of the probability or confidence level of the indirect effect is not based on a "p" value, but on the values resulting from the LLCI-ULCI interval: if the interval does not contain a zero value, the mediation hypothesis is accepted (Hayes, 2009; Hayes 2012a; Mackinnon, 2008).

In view of the high number of TCU respondents in the sample, the mediation test was repeated by excluding the answers of these participants, for comparison with the results obtained from the full sample. Despite the variations in the values of estimated coefficients for the reduced sample, it was found that the calculated direct, indirect and total effects presented similar results and led to statistically significant levels of confidence, such as those obtained from using the full sample.

4.4 Consolidated results

Figure 3 summarizes the results obtained from the mediation test: each path or hypothesis presents the estimated regression coefficient, rounded to two decimal places, as well as their statistical significance.

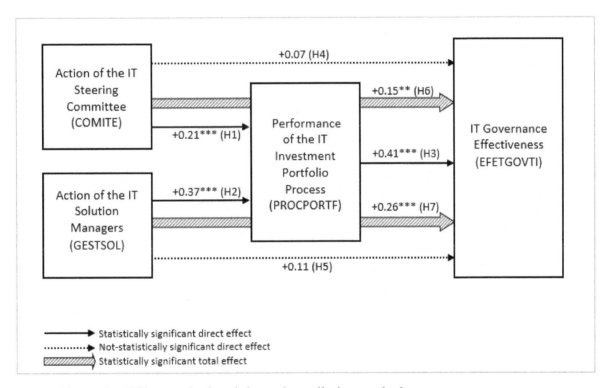

Figure 3 – Effects calculated through mediation analysis

The result of the mediation analysis allows us to discuss how the evaluated IT governance mechanisms relate to each other and with IT governance effectiveness. These relationships and effect sizes, on average, are summarized below on a scale from 0 to 1, which is typical of statistical regression and mediation tests:

a)   Each point of improved performance in the IT investment portfolio process is equivalent to 0.41 point of improvement on IT governance effectiveness (as per H3 in Figure 3);

b)   Each point of improved IT Steering Committee action is equivalent to 0.15 improvement on IT governance effectiveness (as per H6 in Figure 3);

c)   Each point of improved IT Solution Manager action is equivalent to 0.26 point improvement on IT governance effectiveness (as per H7 in Figure 3);

d)   Each point of improved IT Steering Committee action is equivalent to 0.21 point improvement on the performance of the IT investment portfolio process (as per H1 in Figure 3);

e)   Each point of improved IT Solution Manager action results on a 0.37 point improvement on the performance of the IT investment portfolio process (as per H2 in Figure 3).

It should be noted that in the case of COMITE and GESTSOL, this summary has considered the total effects on EFETGOVTI, as the result of the mediation analysis certifies that the effects these mechanisms indirectly exert on IT governance effectiveness, through its influence on the IT investment portfolio, are significant.

These results allow us to reach some important conclusions that can contribute to a better understanding of the specific topic being analyzed herein for the evolution of IT Governance as a field of study, and act as practical guidance for public organization leaders, managers and auditors regarding the implementation of the analyzed governance mechanisms, the planning of derived actions and in identifying training needs.

Because COMITE (H4) and GESTSOL (H5) have not been found to have statistically significant direct effects on EFETGOVTI, but that statistically significant total effects exist, and considering the mediation of PROCPORTF (H6 and H7), an important conclusion is: eventual efforts to improve the action of the IT Steering Committee and/or of IT Solution Managers depend on the existence of an Investment Portfolio Process in order to have relevant effects on IT governance effectiveness.

Finally, it can be concluded that the control entities and best-practice models mentioned in the conceptual sections of the paper are correct to recommend the use of the governance mechanisms analyzed herein, as the present study provides evidence of their contribution to the effectiveness of IT governance.

4.5 Other findings

In addition to the conclusions related to the research question and hypotheses presented in the conceptual model shown in Figure 1, other interesting findings, associated to the different group perceptions, are presented in Appendix B.

Even though these findings are not directly related to the research question and with the primary objective of the study, we took advantage of the opportunity offered by the collected data and carried out some additional exploratory analyses. The results of which are presented next, aiming at encouraging future complementary research on the topic.

In order to carry out these analyses, we used the Microsoft Excel® software and non-parametric tests provided by the XLSTAT add-in.

With regards to the perceived relevance of the three mechanisms for assessing IT governance effectiveness analyzed in the study (COMITE, GESTSOL, PROCPORTF), the evaluation has led to rather high averages for all groups, with a small standard deviation, as can be seen in Table B1, B2 and B3 of Appendix B. Despite unanimous agreement on the relevance of the mechanisms, there is statistically significant evidence of differences in the perception of the groups, namely:

a)   Regarding the relevance of the IT Portfolio Process, there is evidence that groups that have taken a course on IT governance and those that have not do have different perceptions. The same difference exists between IT personnel and IT client personnel, as well as between IT auditors/consultants and non-IT auditors/consultants (Table B1);

b)   Regarding the relevance of the IT Steering Committee, there is evidence of different perceptions between the respondents of other institutions and TCU respondents, as well as between the group that took the IT governance course and the group that did not take the course, as well as between IT auditors/consultants and non-IT auditors/consultants (Table B2);

c)   With regards to the importance of the IT Solution Manager, there is evidence of different perceptions by the group that took the course on IT governance and the group that did not, and also between IT auditors/consultants and non-IT auditors/consultants (Table B3).

There also is evidence of differences in perception between groups regarding the relevance of the eventual causes of non-effectiveness of IT governance that have been evaluated, as shown in Table B4:

a)   Reasonable difference in perception between TCU respondents and the respondents from other institutions regarding the relevance of Cause 1 – insufficient IT personnel, and also regarding Cause 4 – insufficient financial resources;

b)   Reasonable difference in perception between IT personnel and IT client personnel regarding the relevance of Cause 1 – insufficient IT personnel, Cause 2 – lack of technical training by IT personnel, Cause 5 – lack of exploitation of alternatives for the provision of IT solutions, and Cause 6 – lack of management training by IT personnel;

c)   Reasonable   difference   in   perception   between   IT auditors/consultants and non-IT auditors/consultants regarding the relevance of Cause 4 – lack of financial resources.

It is important to note, regarding the results presented in Appendix B, that there is evidence that little difference exists in the perception of the group that exerts a management position and the group that does not carry out this type of activity. This is the case both for the perception about the relevance of the three IT governance mechanisms evaluated (tables B1, B2 and B3), as well as for the perception of the relevance of the six causes of the non-effectiveness of IT governance (table B4) that have been evaluated.

5. CONCLUSIONS

The present study analyzed the relationships between three well-known governance mechanisms and the effectiveness of IT governance in Brazilian federal public institutions. Empirical evidence shows that the performance of the IT Steering Committee and of the IT Solution Manager has a positive influence and considerably affects the performance of the IT Investment Portfolio Process. It also shows that these three mechanisms have a positive influence on the effectiveness of IT governance. The influence of the IT Investment Portfolio Process is direct, quite high, statistically significant and easily detected by means of a simple regression analysis. The direct influences of the IT Steering Committee and of the IT Solution Managers on IT governance effectiveness were not proven at statistically significant levels. Nevertheless, the use of a more robust statistical analysis allowed us to detect statistically significant total effects of these two mechanisms on the effectiveness of IT governance, when the IT Investment Portfolio was considered as a mediator. This suggests that, in order to be effective, efforts to improve the performance of the IT Steering Committee or of IT Solution Managers depend on the existence of the IT Investment Portfolio Process. It should be highlighted that the need to use the mediation analysis technique must not be interpreted as some type of weakness in the effects observed: it only indicates that the mechanisms analyzed interact in a more complex way, thus also requiring more sophisticated techniques for the appropriate analysis of their effects.

It also should be noted that the results of this study should not necessarily be interpreted as a causal relationship between variables, considering that the specific investigation techniques and statistical methods required for providing such evidence were not used (ideally, controlled experiments). Therefore, the terms "influence" and "effect" used in the study in order to facilitate describing the relationships between the governance mechanisms that were evaluated are better interpreted as a factual reflection of the value variations of a variable in relation to the values presented by another variable, irrespective of the identification of the primary cause of this phenomenon.

The performing of this study faced funding and time restrictions that resulted in certain limitations that must be considered when interpreting the results. First, the sample size may be considered limited, given the number of federal public organizations that exist in the country. Second, the disproportional number of respondents per institution may be considered small in some cases and quite large in others, as in the case of TCU, with possible effects on the values estimated by the statistical calculations, a consequence of the different levels of IT governance maturity encountered in the organizations. Third, the fact that the analyzed model did not take into account other IT governance mechanisms, which were intentional, in order to simplify the survey questionnaire and not to discourage respondent participation. However, the absence of other mechanisms implies that other relationships were not evaluated. We suggest that researchers with interest in further deepening the work done in this study may find ways of reducing the aforementioned limitations.

On the other hand, this study has innovated in some important aspects, such as taking into account the opinion of the respondents to assess the relevance of the questions, in addition to the measurement of their fulfillment and the application of the questionnaire to a broad target audience. This audience represented several key IT stakeholders in public organizations, including directors, managers, internal clients and IT technical staff.

Remembering that IT governance is the responsibility of higher-level management, normally the board of directors (Weill & Ross, 2006; ABNT, 2009; BRASIL, 2010b; ISACA, 2012), the results of this study can be used as input for decision-making by public organization leaders regarding the implementation of the governance mechanisms analyzed. They may also support the organization's IT managers and IT governance staff in the identification of training needs and in the planning of communication and educational actions, based on the conclusions presented in Figure 3 – regarding the hypotheses tested based on the conceptual model of Figure 1 – as well as based on the other findings related to the differences in perceptions between groups, as detailed in Appendix B.

REFERENCES

ABNT. **ABNT NBR ISO/IEC 38500/2009 - Governança corporativa de tecnologia da informação,** 2009.

Affeldt, Fabrício S.; Vanti, Adolfo A. Alinhamento estratégico de tecnologia da informação: análise de modelos e propostas para pesquisas futuras. **Journal of Information Systems and Technology Management**, v. 6, n. 2, p. 203-226, 2009.

Albertin, A. L.; Albertin, R. M. M. Tecnologia de Informação e Desempenho Empresarial no gerenciamento de seus projetos: um estudo de caso de uma indústria. Revista de Administração Contemporânea (Printed), v. 12, p. 599-629, 2008a.

Albertin, A. L.; Albertin, R. M. M. Benefícios do uso de Tecnologia de Informação para o desempenho empresarial. Revista de Administração Pública (Printed), v. 42, p. 275-302, 2008b.

Ali, S.; Green, P. Effective information technology (IT) governance mechanisms: An IT outsourcing perspective. **Information Systems Frontiers**, v. 14, n. 2, p. 179-193, 2012.

Archer, N. P.; Ghasemzadeh, F. An integrated framework for project portfolio selection. **International Journal of Project Management**, v. 17, n. 4, p. 207–216, 1999.

Assis, C. B. Governança e gestão da tecnologia da informação: diferenças na aplicação em empresas brasileiras - **dissertação de mestrado**. Escola Politécnica da Universidade de São Paulo (Poli/USP). 2011.

Baron, R. M.; & Kenny, D. A. The moderator-mediator variable distinction in social psychological research: Conceptual, strategic, and statistical considerations. **Journal of Personality and Social Psychology**, v. 51, n. 6, p. 1173-1182, 1986.

BRASIL. Tribunal de Contas da União. Acórdão n° 1.603/2008, Plenário, 2008.

BRASIL. Ministério do Planejamento, Orçamento e Gestão. Secretaria de Logística e Tecnologia da Informação. Instrução Normativa n° 04, de 2010, 2010.

BRASIL. Tribunal de Contas da União. Sumários Executivos - Levantamento de Governança   de   TI   2010,   2010b.

BRASIL. Tribunal de Contas da União. Resolução TCU n° 247/2011, 2011.

BRASIL. Ministério do Planejamento, Orçamento e Gestão. Secretaria de Logística e Tecnologia da Informação. Guia para Criação e Funcionamento do Comitê de TI, 2011b.

BRASIL. Tribunal de Contas da União. Portaria TCU n° 156/2012, 2012.

Castro, H. G. D.; Carvalho, M. M. D. Gerenciamento do portfolio de projetos: um estudo exploratório. **Gestão & Produção**, São Carlos, v. 17, n. 2, p. 283-296, 2010.

Decancq, K.; Lugo, M. A. **Weights in multidimensional indices of well-being:** an overview. Leuven (Be): Center for Economic Studies, 2010.

Dolci, P. C.; Maçada, A. C. G. The dimensions of IT portfolio management (ITPM): an analysis involving IT managers in Brazilian companies. **JISTEM Journal of Information Systems and Technology Management**, São Paulo, v. 8, n. 2, 2011.

GAO. **INFORMATION TECHNOLOGY INVESTMENT MANAGEMENT - A Framework for Assessing and Improving Process Maturity**. Washington, D.C. (USA): United States General Accounting Office, 2004.

Hayes, A. F. Beyond Baron and Kenny: Statistical Mediation Analysis in the New Millennium. **Communication Monographs**, v. 76, n. 4, p. 408-420, 2009.

Hayes, A. F. Mediate. **My Macros and Code for SPSS and SAS**, 2012a.

Hayes, A. F. Process: A Versatile Computational Tool for Observed Variable Mediation, Moderation, and Conditional Process Modeling [White paper]. **My Macros and Code for SPSS and SAS**, 2012b.

ISACA. **Cobit 5 - A Business Framework for the Governance and Management of Enterprise IT**. Rolling Meadows, IL (USA): ISACA, 2012. Available at:

ISACA. **Cobit 5 - Enabling Processes**. Rolling Meadows, IL (USA): ISACA, 2012b.

ITGI. **Board Briefing on IT Governance, 2nd Edition**. Rolling Meadows, IL (USA): IT Governance Institute, 2003. ISBN 1-893209-64-4.

ITGI. **COBIT - Control Objectives for Information and related Technology**. 4.1. ed. Rolling Meadows, IL (USA): Information Technology Governance Institute, 2007.

ITGI. **Enterprise Value Governance of IT Investments - The Val IT Framework 2.0 Extract**. Rolling Meadows, IL (USA): IT Governance Institute, 2008.

Lunardi, G. L.; Becker, J. L.; Maçada, A. C. G. Um estudo empírico do impacto da governança de TI no desempenho organizacional. **Produção**, v. 22, n. 3, p. 612-624, maio/ago 2012.

Machado, C. P. Governança da tecnologia de informação e a efetividade dos sistemas de informação. **Tese de doutorado**. Programa de Pós-Graduação em Engenharia de Produção da Universidade Federal do Rio Grande do Sul. 2007.

Mackinnon, D.P. Introduction to Statistical Mediation Analysis: Multivariate Applications Series. New York (USA): Lawrence Erlbaum Associates, 2008.

Markowitz, H. Portfolio Selection. **Journal of Finance**, v. 7, n. 1, p. 77-91, mar. 1952.

Mcfarlan, F. W. Portfolio approach to information systems. **Harvard Business Review**, v. 59, n. 5, p. 142-150, set-out 1981.

Aug. 9, 2012.

Mello, Gilmar R. Governança corporativa no setor público federal brasileiro. Dissertação (mestrado em ciências contábeis) — Universidade de São Paulo, São Paulo, 2006.

Mendonca, Cláudio Márcio Campos de et al. Governança de tecnologia da informação: um estudo do processo decisório em organizações públicas e privadas. **Rev. Adm. Pública**, Rio de Janeiro, v. 47, n. 2, 2013.

Moraes, R. O.; Laurindo, F. J. B. Um Estudo de Caso de Gestão de Portfolio de Projetos de Tecnologia Da Informação. **G&P Gestão & Produção**, v. 10, n. 3, p. 311-328, dez. 2003.
Accessed on: April 21, 2012.

Peppard, J.; Ward, J.; Daniel, E. Managing the realization of business benefits from IT investments. **MIS Quarterly Executive**, v. 6, n. 1, p. 1-11, 2007.

PMI. **The Standard for Portfolio Management**. 2nd. ed. Newtown Square, Pennsylvania (USA): Project Management Institute, 2008.

Ramos, K. H. C. Governança e Gestão de Tecnologia da Informação: decompondo a organização em componentes com base em arquitetura organizacional orientada a serviços. **Dissertação de Mestrado** em Engenharia Elétrica, PPGENE.DM-410/09, Departamento de Engenharia Elétrica, Universidade de Brasília, Brasília, DF, xii, 203 p. 2009.

Tavakol, M.; Dennick, R. Making Sense of Cronbach's alpha. International Journal of Medical Education, v. 2, p. 53-55, 2011.

Ward, J. M. A Portfolio Approach to Evaluating Information Systems Investments and Setting Priorities. **Journal of Information Technology**, v. 5, p. 222-231, 1990.

Weill, P.; Ross, J. W. **Governança de TI:** Tecnologia da Informação. Revisão Técnica: Tereza Cristina M. B. Carvalho. São Paulo: M. Books do Brasil Editora Ltda., 2006.

Weill, P.; Woerner, S. L.; Mcdonald, M. Managing the IT Portfolio (Updated Circa 2009): Infrastructure Dwindling in the Downturn. **MIT Center for Information Systems Research - Research Briefing**, Cambridge-MA (USA), v. IX, n. 8, Aug. 2009.

Weill, P.; Woerner, S. L.; Rubin, H. A. Managing the IT Portfolio (Updated Circa 2008):It's All About What's New. **MIT Center for Information Systems Research - Research Briefing**, Cambridge-MA (USA), v. VIII, n. 2B, July 2008.

APPENDIX A – Formulated questions and research variables

1. Questions about the IT investment portfolio management process (PROCPORTF):

1.1 The selection and prioritization of proposals for new IT solutions are based on clear and transparent criteria, previously known to all parties involved.

1.2 The selection and prioritization of proposals for new IT solutions take into account the strategic, financial, pro-improved performance and informational benefits that can be generated by each IT solution for the business.

1.3 The selection and prioritization of proposals for new IT solutions take into account the costs related to financial disbursements and the costs associated to their own personnel allocated to develop or contract, support and operate the IT solution, estimated both for the project phase, as well as for the operation phase.

1.4 The analyses associated to the benefits, costs and risks of new IT solutions are recorded/documented, in order to provide input for the monitoring of these elements during the project phase, as well as during the solution's operation phase.

1.5 The responsibilities of the IT area, of the demanding (interested) unit and of the IT steering committee or equivalent body regarding the selection/prioritization stage, as well as the operation and support stage of IT solutions, are well defined.

2. Questions about the IT Steering Committee or equivalent structure (COMITE):

2.1 The organization counts on one (or more) IT steering committee or equivalent structure with representatives from business units that engage in the institution's governance and IT management.

2.2 The representatives of business units in the IT steering committee are heads of organizational units and not advisors or middle-management staff.

2.3 The IT steering committee decides (or is always consulted) on the selection and prioritization of IT projects/initiatives aimed at promoting new IT solutions.

2.4 The IT steering committee follows up/monitors the fulfillment of benefits, costs and risks of the most important IT solutions, during the project phase and during the operation and support phase.

3. Questions about IT solution managers or equivalent mechanism (GESTSOL):

3.1 There is a clearly defined management unit for each one of the IT solutions considered relevant or essential for the institution.

3.2 The IT solution management unit preferably is the owner of the business process affected by the solution or is the demanding unit or is the unit most interested in the solution.

3.3 The management unit defines the functional, non-functional and security requirements of the IT area, as well as the business rules of the IT solution.

3.4 The managing unit, together with the IT area, defines the service levels for the IT solution and monitors their fulfillment for as long as the solution remains in operation.

3.5 The managing unit monitors the fulfillment of benefits, costs and risks during the operation phase of the IT solution.

4. Questions about satisfaction towards IT governance and management (EFETGOVTI):

4.1 The managers of internal units, IT area clients, and other stakeholders are satisfied with the selection and prioritization method for new IT solutions.

4.2 Internal clients and other stakeholders are satisfied with the number of demands per new IT system/solution that have still NOT been met by the IT area (pending requests or backlog).

4.3 Internal clients and other stakeholders are satisfied with the swiftness (deadlines) agreed upon and effectively fulfilled by the IT area for the delivery of new IT solutions.

4.4 Internal clients and other stakeholders are satisfied with the costs agreed upon and effectively fulfilled by the IT area for the delivery of new IT solutions.

4.5 Internal clients and other stakeholders are satisfied with the quality and the level of service presented by the IT solutions currently in operation.

4.6 Internal clients and other stakeholders are satisfied with the fulfillment of strategic, financial, performance improvement and information benefits provided by IT solutions.

APPENDIX B – Other properties of the sample

Group	Qtty	Average	Standard deviation	"p" value (bilateral)
Respondents from other inst.	117	9.2	1.1	
				0.553
TCU respondents	72	9.1	1.0	
Managers	92	9.2	1.0	
				0.551
Non-managers	97	9.1	1.1	
With IT Gov. course	131	9.4	0.8	
				0.036
Without IT Gov. course	58	8.8	1.5	
IT personnel	151	9.1	1.1	
				0.088
IT area clients	38	9.4	0.9	
IT auditors/consultants	84	9.3	0.9	
				0.070
Non IT auditors/consultants	105	9.1	1.2	

Obs.: Because it refers to a non-normal, right-tailed, negative-skewed distribution, the Wilcoxon-Mann-Whitney hypothesis test was used in substitution of Student's t-test.

The hypotheses tested are:

H0: The difference in the position between the two samples/groups is equal to 0.

H1: The difference in the position between the two samples/groups is different from 0

Table B1 – Perception of groups regarding the importance of the IT Portfolio Process

Group	Qtty	Average	Standard deviation	"p" value (bilateral)
Respondents from other inst.	117	9.0	1.3	0.036
TCU respondents	72	8.8	1.1	
Managers	92	9.0	1.1	0.520
Non-managers	97	8.9	1.3	
With course on IT Gov.	131	9.1	1.0	0.050
Without course on IT Gov.	58	8.6	1.5	
IT area personnel	151	9.0	1.2	0.387
IT area client personnel	38	8.9	1.1	
IT auditors/consultants	84	9.2	0.9	0.004
Non-IT auditors/consultants	105	8.7	1.3	

Obs.: Because it refers to a non-normal, right-tailed, negative-skewed distribution, the Wilcoxon-Mann-Whitney hypothesis test was used in substitution of Student's t-test.

The hypotheses tested are:

H0: The difference in the position between the two samples/groups is equal to 0.

H1: The difference in the position between the two samples/groups is different from 0

Table B2 – Perception of groups regarding the importance of the IT Steering Committee

Group	Qtty	Average	Standard deviation	"p" vallue (bilateral)
Respondents from other inst.	117	9.0	1.2	0.218
TCU respondents	72	8.9	1.0	
Managers	92	9.1	0.9	0.428
Non-managers	97	8.9	1.2	
With course on IT Gov.	131	9.1	0.8	0.038
Without course on IT Gov.	58	8.7	1.4	
IT area personnel	151	9.0	1.1	0.496
IT area client personnel	38	9.0	0.9	
IT auditors/consultants	84	9.3	0.8	0.006
Non-IT auditors/consultants	105	8.8	1.2	

Obs.: Because it refers to a non-normal, right-tailed, negative-skewed distribution, the Wilcoxon-Mann-Whitney hypothesis test was used in substitution of Student's t-test.

The hypotheses tested are:

H0: The difference in the position between the two samples/groups is equal to 0.

H1: The difference in the position between the two samples/groups is different from 0

Table B3 - Perception of groups regarding the importance of the IT Solution Manager

Group	Cause 1	Cause 2	Cause 3	Cause 4	Cause 5	Cause 6
TCU respondents	56%	24%	69%	8%	53%	40%
Respondents from other	80%	46%	83%	43%	52%	57%
Managers	76%	39%	76%	35%	52%	49%
Non-managers	67%	38%	80%	26%	53%	52%
With course on IT Gov.	72%	39%	81%	33%	52%	51%
Without course on IT Gov.	71%	37%	71%	25%	54%	50%
IT area personnel	79%	45%	79%	34%	47%	55%
IT area client personnel	42%	9%	76%	18%	76%	33%
IT auditors/consultants	68%	39%	78%	41%	48%	50%
Non-IT	75%	38%	78%	22%	57%	52%

Cause 1: Insufficient IT personnel
Cause 2: Lack of technical training by IT personnel
Cause 3: Lack of or shortcomings in IT governance and management processes
Cause 4: Insufficient financial/budgetary resources
Cause 5: Alternatives regarding the provision of IT solutions are not sufficiently exploited (ex: in-house vs. outsourced development)

Cause 6: Shortcomings in management skills training for IT personnel

Obs: Respondents were allowed to select multiple causes or none of these causes; therefore, the variation possible for <u>each</u> of the causes is 0 to 100% for each stakeholder group.

Table B4 – Perception of groups regarding the main causes of non-effectiveness of IT Governance

6

A CRITICAL REVIEW OF KNOWLEDGE MANAGEMENT IN SOFTWARE PROCESS REFERENCE MODELS

Ernesto Galvis-Lista
Universidad del Magdalena, Santa Marta, Colombia
Jenny Marcela Sánchez-Torres
Universidad Nacional de Colombia, Bogotá, Colombia

ABSTRACT

Knowledge Management (KM) is a critical subject for software development organizations. For this reason, the purpose of this article is to provide a critical review on the way that KM is included in several models of reference of software process (SPRM). For this, five SPRM used in the Latin American countries were selected. Then, an analysis of each process of the SPRM was performed in order to identify features related to the KM. Finally, the KM aspects were mapped in relation to the KM schools (Earl) and the KM capacities (Gold et al). The main contribution of the paper is to show some breaches in SPRM content in relation to KM schools and capabilities.

Keywords: Knowledge Management Process, Knowledge Management in Software Engineering, Software Process Reference Models, Software Process Improvement

1. INTRODUCTION

The software development organizations (SDO) have been interested in achieving levels of capability in their processes to obtain organizational maturity. For this reason, researchers and professional organizations in the Software Engineering discipline (SE) have developed an increasing number of Software Process Reference Models (SPRM) and Processes Assessment Models. These models have emerged to provide the necessary elements to implement or assess SDO processes. Most of the SPRM are based on the ISO/IEC 15504 Standard (ISO/IEC, 2004), through which their constitutive elements are established. This means that all models based on this standard have a common structure even though they have been proposed for processes of diverse natures. Moreover, the content of most of SPRM used in the industry covers engineering, management and support processes, whose bases are all the disciplines of SE (Abran, Bourque, Dupuis, & Moore, 2001).

Address for correspondence / Endereço para correspondência

Ernesto Galvis-Lista, Assistant Professor, Faculty of Engineering, Universidad del Magdalena, Calle 32 22-08, Santa Marta, Colombia

Jenny Marcela Sánchez-Torres, Associate Professor, Faculty of Engineering Universidad Nacional de Colombia   Carrera 45 26-85, Bogotá, Colombia.

On the other hand, in the last decade, Knowledge Management (KM) has become one of the management processes within SE. An increasing number of publications have treated this subject from diverse perspectives. A synthesis of the scientific work on KM in SE can be found in the systematic review performed (Bjørnson & Dingsøyr, 2008). In this work, it is found a predominant interest in subjects like codification, storage and recovery of knowledge using information technologies (IT). Subjects like the creation, transfer and application of knowledge, however, have not been treated extensively by the academic community. Furthermore, the authors conclude that the majority of the empirical research works are focused on the KM application in the software process improvement (SPI).

In this line of argument, KM in SPI is, in terms of (Aurum, Daneshgar, & Ward, 2008), an important research subject since the SPI initiatives have KM as their main component. Also, these authors argue that KM is useful in the definition of the software process in the application of a processes approach for SE and in the adaptation of software processes for future uses. However, a detailed review of papers published in the last five years, whose main subject is KM in SPI, led to the conclusion that the predominant approach is the knowledge codification, as it is found in (Alagarsamy, Justus, & Iyakutti, 2007, 2008a, 2008b; Capote, Llantén, Pardo, Gonzalez, & Collazos, 2008; Cruz Mendoza et al., 2009; Ivarsson & Gorschek, 2011; Montoni, Cerdeiral, Zanetti, & Cavalcanti da Rocha, 2008). Besides, there are works that treat the organizational knowledge mapping from the building of knowledge directories, as can be found in (Alagarsamy et al., 2008b; Li, Huang, & Gong, 2008), and in the creation and empowerment of organizational structures to promote the exchange and transfer of knowledge, as it is found in (Basri & O'Connor, 2011; Capote, Llantén, Pardo, & Collazos, 2009; Li et al., 2008; Nielsen & Tjørnehøj, 2010).

In synthesis, research works on KM in SPI have been focused on the application of KM as a technological and management tool in SPI initiatives and projects. Nevertheless, there are no approaches related to KM like a process included in SPI initiatives. For this reason, the purpose of this paper is to present a critical review about how KM has been included as a defined process within several SPRM used in the software industry in Latin America. It is important to say that the SPRM provide the basis for SPI initiatives as they contain the definition of all SE processes that SDO would have to implement and improve in order to achieve better levels of capability in their processes to obtain organizational maturity.

To present the results of the review, this paper was structured in the following way: The second section shows the KM theoretical foundations needed to compare, in accordance with a frame of common ideas, the diverse approaches on KM within the analyzed SPRM. In the third section the methodology used for the review is described. In the fourth section the review results are shown in accordance with selected theoretical foundations. Finally, the conclusions and references used in the preparation of the paper are discussed.

2. THEORETICAL FOUNDATIONS

By considering the recent appearance and the conceptual diversity of the KM field, one way to identify a first perception of what KM means is to address the analysis through approaches and schools of thought. For this reason, seven proposals of classification for the KM approaches were identified, as shown in Table 1. Each one of these proposals was studied in order to select the most suitable to serve the objective of this review.

Authors	Proposed categories
(Sieber & Andreu, 1999)	1) Information perspective 2) Technological perspective 3) Cultural perspective
(McAdam & McCreedy, 1999)	1) Models of categorization of knowledge 2) Intellectual capital models 3) Models of Social Construction of knowledge
(Apostolou & Mentzas, 1999)	1) Approach in knowledge creation 2) Approach in knowledge processes 3) Technological approach 4) Holistic approach
(Alvesson & Kärreman, 2001)	1) KM like spread out libraries 2) KM like community 3) KM like regulatory control 4) KM like action templates
(Takeuchi, 2001)	1) Approach of knowledge measuring 2) Knowledge management approach 3) Knowledge Creation Approach
(Earl, 2001)	1) Technocratic schools 2) Economic schools 3) Behavioral Schools
(Choi & Lee, 2003)	1) Passive style 2) System-oriented style 3) People-oriented style 4) Dynamic style
(Kakabadse & Kakabadse, 2003)	1) Models based on philosophy 2) Cognitive models 3) Network models Models of communities of practice 4) Quantum Models
(Rodríguez Gómez, 2007)	1) Storage, access and transfer approaches 2) Sociocultural approaches 3) Technological approaches
(Barragán Ocaña,, 2009)	1) Philosophical, theoretical and conceptual models 2) Intellectual capital and cognitive models 3) Models of social and work networks 4) Technological and scientific models 5) Holistic models

Table 1 Proposals of classification of the KM approaches

In this sense, the first theoretical referent considered was the taxonomy of KM strategies proposed by (Earl, 2001). The selection of this taxonomy is based on the fact that it was built on a research that included: (1) six case studies in organizations, (2) direct research with twenty chief knowledge officers, (3) a workshop about KM programs in organizations with the network of knowledge managers from the United Kingdom, and (4) the analysis of KM programs published in academic and professional journals.

Furthermore, in relation to the content, it is believed that this taxonomy is the most detailed and, unlike others, the conceptual component is complemented by empirical studies. In addition, it is important to point out that although each school represents a particular purpose or approach, they are not competitive between themselves. On the contrary, in practice, KM programs are composed of strategies and tools from several schools. The identified KM schools are categorized as "technocratic", "economic", and "behavioral."

The technocratic schools are the systems, cartographic and engineering schools. The systems school is focused on the IT tools for codifying and exchanging of knowledge using a knowledge base. The cartographic school is focused on the creation and maintenance of maps or knowledge directories that belong to the organization. The engineering school is focused on the implementation of knowledge processes and flows within the organization.

The economic schools are focused on the exploitation of organizational knowledge like intellectual capital that allows the creation of flows of income for the organization. In this category, Earl identified only the commercial school.

The behavioral schools are focused on the promotion of knowledge creation and exchange, as well as all organizational and personal aspects involved in the use of knowledge as an organizational resource. In this third category, there are three schools: organizational, spatial and strategic schools. The organizational school is focused on the creation of formal and informal networks to exchange knowledge. The spatial school is focused on the design of physical workspaces to promote and improve the exchange of knowledge. The strategic school is focused on the design and implementation of all the organizational strategy taking knowledge as its essence. A summary of Earl's taxonomy is shown in Table 2.

Category	School	Core principle	Basic Ideas
Technocratic	Systems	Knowledge Codification of a specific domain	Codification of specialized knowledge in knowledge bases to be used by other specialists or qualified personnel
	Cartographic	People connectivity	Identification and mapping of the organizational knowledge for its promotion and utilization, ensuring that people with knowledge in the organization are accessible by others for consultancy and queries
	Engineering	Flows of knowledge to improve central capabilities of the organization	Supply staff with enough knowledge about their work Processes formalization of provision of contextual knowledge and better practices to the administrative and management staff
Economic	Commercial	Marketing of Intellectual or knowledge property	The protection and exploitation of the intellectual or knowledge assets in an organization to produce incomes
Behavioral	Organizational	Increase of the connectivity between the workers of knowledge	Use of organizational structures or networks to share knowledge Communities where knowledge is exchanged and shared in a, not common, personal and less structured way
	Spatial	Design of physical spaces to boost the contact and the activity of knowledge	Design and use of spaces to facilitate knowledge exchange Promotion of socialization as a way of knowledge exchange
	Strategic	Become aware about possibilities of value creation by recognizing knowledge as a resource.	Knowledge like an essential dimension of the competitive strategy The company is conceptualized like a business of knowledge The actions of knowledge management are varied and can frame in the other schools

Table 2 Classification of GC schools. (Earl, 2001)

As a complementary perspective to the Earl's approach, the work done by (Gold, Malhotra, & Segars, 2001) was taken. In this proposal, the authors argue that organizations should take advantage of the knowledge they possess and create new knowledge to compete in their markets. To achieve this, organizations must develop two types of KM capabilities: knowledge infrastructure capabilities and knowledge processes capabilities.

Infrastructure capabilities enable maximization of the social capital, defined as "the sum of current and potential embedded resources, available through, and derived from the network of relations that a social unit has (Gold et al., 2001). In a complementary form, process capabilities are dynamic elements that take advantage of infrastructure capabilities to convert knowledge into an active organizational resource. As illustrated in Figure 1, in terms of (Gold et al., 2001), the dimensions of infrastructure and processes reflect an additive capability to release and maintain over time an organizational change program through KM, in order to achieve organizational effectiveness.

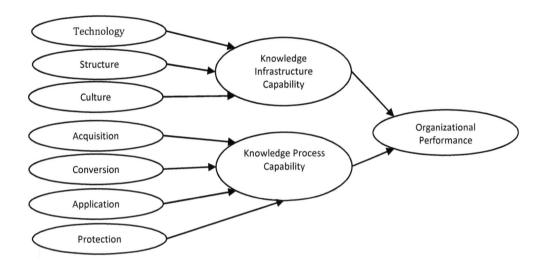

Figure 1 Knowledge Management Capabilities and Organizational Effectiveness. (Gold et al., 2001)

The three infrastructure capabilities are the technology capability, the structure capability and the culture capability. The technology capability addresses tools and means that enable flows of knowledge efficiently. The structure capability focuses on the existence of rules, trust mechanisms and formal organizational structures that encourage the creation and exchange of knowledge between people in the organization. The cultural dimension refers to the presence of shared contexts within the organization.

The four knowledge processes capabilities are knowledge acquisition, knowledge conversion, knowledge application and knowledge protection. The knowledge acquisition process is aimed at the gain of knowledge from various sources both within and outside the organization. The knowledge conversion process focuses on making existing knowledge useful from its encoding, combination, coordination and distribution. The knowledge application process is addressed to the real use of the knowledge in the daily practices of the organization. And the knowledge protection process is designed to define and implement the strategies to protect the organizational knowledge of theft or improper or illegal uses. Table 3 summarizes the KM capabilities proposed by (Gold et al., 2001).

Categories	Capabilities	Main principle
Infrastructure	Technology	The IT systems determine the way in which knowledge is transferred and accessed.
	Structure	The organizational structures, formal and informal, can inhibit or facilitate interaction between people, essential in the KM.
	Culture	The organizational culture must support and enhance the activities of knowledge.
Processes	Acquisition	The location and Acquisition of knowledge or creation of knowledge through the collaboration between individuals and business partners.
	Conversion	Knowledge must be organized and structured in a way that facilitates their distribution and use within the organization.
	Application	Knowledge must be used to adjust the direction, strategy, solve new problems and improve efficiency.
	Protection	Knowledge must be protected from inappropriate use, or unauthorized exploitation.

Table 3 Knowledge Management Capabilities: Infrastructure and Processes

3. METHODOLOGY

The review methodology designed to perform this work consists of three stages. In the first, SPRM (Software Process Reference Models) were selected for analysis in the practice of revision. For this, a set of publications by authors from Latin America over the past decade have been analyzed, whose main subject was the improvement of software processes. The analysis consisted in the identification and quantification of the worked or used SPRM as a foundation in the publications, with the purpose to select the five more worked SPRM.

In the second stage, the processes related to KM were identified in each of the SPRM included in the review. Here, the specification of each process was studied, in other words, the statement of the purpose and expected outcomes of the process. With this analysis, a subset of processes were selected which have related aspects with KM.

In the third stage, the processes identified in the second stage were analyzed in relation to the KM schools (Earl, 2001) and the KM capabilities (Gold et al., 2001). In this sense, each of the identified aspects was located in schools and corresponding capabilities. Table 4 describes each one of the steps of the methodology used in this study.

Stage	Name	Objective	Activities
1	**Selection of SPRM**	Select a set of SPRM used in Colombian and Latin American contexts.	• The search of papers on the improvement of software processes, published in the last decade, with origins in any of the countries of Latin America using SCOPUS and ISI Web of Knowledge. • Identification of the SPRM in the article, based on the reading of the metadata of the publication. • Data analysis to identify and select the most mentioned SPRM in academic publications. • The search of primary documents, with the description of the processes involved in each selected SPRM.
2	**Identification of processes**	Identify the processes, defined within the selected SPRM, that contained aspects related with the KM.	• Extraction of the description of the purpose and the results of each process in a database. • The search and record of key statements related to KM in the description of the purpose of the process. • The search and record of key statements related to KM in the description of the expected results of the process. • Selection of processes identified with relative aspects of KM.
3	**Mapping of processes**	Relate the relative aspects of the KM, from the processes identified in step two, with the schools of KM and the organizational capabilities of KM.	• Location of each key statement identified in step two in the corresponding KM school. • Development of mapping of the processes against KM schools. • Location of each key statement identified in step two in the corresponding KM capabilities. Development of mapping of the processes against the capabilities of KM. Summary and discussion of the obtained results.

Table 4 Stages of the methodology

4. RESULTS

By following the steps of the methodology, the main results were: 1) the selection of five SPRM, 2) the identification of 19 processes related to the KM in the SPRM, and 3) the mapping of the 19 processes in relation to KM schools and the KM capabilities. In the following three subsections the results of each stage are described in detail.

1. Selection of SPRM

The selection of SPRM began with the definition of the search equations used in the ISI Web of Knowledge and SCOPUS databases. These equations are composed of phrases in English about improvement, capability and maturity of processes of software engineering. Table 5 shows the search equations and the results obtained from 2001 to 2012.

Source	Search Equations	Results
ISI Web of Knowledge	(TS=((("software process" OR "software engineering") AND ("improvement" OR "capability" OR "maturity" OR "reference model")) OR "ISO/IEC 15504")) AND (CU=("Argentina" OR "Bolivia" OR "Brazil" OR "Chile" OR "Colombia" OR "Costa Rica" OR "Ecuador" OR "El Salvador" OR "Guatemala" OR "Honduras" OR "Mexico" OR "Nicaragua" OR "Panama" OR "Paraguay" OR "Peru" OR "Portugal" OR "Spain" OR "Trinidad and Tobago" OR "Uruguay" OR "Venezuela"))	65
SCOPUS	TITLE-ABS-KEY((("software process" OR "software engineering") AND ("improvement" OR "capability" OR "maturity" OR "reference model")) OR "ISO/IEC 15504") AND (AFFILCOUNTRY("Argentina" OR "Bolivia" OR "Brazil" OR "Chile" OR "Colombia" OR "Costa Rica" OR "Ecuador" OR "El Salvador" OR "Guatemala" OR "Honduras" OR "Mexico" OR "Nicaragua" OR "Panama" OR "Paraguay" OR "Peru" OR "Portugal" OR "Spain" OR "Trinidad and Tobago" OR "Uruguay" OR "Venezuela"))	450

Table 5 Search Equations

By eliminating duplicates, 424 items were obtained. Subsequently, on a first reading to exclude unrelated thematic articles a set of 124 articles to execute the data extraction were obtained as a result. The data extraction focused on classifying the articles according to the referenced SPRM in the content as part of the theoretical foundation or as methodological sustenance. The result of the classification is shown in Figure 2.

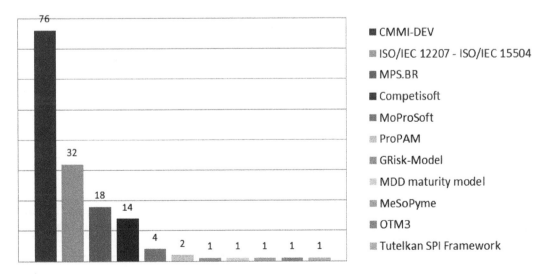

Figure 2 Identification of the SPRM in the Analyzed Articles

After the analysis, the first result was the selection of five SPRM: 1) the international standard, ISO / IEC 12207, 2) the Brazilian SPRM called MPS.BR by the acronym from the Portuguese expression " Melhoria de Processo do Software Brasileiro " or Improvement of Processes of the Brazilian Software, 4) The Process Model of the Mexican Software Industry (MoProSoft) and 5) the process model defined as part of the Process Improvement Program to Enhance the Competitiveness of Small and Medium Software Industry in Latin America - COMPETISOFT. Table 6 describes the selected SPRM.

SPRM	Year	Institution	Country	Processes	Used References
CMMI-DEV	2011	Software Engineering Institute	United States	22	(CMMI Product Team, 2010) (Chrissis, Konrad, & Shrum, 2011) (SCAMPI Upgrade Team, 2011)
ISO/IEC 12207	2008	International Organization for Standardization	International	43	(Pino, García, Ruiz, & Piattini, 2005); (Pino, Garcia, Ruiz, & Piattini, 2006); (ISO/IEC, 2006); (ISO/IEC, 2008); (Baldassarre, Piattini, Pino, & Visaggio, 2009);
MPS.BR	2011	Asociación para la Promoción de la Excelencia del Software Brasilero	Brazil	19	(Weber et al., 2005) (Santos et al., 2010) (SOFTEX, 2011a) (SOFTEX, 2011b)
Competisoft	2008	COMPETISOFT Project	Latin America	9	(Oktaba et al., 2007) (Competisoft, 2008a) (Competisoft, 2008b) (Oktaba, 2009) (Aguirre, Pardo Calvache, Mejía, & Pino, 2010)
MoProSoft	2005	Asociación Mexicana para la Calidad en Ingeniería de Software - AMCIS	Mexico	8	(Oktaba et al., 2005a) (Oktaba et al., 2005b) (Oktaba et al., 2006) (Oktaba, 2006)

Table 6 Description of the selected SPRM

2.   Identification of related processes with KM in the SPRM

The process analysis to identify those that contain aspects related to KM resulted in a set of 19 processes out of 101 processes from the five selected SPRM. Table 7 shows the identified processes in each SPRM.

Model	Related processes to the KM
ISO 12207	Management of the Software Configuration. Process of Resolution of Software problems. Management of the Cycle of Life model. Management of Human Resources. Management of Reuse of Assets. Domain Engineering.
CMMI-DEV	Management of the Configuration. Definition of the Organizational Process. Organizational training.
MPS.BR	Management of the Configuration. Definition of the Organizational Process. Management of Human Resources. Development for the Reutilization.
MoProSoft	Management of the Process. Management of Human Resources and of the Work Environment. Organizational Knowledge.
Competisoft	Management of the Process. Management of Human Resources and of the Work Environment. Organizational Knowledge.

Table 7 Processes that contain KM aspects

3. Mapping of processes in relation to km schools and capabilities

In relation to the analysis of the SPRM regarding the KM schools it was discovered that most of the identified aspects are related to the school system. In other words, the dominant approach is the encoding of knowledge. In fact, although in several SPRM there is an explicit reference to the KM (MoProSoft, Competisof), the scope of this process is limited to manage a repository of organizational knowledge. The contents of this repository of knowledge are, primarily, best practices, records of learned lessons, knowledge artifacts resulting from activities of software construction, and knowledge regarding the definition of the processes of the organization. Added to this, the ISO / IEC 12207, CMMI-DEV and MPS.BR models include the concept of repository of the organizational knowledge within the management processes of configuration and definition of the organizational process.

Also, all SPRM include aspects related to the engineering school. In particular, this school is materialized in the form of training activities and the provision of qualified personnel to carry out the activities of knowledge. These proposals become part of the processes of human resource management. Table 8 shows the relationships between the processes of the selected SPRM and KM schools.

Model	Related Processes to KM	Systems	Cartographic	Engineering	Commercial	Organizational	Spatial	Strategic
		KM Schools						
ISO 12207	Management of the Configuration.	X	-	-	-	-	-	-
	Resolution of Software problems	X	-	-	-	-	-	-
	Management of the Cycle of Life model	-	-	X	-	-	-	-
	Management of Human Resources	X	-	X	-	-	-	-
	Management of Reuse of Assets	X	-	-	-	-	-	-
	Domain Engineering	X	-	-	-	-	-	-
CMMI-DEV	Management of the Configuration	X	-	-	-	-	-	-
	Definition of the Organizational Process.	X	-	-	-	-	-	-
	Organizational training.	-	-	X	-	-	-	-
MPS.BR	Management of the Configuration.	X	-	-	-	-	-	-
	Definition of the Organizational Process.	X	-	-	-	-	-	-
	Management of Human Resources.	-	-	X	-	-	-	-
	Development for the Reutilization.	X	-	-	-	-	-	-
MoProSoft	Management of the Process.	X	-	-	-	-	-	-
	Management of Human Resources and of the Work Environment.	-	-	X	-	-	-	-
	Organizational Knowledge.	X	-	-	-	-	-	-
Competisoft	Management of the Process.	X	-	-	-	-	-	-
	Management of Human Resources and of the Work Environment.	-	-	X	-	-	-	-
	Organizational Knowledge	X	-	-	-	-	-	-

Table 8 Relationship between the SPRM processes and KM schools

The analysis of the SPRM regarding the organizational KM capabilities resulted in the fact that most of the aspects of KM identified in the processes are related to the technological infrastructure capability and the knowledge conversion process capability. This is coherent with the emphasis on the systems school. In addition, another important element is that all SPRM have, at least, a process concerning the design and implementation of an organizational structure with a processes approach. Also, the knowledge acquisition and application processes are explicitly covered within the models. The relationship between the SPRM processes and KM capabilities is shown in Table 9.

Model	Related Processes to KM	KM Capabilities						
		Technology	Culture	Structure	Acquisition	Conversion	Application	Protection
ISO 12207	Management of the Configuration.	X	-	-	-	X	-	-
	Resolution of Software problems	X	-	-	-	X	-	-
	Management of the Cycle of Life model	-	-	X	X	-	-	-
	Management of Human Resources	-	-	-	X	-	-	-
	Management of Reuse of Assets	X	-	-	-	X	X	-
	Domain Engineering	X	-	-	X	X	-	-
CMMI-DEV	Management of the Configuration	X	-	-	-	X	-	-
	Definition of the Organizational Process.	X	-	X	-	X	-	-
	Organizational training.	-	-	-	X	-	-	-
MPS.BR	Management of the Configuration.	X	-	-	-	X	-	-
	Definition of the Organizational Process.	X	-	X	-	X	-	-
	Management of Human Resources.	-	-	-	X	-	-	-
	Development for the Reutilization.	X	-	-	-	X	X	-
MoProSoft	Management of the Process.	X	-	X	-	X	-	-
	Management of Human Resources and of the Work Environment.	-	-	-	X	-	-	-
	Organizational Knowledge.	X	-	-	-	X	-	-
Competisoft	Management of the Process.	X	-	X	-	X	-	-
	Management of Human Resources and of the Work Environment.	-	-	-	X	-	-	-
	Organizational Knowledge	X	-	-	-	X	-	-

Table 9 Relationship between the SPRM processes and capabilities of KM

5.   CONCLUSIONS

From the perspective of the KM schools, the subjects included in the SPRM are limited to systems and engineering schools. Therefore, any SDO that works on a SPI initiative based on the analyzed SPRM could not include strategies from other KM schools within the certification of their processes. For example, the design of the physical spaces to promote the creation and exchange of knowledge, from the spatial school, is not included in the studied SPRM, although a growing number of companies have been applying it in practice.

In addition, several authors argue that the software industry is a knowledge-intensive industry. Therefore, it is surprising and regrettable that the commercial school's approaches are not explicitly included in the studied SPRM. It s also noteworthy that the approaches of the organizational and strategic schools are not included in the studied SPRM, since these schools have a very close relationship with the principles and practices of the agile methods for software development which have an important influence on the software industry.

Concerning the organizational KM capabilities, the studied SPRM explicitly exclude the culture capability. However, in recent years the scientific literature on design and process improvement, and especially the movement of agile methods, has emphasized the crucial role of the organizational culture for SDO. For this reason, this absence is a gap that must be addressed soon. Moreover, the studied SPRM do not include two process capabilities that are crucial for any organization: knowledge application and protection.

In this order of ideas, the present paper shows that the studied SPRM include within their scope some aspects of KM. This fact reaffirms the importance of KM for SDO, and in particular, the importance of KM in SPI. Mainly, the subjects of interest about KM in the SPRM are: 1) the encoding of knowledge, 2) the use of knowledge repositories, and 3) the organizational training. These topics of interest are located, in terms of (Buono & Poulfelt, 2005), in a first-generation KM. In this type of KM, knowledge is considered as a possession or something that can be captured and stored in repositories of knowledge-based technology. On the contrary, in the second-generation KM, knowledge is considered a complex phenomenon related to socio-cultural, political and technological aspects. For such a reason, a gap is evident in the content of the analyzed SPRM as these do not take into account elements of the second-generation KM.

The previous arguments encourage the formulation of three questions that serve as a source of motivation for future investigations: 1) what KM purposes and results should be incorporated into existing SPRM to have a more complete reference in the design, implementation, evaluation and improvement of processes within SDO? 2) Is it possible to incorporate these KM purposes and results as a new process within the existing SPRM? Or perhaps a reference model of KM processes for SDO is needed? 3) If the resulting reference model of KM processes could be used in an initiative for determining the levels of capability of SDO processes, what should the corresponding evaluation model of KM processes be like? The answers to these questions are highly valued in KM research and may be a significant contribution to the field since they are aligned with KM research trends identified by (Dwivedi, Venkitachalam, Sharif, Al-Karaghouli, & Weerakkody, 2011). They argue that the future research in the KM field requires studies related to the unification of the various KM models that exist today in the literature, and the understanding of the determinants of the evolution of KM in organizations. Also, studies are deemed relevant to the effectiveness of the KM and the necessary organizational and technological support to achieve it.

In summary, this study constitutes an important reference for research and practice as it represents a synthesis of the KM subjects included in the SPRM, and helps SDO to identify the fundamentals and the existing options for implementing KM initiatives. Moreover, this study helps researchers to identify trends and subjects to develop new research projects about the inclusion of the different "varieties" of KM in the SPRM, or to develop a reference model of KM processes for SDO.

ACKNOWLEDGEMENTS

The authors express their gratitude to COLCIENCIAS by its support through "Generación del Bicentenario" program and to the Universidad del Magdalena by its support through the "Formación Avanzada para la Docencia" program. These two programs are funding doctoral studies of the first author.

REFERENCES

Abran, A., Bourque, P., Dupuis, R., & Moore, J. W. (Eds.). (2001). *Guide to the Software Engineering Body of Knowledge - SWEBOK*. IEEE Press.

Aguirre, A. F., Pardo Calvache, C. J., Mejía, M. F., & Pino, F. J. (2010). Reporte de experiencias de la aplicación de Competisoft en cinco mipymes colombianas. *Revista EIA*, (13), 107–122.

Alagarsamy, K., Justus, S., & Iyakutti, K. (2007). The knowledge based software process improvement program: A rational analysis. In *2nd International Conference on Software Engineering Advances - ICSEA 2007*.

Alagarsamy, K., Justus, S., & Iyakutti, K. (2008a). On the implementation of a knowledge management tool for SPI. In *Proceedings - International Conference on Computational Intelligence and Multimedia Applications, ICCIMA 2007* (Vol. 2, pp. 48–55).

Alagarsamy, K., Justus, S., & Iyakutti, K. (2008b). Implementation specification for software process improvement supportive knowledge management tool. *IET Software*, *2*(2), 123–133.

Alvesson, M., & Kärreman, D. (2001). Odd Couple: Making Sense of the Curious Concept of Knowledge Management. *Journal of Management Studies*, *38*(7), 995–1018. doi:10.1111/1467-6486.00269

Apostolou, D., & Mentzas, G. (1999). Managing corporate knowledge: a comparative analysis of experiences in consulting firms. Part 1. *Knowledge and Process Management*, *6*(3), 129–138. doi:10.1002/(SICI)1099-1441(199909)6:3<129::AID-KPM64>3.0.CO;2-3

Aurum, A., Daneshgar, F., & Ward, J. (2008). Investigating Knowledge Management practices in software development organisations - An Australian experience. *Information and Software Technology*, *50*(6), 511–533. doi:10.1016/j.infsof.2007.05.005

Baldassarre, M. T., Piattini, M., Pino, F. J., & Visaggio, G. (2009). Comparing ISO/IEC 12207 and CMMI-DEV: Towards a mapping of ISO/IEC 15504-7. In *Proceedings of the ICSE Workshop on Software Quality, 2009. WOSQ '09* (pp. 59–64). Presented at the ICSE Workshop on Software Quality, 2009. WOSQ '09, IEEE. doi:10.1109/WOSQ.2009.5071558

Barragán Ocaña,, A. (2009). Aproximación a una taxonomía de modelos de gestión del conocimiento. *Intangible Capital*, *5*(1), 65–101.

Basri, S. B., & O'Connor, R. V. (2011). Knowledge Management in Software Process Improvement: A Case Study of Very Small Entities. In *Knowledge Engineering for Software Development Life Cycles: Support Technologies and Applications* (p. 273). IGI Global.

Bjørnson, F. O., & Dingsøyr, T. (2008). Knowledge management in software engineering: A systematic review of studied concepts, findings and research methods used. *Information and Software Technology*, *50*(11), 1055–1068. doi:10.1016/j.infsof.2008.03.006

Buono, A. F., & Poulfelt, F. (2005). *Challenges and issues in knowledge management* (Vol. 5). Information Age Pub Inc.

Capote, J., Llantén, C. J., Pardo, C., & Collazos, C. (2009). Knowledge management in a software process improvement program in micro, small and medium-sized enterprises: KMSPI Model. *Revista Facultad de Ingenieria*, (50), 205–216.

Capote, J., Llantén, C. J., Pardo, C., Gonzalez, A., & Collazos, C. (2008). Gestión del conocimiento como apoyo para la mejora de procesos software en las micro, pequeñas y medianas empresas. *Ingenieria e investigacion*, *28*.

Choi, B., & Lee, H. (2003). An empirical investigation of KM styles and their effect on corporate performance. *INFORMATION & MANAGEMENT*, *40*(5), 403–417.

Chrissis, M. B., Konrad, M., & Shrum, S. (2011). *CMMI for Development®: Guidelines for Process Integration and Product Improvement (3rd Edition)* (3rd ed.). Addison-Wesley Professional.

CMMI Product Team. (2010). *CMMI® for Development, Version 1.3* (CMU/SEI-2010th-TR-033 ed.). Pittsburgh, PA, USA: Carnegie Mellon University.

Competisoft. (2008a). *COMPETISOFT. Mejora de Procesos para Fomentar la Competitividad de la Pequeña y Mediana Industria del Software de Iberoamérica.*

Competisoft. (2008b). COMPETISOFT. Mejora de Procesos de Software para PEqueñas Empresas. Retrieved August 20, 2011, from http://alarcos.inf-cr.uclm.es/Competisoft/framework/

Cruz Mendoza, R., Morales Trujillo, M., Morgado C, M., Oktaba, H., Ibarguengoitia, G. E., Pino, F. J., & Piattini, M. (2009). Supporting the Software Process Improvement in Very Small Entities through E-learning: The HEPALE! Project. In *2009 Mexican International Conference on Computer Science (ENC)* (pp. 221–231). Presented at the 2009 Mexican International Conference on Computer Science (ENC), IEEE. doi:10.1109/ENC.2009.33

Dwivedi, Y. K., Venkitachalam, K., Sharif, A. M., Al-Karaghouli, W., & Weerakkody, V. (2011). Research trends in knowledge management: Analyzing the past and predicting the future. *Information Systems Management*, *28*(1), 43–56.

Earl, M. (2001). Knowledge Management Strategies: Toward a Taxonomy. *J. Manage. Inf. Syst.*, *18*(1), 215–233.

Gold, A. H., Malhotra, A., & Segars, A. H. (2001). Knowledge management: An organizational capabilities perspective. *Journal of Management Information Systems*, *18*(1), 185–214.

ISO/IEC. (2004). *ISO/IEC 15504-1:2004, Information technology - Process assessment - Part 1: Concepts and vocabulary*. Ginebra, Suiza: International Organization for Standardization.

ISO/IEC. (2006). *ISO/IEC 15504-5:2006, Information technology - Process Assessment - Part 5: An exemplar Process Assessment Model*. Ginebra, Suiza: International Organization for Standardization.

ISO/IEC. (2008). *ISO/IEC 12207:2008, Standard for Systems and Software Engineering - Software Life Cycle Processes.*

Ivarsson, M., & Gorschek, T. (2011). Tool support for disseminating and improving development practices. *Software Quality Journal*. doi:10.1007/s11219-011-9139-6

Kakabadse, N. K., & Kakabadse, A. (2003). Reviewing the knowledge management literature: towards a taxonomy. *Journal of Knowledge Management*, *7*(4), 75–91. doi:10.1108/13673270310492967

Li, Z., Huang, S., & Gong, B. (2008). The knowledge management strategy for SPI practices. *Chinese Journal of Electronics*, *17*(1), 66–70.

McAdam, R., & McCreedy, S. (1999). A critical review of knowledge management models. *The Learning Organization*, *6*(3), 91–101. doi:10.1108/09696479910270416

Montoni, M. A., Cerdeiral, C., Zanetti, D., & Cavalcanti da Rocha, A. R. (2008). A Knowledge Management Approach to Support Software Process Improvement Implementation Initiatives. In R. V. O'Connor, N. Baddoo, K. Smolander, & R. Messnarz (Eds.), *Software Process Improvement* (Vol. 16, pp. 164–175). Berlin, Heidelberg: Springer Berlin Heidelberg.

Nielsen, P. A., & Tjørnehøj, G. (2010). Social networks in software process improvement. *Journal of Software Maintenance and Evolution: Research and Practice*, *22*(1), 33–51. doi:10.1002/smr.452

Oktaba, H. (2006). MoProSoft®: A Software Process Model for Small Enterprises. In *Proceedings of the 1st International Research Workshop for Process Improvement in Small Settings* (pp. 93–110). Presented at the International Research Workshop for Process Improvement in Small Settings, Software Engineering Institute.

Oktaba, H. (2009). *Competisoft : mejora de procesos software para pequeñas y medianas empresas y proyectos* (1a ed.). México D.F.: Alfaomega.

Oktaba, H., Esquivel, C., Su Ramos, A., Martínez, A., Quintanilla, G., Ruvalcaba, M., … Fernández, Y. (2005a). *Modelo de Procesos para la Industria de Software MoProSoft Version 1.3*. México: Secretaría de Economía.

Oktaba, H., Esquivel, C., Su Ramos, A., Martínez, A., Quintanilla, G., Ruvalcaba, M., … Fernández, Y. (2005b). *Modelo de Procesos para la Industria de Software MoProSoft Version 1.3 Por Niveles de Capacidad de Procesos*. México: Secretaría de Economía.

Oktaba, H., Esquivel, C., Su Ramos, A., Martínez, A., Quintanilla, G., Ruvalcaba, M., … Fernández, Y. (2006). *Software Industry Process Model MoProSoft Version 1.3. 2*. México: Ministry of Economy.

Oktaba, H., García, F., Piattini, M., Ruiz, F., Pino, F. J., & Alquicira, C. (2007). Software Process Improvement: The Competisoft Project. *Computer*, *40*, 21–28. doi:10.1109/MC.2007.361

Pino, F. J., Garcia, F., Ruiz, F., & Piattini, M. (2006). Adaptation of the standards ISO/IEC 12207:2002 and ISO/IEC 15504:2003 for the assessment of the software processes in developing countries. *IEEE Latin America Transactions*, *4*, 85–92. doi:10.1109/TLA.2006.1642455

Pino, F. J., García, F., Ruiz, F., & Piattini, M. (2005). Adaptación de las normas ISO/IEC 12207: 2002 e ISO/IEC 15504: 2003 para la evaluación de la madurez de procesos software en países en desarrollo. In *Proceedings of JISBD'05* (pp. 187–194). Presented at the JISBD'05, IEEE.

Rodríguez Gómez, D. (2007). Modelos para la creación y gestión del conocimiento : una aproximación teórica. *Educar*, (37), 25–39.

Santos, G., Kalinowski, M., Rocha, A. R., Travassos, G. H., Weber, K. C., & Antonioni, J. A. (2010). MPS.BR: A Tale of Software Process Improvement and Performance Results in the Brazilian Software Industry (pp. 412–417). IEEE. doi:10.1109/QUATIC.2010.75

SCAMPI Upgrade Team. (2011). *Standard CMMI® Appraisal Method for Process Improvement (SCAMPI SM) A, Version 1.3: Method Definition Document* (CMU/SEI-2011th-HB-001 ed.). Pittsburgh, PA, USA: Carnegie Mellon University.

Sieber, S., & Andreu, R. (1999). La gestion integral del conocimiento y del aprendizaje. (With English summary.). *Economia Industrial*, (2), 63–72.

SOFTEX. (2011a). *MPS.BR - Mejora de Proceso del Software Brasileño - Guía de Evaluación*. Brasil: SOFTEX.

SOFTEX. (2011b). *MPS.BR - Mejora de Proceso del Software Brasileño - Guía General*. Brasil: SOFTEX.

Takeuchi, H. (2001). Towards a Universal Management Concept of Knowledge. In *Managing industrial knowledge* (p. 315). Sage.

Weber, K. C., Araújo, E. E. R., Rocha, A. R. C., Machado, C. A. F., Scalet, D., & Salviano, C. F. (2005). Brazilian Software Process Reference Model and Assessment Method. In pInar Yolum, T. Güngör, F. Gürgen, & C. Özturan (Eds.), *Computer and Information Sciences - ISCIS 2005* (Vol. 3733, pp. 402–411). Berlin, Heidelberg: Springer Berlin Heidelberg.

7

METHOD FOR MEASURING THE ALIGNMENT BETWEEN INFORMATION TECHNOLOGY STRATEGIC PLANNING AND ACTIONS OF INFORMATION TECHNOLOGY GOVERNANCE

Lúcio Melre da Silva
João Souza Neto
Catholic University of Brasilia, Brasília, Distrito Federal, Brazil

ABSTRACT

The purpose of this research is to present a method for measuring the degree of alignment between Strategic Planning and Information Technology Management practices and Information Technology Governance. A survey of IT governance maturity at the High Courts and the Supreme Court was carried out in order to reach this aim. The Attribute Table of the COBIT 4.1 was used both as a model for maturity analysis as for the degree of alignment of IT strategic plans of these bodies with the IT Strategic Planning established by the National Judiciary Council (CNJ). It was assessed the maturity of thirty four processes, according to six attributes, in the four COBIT domains. The proposed method, named COMPLAN-GTI, allows the linking of the guidelines of the strategic planning to the COBIT processes. The field research above mentioned shows that the alignment between the planning established by the CNJ and those established by the High Courts and Supreme Court is around 68%, leading to the conclusion that the policies and actions established by the National Council of Justice for the Judiciary are being followed. The application of the method is also used to confirm whether the management practices and the IT Governance are consistent with the strategic plan established by the organization. It was observed in the research carried out in the Courts that the average convergence between PETIs and management practices and Governance lies around 70%, leading to the conclusion that the strategic plans exerted influence on the action planning of these organizations.

Keywords: Information Technology Governance; Strategic Planning; COBIT.

Address for correspondence / Endereço para correspondência

Lúcio Melre da Silva. Master in Information Technology and Knowledge Management – MGCGI/UCB, Catholic University of Brasilia, Researcher at Catholic University of Brasilia in Metamodels of IT frameworks, Campus Avançado, SGAN 916 Asa Norte - Modulo B - Sala A111 - CEP: 70.790-160 Brasília – DF, Brasil

João Souza Neto, Doctor of Science in Electrical Engineering, University of Brasilia – UNB, Professor at Catholic University of Brasilia, on the Master's degree Program in Information Technology and Knowledge Management, Campus Avançado, SGAN 916 Asa Norte - Modulo B - Sala A121 - CEP:70.790-160 Brasília – DF, Brasil

1.   INTRODUCTION

The Brazilian Constitution, in its Second Article, states that the Legislative, the Executive and the Judiciary are branches of the government, independent and harmonious among themselves. Chapter III deals specifically with the Judiciary, and determines its composition, principles, the responsibilities of the several agencies that comprise it, as well as the guarantees of the Judiciary members and the Judiciary administrative and financial autonomy.

The Judiciary is constituted by the Supreme Court, the Superior Court, the Federal Regional Courts and their Federal Judges, Labor, Electoral and Military Courts and their respective Judges and the Courts and Judges of the States.

The Constitutional Amendment No. 45, dated December 30th, 2004, laid the foundations for the accomplishment of a comprehensive reform in the Brazilian Judiciary. One of the innovations introduced by the reform of the Brazilian Constitution was the creation of the National Council of Justice – CNJ (*Conselho Nacional de Justiça*), whose mission is to contribute to a decision made with morality, efficiency and effectiveness, for the benefit of justice.

The CNJ is an agency focused on the reformulation of the Judiciary's officials and the judicial procedures, especially regarding the administrative and procedural control and transparency, and it was set up in conformance with the Federal Constitution, in particular pursuant to article 103-B. It has a Standing Committee of Information Technology and Infrastructure, which proposes actions to:

- Implement adequate infrastructure for the intended operation of the Judiciary;

- Create the Information Technology Strategic Planning to ensure the appropriate technology for the proper performance of the activities of the Courts, the interoperability between different systems, and the improvement and implementation of the electronic judicial process, and

- Deploy the electronic judicial process.

In order to assist the CNJ in the Information Technology (IT) management and Governance activities, it was created a committee which has done relevant work on the Information Technology Strategic Planning for the Judiciary. This committee was approved by the Resolution No. 99 of November 24th, 2009, which established its mission, vision and attributes as well as the strategic objectives to be achieved by the Judiciary.

This research was conducted at the Superior Courts and at the Supreme Court and, although the Supreme Court it is not obliged to follow the recommendations of the CNJ, it has adopted all the practices related to the IT management and Governance.

The Supreme Court is also a member of the National Committee of Information Technology and Communications of the Judiciary.

2.   THEORETICAL REFERENCE

2.1.   Strategic Planning

In 2011 a research called Global Status Report on the Governance of Enterprise IT was conducted by ITGI. The research aimed to identify trends regarding the importance of the Information Technology and more than 800 IT executives from organizations located in twenty-one countries participated. The same survey was conducted in 2004, 2006 and 2008, in order to identify the growth or decline in the trends. This research showed that the vast majority of respondents see IT as an issue to the business strategies, thus confirming that IT increases the competitiveness of enterprises. (ITGI, 2011).

Strategic planning is critical to the survival of public and private organizations, since it establishes a guideline for the actions that should be followed by all units of the organization, aiming at the achievement of enterprise targets. It is a dynamic, systemic, participatory and collective process used to determine the goals, strategies and actions of the organization. The process starts with the identification of the problems within the organization. (REZENDE, 2011).

In order to meet its goals and objectives it is crucial for an organization to have its Information Technology projects and activities aligned with the demands and needs of the business. Some authors, as Henderson and Venkatraman (1993), have discussed the importance of the Information Technology for streamlining the activities of the organization, stating that this role requires the deployment of an efficient IT platform (including hardware, software and communication systems) for the management and control of all processes.

However, three scenarios are still observed in the relationship between IT and the business:

1.   Focus on operational services and infrastructure of the organization;

2.   Delivery of the IT solutions and support to enterprise strategies, without participation in strategy making;

3.   Full integration of the IT activities with the business objectives and strategic goals of the company.

Scenario 3, which is considered the most suitable one for the delivery of the desired business value, can be achieved with the adoption of an IT strategic planning (PETI – Plano Estratégico de TI), which should be aligned and integrated with the institutional strategic planning. PETI is a dynamic and iterative process that defines, in a strategic level, the organizational information, the IT resources (hardware, software, data and information management, and information systems), the people involved in the process and the infrastructure necessary to meet all the goals and objectives established by the organization. (REZENDE, 2011).

2.2. Information Technology Governance

The Governance of Information Technology is part of the Corporate Governance and it consists of the leadership, the organizational structures and the processes that ensure the IT organization to sustain and extend the organization's strategies and goals, based on the guidelines of the strategic planning.

It is necessary to discuss the Corporate Governance, since all definitions of the Information Technology Governance are directly or indirectly related to it.

The Code of Best Practices for Corporate Governance, published by the Instituto Brasileiro de Governança Corporativa, *(Brazilian Institute of Corporate Governance)* states that Corporate Governance is the system by which organizations are directed, monitored and encouraged, involving the relationships among the owners, the board of directors, the management and the control bodies. Good Corporate Governance practices translate principles into objective recommendations, aligning interests in order to enhance and preserve the value of the organization, facilitating its access to the resources and contributing to its longevity. (IBGC, 2009).

This is not a new subject, but it deserved special mention in the press after the financial scandals at the beginning of this century, when important U.S. companies such as Enron, WorldCom and Tyco led thousands of customers into bankruptcy due to accounting manipulations and financial disruptions.

Weill and Ross (2006) proposed a framework to link corporate governance to IT governance. There are two groups in this framework. The first group describes the relationships of the board with the shareholders and other stakeholders. The senior executive team acting as an agent of the board is responsible for articulating strategies and behaviors to carry out the directions of the board. The other group encompasses the seven main assets (human, financial, physical, intellectual property, relationship, information, and IT), and, through them, the companies accomplish their strategies and generate business value. According to these authors, companies with common mechanisms for various assets present a better performance.

IT governance involves many aspects related to the practices established and consolidated in the market. IT governance development strategies should take into account aspects related to the available resources, the structure and the business of each organization. The proper goal setting and decision making should result in benefits for the organization.

In order to be considered effective, and according to Weill and Ross (2006), IT governance must answer three questions:

1.   Which IT decisions must be made to ensure the effective management and use of IT?

2.   Who should make such decisions?

3.   How will these decisions be made and monitored?

To answer the first two questions, the authors proposed an array of governance arrangements, that relates five IT key decisions (IT principles, IT architecture, IT infrastructure, needs for business applications and IT investment and prioritization) to seven organizational archetypes (business monarchy, IT monarchy, feudalism, federalism, duopoly, and anarchy). The IT key decisions concern to the major decisions to be taken in the domain of the IT governance, while the archetypes typify the decision makers.

The IT principles clarify the business role of IT; the architecture defines the requirements for integration and standardization; the infrastructure determines the shared services and the support services; the need for business applications specify the business needs for IT applications, which were acquired or developed internally, and the investments and prioritization of IT indicate which initiatives to fund and how much to spend on them.

Regarding the archetypes, the responsibilities of those who make the decisions are passed on to the senior management in business monarchy to IT managers in IT monarchy, to the managers of the business units in feudalism, to the headquarters and branches managers in federalism. In the case of IT duopoly, IT managers and some other group are the decision makers and, finally, in anarchy, the decisions are made individually or in small groups.

The ITGI (2007) defines the following focus areas in the IT Governance:

1.   Strategic Alignment: align the IT operations with the organization's strategic objectives. It is responsible for ensuring alignment and prioritization of projects based on the strategic goals of the organization;

2.   Value Delivery: ensures that IT delivers to the business the benefits foreseen in the IT strategy. It is responsible for the cost optimization and the provision of the IT intrinsic value;

3.   Resource Management: focuses on the better use of investments and on the appropriate management of the critical IT resources: applications, information, infrastructure and people;

4.   Risk Management: emphasizes a clear understanding of the organization's appetite for risk as well as the compliance requirements, the transparency about the significant risks to the organization and the inclusion of risk management into the routine activities;

5.   Performance Measurement: tracks and follows up the implementation of the strategies, the progress of projects, the use of the resources, the delivery and the support services performance.

In the public sector some difficulties arise when it adopts the frameworks developed specifically for private companies. Therefore, Weill and Ross (2006) proposed a specific framework for nonprofits organizations, being categorized as government organizations which include defense, immigration, public services, police, education and health, as well as NGOs.

According to the authors, four major challenges of nonprofit organizations were identified: measurement of value and performance, investments in IT infrastructure, coproduction and architectures, and citizens, clients and buyers.

The measurement of value is difficult to implement because some factors like profit or cost reduction are not involved. Thus, the measurement of value should be made taking into account other parameters such as the customer satisfaction, the quality of the product delivered and the quality of the support to the customer in the public sector, the customer is the citizen).

According to the authors, the investments in infrastructure can be justified in three ways: by holding office, i.e., without the need to submit justification; by expense reduction, that can be quantified and assessed; and by the enablement of new capabilities.

Co-production refers to the capacity of nonprofit organizations to encourage or compel the co-producers to commit to creating public value to a wider audience. Such capacity can bring direct benefits to the citizens as much as it allows reducing deadlines and anticipating the delivery of services to the society.

Citizens, customers and buyers should be identified in the provision of services by nonprofit organizations, since the treatment devoted to each one of them may be different due to the goals to be achieved.

The identification of these four major challenges, in association with others, influences how the organization implements its IT governance, thus justifying the importance of this identification.

Research developed by Xavier (2010) in the Federal Public Administration agencies concluded that the COBIT ® (Control Objectives for Information and related Technology) may serve as reference for the implementation of improvements aiming at the establishment of IT goals and indicators. Also, it allows monitoring the evolution of the IT governance maturity level in the agencies of the Brazilian Public Sector.

2.2.1 The COBIT Framework

The COBIT framework was developed by ITGI and the current version is number 5. This version was published in mid-April 2012 and it is a significant update to COBIT. However, the previous version, the 4.1, used in this study, still has wide acceptance due to its large knowledge base application.

COBIT 4.1 provides best practices for IT Governance using a model which consists of domains, processes and activities presented in a manageable and logical structure (ITGI, 2007). It provides a framework to manage and control IT activities and presents five key characteristics: focus on business, process orientation, overall acceptability, compliance requirements and common language.

The COBIT framework is based on the premise that IT has to deliver the information required by the business to help it achieve its goals. It provides a framework and a guide to implement IT governance, allowing the prioritization of IT processes that should be improved. The model combines the business requirements for information with the objectives of the IT function.

Thus, the basic principle of the COBIT framework can be summarized as IT resources which are managed by IT processes to achieve IT goals which, in turn, respond to business requirements (ITGI, 2007). This principle is illustrated in Figure 1, in the COBIT cube. In each dimension of the cube, in this figure, are shown the IT processes (thirty-four, divided into four domains), the IT resources (applications, information, infrastructure and people) and the business requirements (effectiveness, efficiency, confidentiality, integrity, availability, compliance and reliability of information).

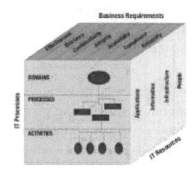

Figure 1 – The COBIT Cube
Source: (ITGI, 2007, p. 27)

IT processes are organized into four areas and divided into two hundred and ten activities. Each domain has its own set of control objectives and scope. They are the following: Plan and Organize (PO), Acquire and Implement (AI), Deliver and Support (DS) and Monitor and Evaluate (ME).

The maturity analysis of each COBIT process allows the organization to identify its current stage, the current state of the market (benchmarking), the maturity desired and the path to be traversed to go from the current situation to the future one. Each COBIT process is rated on a generic and complex scale, requiring a complete and systemic view of the organization (XAVIER, 2010). The scale used is shown in Table 1 that describes the general characteristics of the degrees of maturity.

Table 1 - Maturity Scale of COBIT 4.1	
0 - Non-Existent	Complete lack of a recognized process. The organization does not even acknowledge that there is an issue to be worked on.
1 - Initial / Ad hoc	There is evidence that the organization has recognized that there are issues which need to be addressed. However, there is no standardized process, but rather, an ad hoc approach which tends to be applied individually or on a case-by-case basis. The general approach to management is disorganized.
2 - Repeatable but Intuitive	Processes have evolved to a stage where similar procedures are followed by different people doing the same task. There is no formal training or communication of standard procedures, and the responsibility is left to the individuals. There is a high degree of confidence in the individuals' knowledge , and, consequently, errors may occur.

3 - Defined	Procedures were standardized, documented and communicated through training. It is mandatory that these processes are followed up. However, there is a possibility that deviations will not be detected. The procedures are not sophisticated, but there is a formalization of existing practices.
4 - Managed and Measurable	The management monitors and measures adherence to the procedures and takes action when the processes are not working well. The processes are constantly improved and, thus, they provide good practices. The use of automation and tools is limited or fragmented.
5 - Optimized	The processes have been refined to a level of good practice and are continually improved. IT is used as an option to automate the workflow, providing tools to improve quality and effectiveness, thus helping the organization to adapt quickly.

Source: (ITGI, 2007, p.21). Adapted by the authors.

The proposed measure of maturity, presented here, is supported by the study entitled IT Governance and Process Maturity of ITGI. This proposal is linked to COBIT, and it shows a simpler maturity evaluation process, compared to the maturity assessment mechanisms commonly employed (ITGI, 2008). The IT Governance and Process Maturity publication shows the details of a study involving fifty-one institutions in North America, Asia and Europe, which are organized, among other criteria, by area. These areas of expertise include capital-intensive industries (high cost of capital assets), utilities (infrastructure for public services), service industries, financial institutions, and finally, government and non-profit organizations.

The use of attributes attached to processes allowed the design of a methodology to assess the maturity in a simpler and more straightforward way. The original approach of the COBIT presents a specific model that provides a maturity scale for each of the thirty-four processes. Thus, each process has its own maturity model, which has been generated from a generic model.

This generic model provides for the identification of referential attributes (Awareness and Communication; Policies, Plans and Procedures; Tools and Automation; Skills and Expertise; Responsibility and Accountability and Goal Setting and Measurement). Such attributes are organized in a 0 to 5 scale (0 = non-existent, 1 = initial or ad hoc, 2 = repeatable but intuitive, 3 = defined, 4 = managed and measured and 5 = optimized) that allows its application to any process, i.e., there is no need, when evaluating the maturity of a given process, to use a specific maturity model linked to it, but to use only the Attributes Maturity Table (Table 2), where the generic model is presented.

Recognition of the need for the process is emerging	There are *ad hoc* approaches to processes and practices	Some tools may exist; usage is based on standard desktop tools	Skills required for the process are not identified.	There is no definition of accountability and responsibility.	Goals are not clear and no measurement takes place
There is sporadic communications about the issues	The process and policies are undefined	There is no planned approach to the tool usage	A training plan does not exist and no formal training occurs	People take ownership of issues based on their own initiative on a	

Source: (XAVIER, 2010)

Each maturity level, in this generic model, presents what is expected for each attribute. Indeed, there is a range of maturity levels for each one of the six attributes. According to this scale, it becomes easy to identify the level of maturity of each process simply locating the situation that best fits the current situation of the process in the Attributes Maturity Table.

3.   METHOD TO COMPARE STRATEGIC PLANS AND IT GOVERNANCE ACTIONS - COMPLAN – GTI

The COMPLAN - GTI method was created to check the alignment between the strategic plans of the Courts and the plan established by the National Judicial Council for the Judiciary, as well as the alignment of IT governance and management practices with the related strategic planning.

This method proposes an objective analysis of the strategic planning of an organization by comparing and listing of all objectives, actions and goals of the strategic planning to the COBIT processes. It also evaluates whether management and IT governance practices are performed by the organizations in accordance with its strategic planning.

The step of the method dedicated to comparing the actions and goals of the strategic planning to the COBIT processes is justified by the fact that the Courts which have been evaluated had recently done a COBIT maturity evaluation that pointed out their strengths and weaknesses. The outcome of this evaluation casta doubt on whether the Courts were planning objective actions to overcome their shortcomings. Therefore, this is the purpose of this step of the COMPLAN-GTI method, i.e., to assess whether the planned strategic actions have support in the reality exposed by the COBIT maturity assessment.

A strategic plan aims to establish a guideline for the actions that should be followed by all units of the organization in order to reach its targets. The National

Council of Justice established, pursuant to Resolution No. 99 of November 24th 2009, the IT Strategic Planning for the Judiciary (BRAZIL, 2009), but it did not indicate, among the established objectives, which ones had the highest priority. Consequently, all actions must be undertaken with the same degree of importance.

The application of this method requires a previous analysis of the IT Strategic Planning of the organization in order to identify the themes (or perspectives) and the strategic objectives related to the lines of action to be carried out. The method seeks to relate every proposed action to accomplish a strategic planning goal to the COBIT processes. To achieve this, the following actions must be taken:

1. Identify the keywords of the proposed action;

2. Search the occurrence of the keywords in the whole set of processes (thirty-four) and in the detailed control objectives (two-hundred and ten) of the COBIT. If there is a match, it has to be assessed whether the process or the detailed control objective relates to the proposed action. This assessment, although subjective, should be performed by an appraiser with the following competencies, skills and characteristics:

2.1. Professional experience: he/she should be a technical professional or a participant of the managerial staff of the Court; this person should have practical experience in the area of the evaluated process and he/she should know about the IT management processes practiced in the Court;

2.2. Knowledge of the COBIT 4.1 framework, processes and detailed control objectives;

2.3. Ability to relate the actions taken by the Court to the indicated COBIT processes;

2.4. Ability to work in a team, if the assessment is carried out by more than one professional.

3. The identified process should comprise the column Related COBIT Process – Priority COBIT Process;

4. In case there is no match between one of the keywords and the processes and the detailed control objectives of COBIT, synonyms should be used in the conducted search in order to exhaust all the possibilities of relationship with those COBIT components.

Steps 1 to 4 must be repeated for all actions related to the strategic planning in order to identify all the COBIT processes related to the specific actions of the IT Strategic Plan (PETI).

This method was also applied to the IT strategic planning of each one of the Courts under study, therefore allowing the identification of the COBIT processes related to each theme or strategic objective listed in the IT strategic planning of the organization.

After the identification of the COBIT processes related to the actions set out in the IT strategic planning of both CNJ and the Court, it is possible to create a map to indicate the presence of these processes in the two plans.

This study identified four scenarios in the relationship between the strategic planning of the CNJ and the nth Court being analysed (TRIBUNALn):

i)   COBIT process present in PETI - CNJ and present in PETI - TRIBUNALn (Scenario 1),

ii) COBIT process present in PETI - CNJ and absent in PETI - TRIBUNALn (Scenario 2),

iii) COBIT process present in PETI - TRIBUNALn and absent in PETI - CNJ (Scenario 3) and

iv) COBIT process absent in both strategic planning (Scenario 4).

The percentage of alignment is obtained by relating the quantity of processes belonging to scenarios 1 and 2. These are the scenarios where the COBIT process is present in the IT strategic planning established by the CNJ for the Judiciary. Then, it was decided that if the percentage of alignment exceeds 50%, the plans should be considered aligned. In order to obtain this percentage, the following formula was used:

$$\% alignment = \frac{Scenario\ 1}{(Scenario1 + Scenario\ 2)} * 100$$

The application of the research questionnaire is also part of the method. The questionnaire identifies the maturity of each one of the COBIT processes in the Court which are analyzed according to six attributes (Awareness and Communication; Policies, Plans and Procedures; Tools and Automation; Skills and Expertise; Responsibility and Accountability and Goal Setting and Measurement).

The Process Maturity (MatProc) is the integer value obtained by truncation of the arithmetic mean of the values of each of the attributes related to that process. XAVIER (2010, p. 59). Thus,

$$MatProc = \frac{\sum_{n=1}^{6} Atributtes}{6}$$

Every process was evaluated according to its current status at the time and what is expected two years from now (future status). All thirty-four COBIT processes were evaluated.

To check the alignment between the strategic planning of the Court and its IT governance and management practices, a table was created. It shows the current and future maturities of all COBIT processes and the improvement of the maturity necessary for the achievement of the future situation. To calculate this increase in maturity, the current maturity is subtracted from the future maturity. The application of this criterion aims to identify which processes will be subject to greater attention by the Court in the actions to be undertaken in the next two years. Such efforts are related to the status of the COBIT processes.

The actions to be taken concerning the processes of scenarios 1 and 2 are those related to the strategic planning of the CNJ. Thus, these efforts should be prioritized as they aim to enforce the provisions of the CNJ. Processes related to scenarios 3 and 4 are not part of the PETI-CNJ because the processes of scenario 3 are listed only in the PETI of the Court and the processes of scenario 4 are not present in any of the strategic plans. Thus, the percentage of alignment of IT governance and management practices with strategic planning is obtained by applying the formula:

$$\%Alignment\ COBITxPETI = \frac{Esf\ Sit\ 1 + Esf\ Sit\ 2}{Esf\ Sit\ 1 + Esf\ Sit\ 2 + Esf\ Sit\ 3 + Esf\ Sit\ 4}$$

where: *EsfSit n = Increase of Maturity for Scenario n*

If the alignment percentage exceeds 50%, it was decided that the IT governance and management practices should be considered aligned with the strategic planning of the Court, since more than half of the efforts are directed to the guidelines set out in the IT strategic planning.

4. APPLICATION OF THE COMPLAN–GTI METHOD

The method was applied to the IT strategic planning of the Brazilian Superior Courts and the Supreme Court as well as to the PETI established by the CNJ for the Judiciary. It was also used to evaluate the IT governance and management practices of the Courts through the assessment of the priorities given to the COBIT processes. To protect the information provided by the Courts, they were identified only as TRIBUNALn , where n ranges from 1 to 5, since five Courts were surveyed.

The following values were set by the CNJ on the IT Strategic Planning for the Judiciary: speed, modernity, accessibility, transparency, social and environmental responsibility, fairness, ethics and probity. Thirteen strategic objectives were grouped into eight themes, which are presented in Table 3, with the lines of action established by the CNJ for its implementation. For each of the actions listed in PETI-CNJ the COMPLAN-GTI method was applied in order to identify the COBIT related processes.

The analysis of the PETI-CNJ identified major strategic objectives and actions to be undertaken for the achievement of themes. The themes identified by CNJ were: efficiency, access to the main Judicial information system; social responsibility; alignment and integration, institutional performance, people management, infrastructure and technology budget. Each theme had one or more related strategic objectives, with their respective actions.

For every action, keywords with their synonyms were identified and they were called search expressions. These expressions have been searched in the process table and in the detailed control objectives of the COBIT. On the selected processes, a subjective analysis was performed by the assessor to evaluate whether the process or the detailed control objective was actually related to the proposed action.

The method COMPLAN-GTI was applied to the IT strategic planning of the Courts. According to studies performed in the strategic planning of the Court, the main themes/perspectives, the strategic objectives and the lines of action to be undertaken by the Court were identified.

After collecting the actions and the lines of action, a method to identify the COBIT processes related to each action was applied, as shown in Table 3.

The planning established by CNJ (BRAZIL, 2009) stated in its 2nd Article that: "The National Council of Justice and the Courts indicated in sections 11 to 92 of Article VII of the Constitution will establish their respective information technology and communications (ITC) strategic plans aligned with the National ICT Strategic Plan, with a minimum coverage of five years and it shall be approved in its plenary and special organs until March 31, 2009."

Thus, all the goals and targets set in the strategic planning of the Court under analysis must be aligned to the goals and targets set by the National Council of Justice.

5.   ANALYSIS OF THE RESULTS

The results were organized according to three criteria, as follows: qualitative data analysis of the Courts; alignment between the IT strategic planning of the Courts and that same alignment concerning the National Judicial Council for the Judiciary and, finally, the analysis of the IT actions undertaken by the Courts in light of their IT strategic planning.

5.1   Alignment between PETI-CNJ and PETI-TRIBUNAL

To check the alignment between the strategic planning of the Courts and the one established by the CNJ for the Judiciary, a table was created. In this table, called Table 3, all the COBIT processes were listed and their presence or absence in the strategic planning of CNJ and the Courts was marked. The COBIT processes were selected using the COMPLAN-GTI method as described in Chapters 3 and 4.

The columns "CNJ" and "TRIBUNAL N" show the "yes" status if the related process is present in their strategic planning according to the four scenarios that may occur in the relationship between the strategic planning of the CNJ and the COURT.

PROCESSO	CNJ	TRIB.1	Sce. Trib 1	TRIB.2	Sce. Trib 2	TRIB.3	Sce. Trib 3	TRIB.4	Sce. Trib 4	TRIB.5	Sce. Trib 5
PO01	yes	yes	Scenario 1	yes	Scenario 1	yes	Scenario 1	yes	Scenario 1	yes	Scenario 1
PO02	yes		Scenario 2		Scenario 2	yes	Scenario 1		Scenario 2		Scenario 2
PO03	yes	yes	Scenario 1	yes	Scenario 1	yes	Scenario 1	yes	Scenario 1	yes	Scenario 1
PO04	yes	yes	Scenario 1	yes	Scenario 1	yes	Scenario 1	yes	Scenario 1	yes	Scenario 1
PO05	yes	yes	Scenario 1	yes	Scenario 1	yes	Scenario 1	yes	Scenario 1	yes	Scenario 1
PO06	yes		Scenario 2	yes	Scenario 1	yes	Scenario 1		Scenario 2	yes	Scenario 1
PO07	yes	yes	Scenario 1	yes	Scenario 1	yes	Scenario 1		Scenario 2	yes	Scenario 1
PO08	yes	yes	Scenario 1	yes	Scenario 1	yes	Scenario 1	yes	Scenario 1	yes	Scenario 1
PO09	yes	yes	Scenario 1	yes	Scenario 1		Scenario 2	yes	Scenario 1		Scenario 2
PO10	yes	yes	Scenario 1	yes	Scenario 1	yes	Scenario 1	yes	Scenario 1	yes	Scenario 1
AI01			Scenario 4		Scenario 4	yes	Scenario 3		Scenario 4	yes	Scenario 3
AI02	yes		Scenario 2		Scenario 2	yes	Scenario 1		Scenario 2		Scenario 2
AI03	yes	yes	Scenario 1		Scenario 2	yes	Scenario 1	yes	Scenario 1	yes	Scenario 1
AI04	yes	yes	Scenario 1	yes	Scenario 1	yes	Scenario 1	yes	Scenario 1	yes	Scenario 1
AI05	yes		Scenario 2		Scenario 2	yes	Scenario 1		Scenario 2		Scenario 2
AI06		yes	Scenario 3		Scenario 4	yes	Scenario 3	yes	Scenario 3		Scenario 4
AI07	yes	yes	Scenario 1		Scenario 2	yes	Scenario 1	yes	Scenario 1		Scenario 2
DS01	yes	yes	Scenario 1		Scenario 2	yes	Scenario 1	yes	Scenario 1	yes	Scenario 1
DS02			Scenario 4		Scenario 4	yes	Scenario 3		Scenario 4		Scenario 4
DS03	yes		Scenario 2		Scenario 2	yes	Scenario 1	yes	Scenario 1		Scenario 2
DS04	yes	yes	Scenario 1	0	Scenario 2	yes	Scenario 1		Scenario 2	yes	Scenario 1
DS05	yes	yes	Scenario 1	yes	Scenario 1	yes	Scenario 1		Scenario 2	yes	Scenario 1
DS06		yes	Scenario 3	yes	Scenario 3		Scenario 4	yes	Scenario 3	yes	Scenario 3
DS07	yes	yes	Scenario 1	yes	Scenario 1	yes	Scenario 1		Scenario 2	yes	Scenario 1

Table 3 – Alignment of the PETI of the Courts with the PETI-CNJ

PROCESSO	CNJ	TRIB.1	Sce. Trib 1	TRIB.2	Sce. Trib 2	TRIB.3	Sce. Trib 3	TRIB.4	Sce. Trib 4	TRIB.5	Sce. Trib 5
DS08	yes	yes	Scenario 1		Scenario 2		Scenario 2	yes	Scenario 1	yes	Scenario 1
DS09		yes	Scenario 3		Scenario 4	yes	Scenario 3		Scenario 4		Scenario 4
DS10		yes	Scenario 3		Scenario 4		Scenario 4	yes	Scenario 3		Scenario 4
DS11			Scenario 4		Scenario 4		Scenario 4		Scenario 4		Scenario 4
DS12			Scenario 4		Scenario 4		Scenario 4		Scenario 4		Scenario 4
DS13		yes	Scenario 3		Scenario 4	yes	Scenario 3		Scenario 4		Scenario 4
ME01	yes	yes	Scenario 1		Scenario 2	yes	Scenario 1	yes	Scenario 1	yes	Scenario 1
ME02		yes	Scenario 3	yes	Scenario 3		Scenario 4	yes	Scenario 3	yes	Scenario 3
ME03	yes		Scenario 2		Scenario 2		Scenario 2		Scenario 2		Scenario 2
ME04	yes	yes	Scenario 1	yes	Scenario 1	yes	Scenario 1	yes	Scenario 1	yes	Scenario 1

Graph **1** portraits the result of the analysis of the alignment between the PETI-CNJ and the IT strategic planning of the Courts (formula *% alignment*).

Graph 1 – Alignment between PETI-CNJ and PETI of the Courts

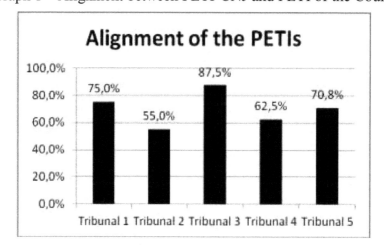

Graph 1 points out that all Courts had alignment percentages exceeding 50%, what indicates, as defined, that the strategic plans of these Courts are aligned with the strategic plans of the CNJ. These results answer "yes" to the first research question which is: Are the guidelines and recommendations of the National Council of Justice being met? In order to answer this question, it is necessary to have in mind that those guidelines and recommendations aim to meet the guidelines of the controlling agencies, and, also, they especially aim to make the agencies of the Judiciary act with greater effectiveness and efficiency.

This result was expected because Resolution No. 99, in its 2nd Article, imposed that the Courts specified in sections 11 to 92 of Article VII of the Constitution (including the High Courts) would have "to develop their information technology and communications strategic planning **aligned with the National ICT Strategic Plan**, with a minimum coverage of five years [...]" (BRAZIL, 2009, authors' emphasis) .

On average, the High Courts and the Supreme Court had a percentage of 70.16% of alignment of their IT strategic planning with the planning established by the CNJ for the Judiciary. Nevertheless, this alignment is not complete due to the diversity of priorities set by the management of the Courts, and such management lasts only two years. Thus, all Courts undertake information technology actions not only to achieve the goals set by the CNJ but, also, to meet the guidelines of their respective administrations.

5.2 Application of the survey questionnaire of IT governance

The survey questionnaire was applied to the five Courts in order to assess the maturity of the IT governance using the COBIT attribute table, as explained in the description of the data collection phase.

Each process was evaluated according to the six attributes of the COBIT (Awareness and Communication; Policies, Plans and Procedures; Tools and Automation; Skills and Expertise; Responsibility and Accountability, and Goal Setting and Measurement) on current and future perspectives. The maturity of the process was calculated with basis on the values obtained.

This research also aims to provide some information to the Courts in order to enable them to work out benchmarking. Graphs 2 and 3 show the maturities of all Courts, as well as the global average maturity. Thus, this data can be used by managers and administrators to conduct analysis to identify the position of one Court compared to the position of other Courts, and to search for creative solutions to solve common problems. The average maturity, per process, is also shown in the graphs in order to facilitate their identification.

Graph 2 – Current Average Maturity. Processes PO1 to AI7

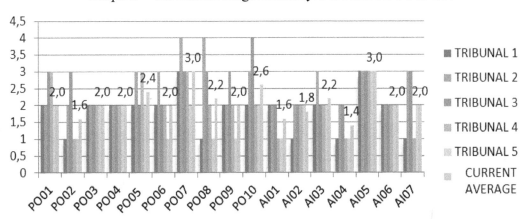

Graph 3 – Current Average Maturity. Processes DS1 to ME4

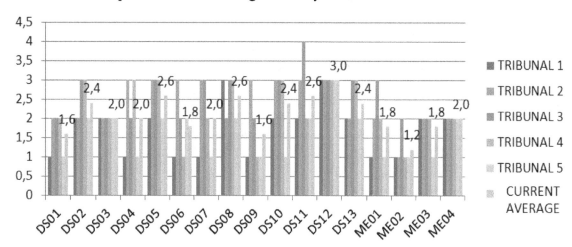

The global average maturities, the average maturity of each of the High Courts and the average maturity of the Supreme Court were calculated in the current and future scenario. The maturity level values were calculated to one decimal place to allow a better understanding of the differences found between the Courts, although for the COBIT 4.1, these values should be presented in integer format without decimal places.

The maturities shown are the integer values obtained for each process, according to the set of attributes of the COBIT. The arithmetic mean was calculated for each process.

The following formula was used to calculate the average maturity, the current and future average maturity of each Court.

$$Maturity = \frac{\sum_{n=1}^{34} Maturity\, n}{34}$$

Graph 4 was plotted with the values obtained above.

Graph 4 – Current and Future Maturities of the Courts

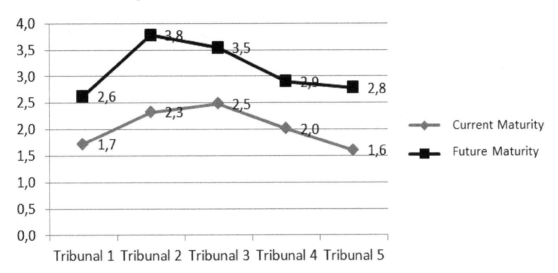

The average maturity of the Courts was obtained applying the formula:

$$Average\ Maturity = \frac{\sum_{n=1}^{5} Maturity\ Court\ n}{5}$$

The current and future average maturity of the High Courts and the Supreme Court was:

Current average maturity   = 2.0
Future average maturity   = 3.1

The current maturity value, 2.0, shows that the management and the IT governance processes of the Superior Courts, although repeatable, are not documented and are just intuitive. Processes have evolved to a stage where similar procedures are followed and executed by different people. However, there are no formal training standard procedures and the official communication is not yet institutionalized. There is a tendency to focus the responsibilities on the individual, with the corresponding increase risk of errors.

The fact that the courts wish to reach a level of maturity in the next two or three years shows that the upper administration of the Courts is confident in sponsoring the IT projects. To reach this level of maturity, it is necessary that the IT governance practices are effectively sponsored by the high authorities of the Courts who should prioritize the creation of IT governance Committees, and, also, they should prioritize the actions related to the strategic alignment of IT with business and the delivery of value. It is expected that in two years from now the procedures be standardized, documented and formally communicated as well as the monitoring of the adherence to the standard procedures be in effect.

5.3   Alignment between PETI-TRIBUNAL and IT governance

The application of the method to survey the alignment among the IT governance (ITG), the management practices and the strategic planning have identified which processes should be object of greater attention by the Court in the actions to be undertaken in the next two years. Such efforts are related to the situation of the COBIT process.

Graph 5 shows the percentage of effort dedicated to the actions related to scenarios 1 and 2, above 50%.

Graph 5 - %Alignment ITG and PETI–TRIBUNAIS

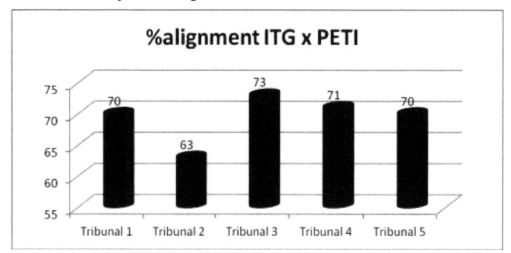

The average value found is 70%, what justifies the statement that the IT governance and the management practices of the Courts are in line with their strategic planning. These results answer the second research question: *Are the actions prioritized by the Courts aligned with their strategic planning?*

It is important to remark that effort calculations were performed in absolute terms, with each unity of maturity increase (future status - current status) corresponding to one unity of effort, regardless of the complexity of the process evaluated. Some COBIT processes require greater efforts than others in order to increase one unit into the maturity level. The framework COBIT 4.1 provides an annex, named Linking IT Processes to IT Goals, where the thirty-four COBIT processes are related to twenty-eight IT Goals. It is possible to confirm that some processes influence a larger number of goals (ITGI, 2007). For example, when analyzing IT Goals achieved by the process ME4 - Provide IT governance (five goals), it seems that these goals are more complex than the process AI1 - Identify Automated Solutions (only two goals). However, for the purposes of this research, these efforts were equally carried out.

6. CONCLUSION

The aim of this work is to propose a method to assess whether the guidelines of an information technology strategic planning (PETI) are observed on the IT governance and management practices, and to verify the alignment between IT strategic plans. In order to evaluate the applicability of the method the IT strategic planning of the Superior Courts and the Supreme Court were analyzed, and also the PETI established by the National Judicial Council for the Judiciary. As a model for maturity analysis, it was undertaken a survey of IT governance maturity of the Superior Courts and the Supreme Court using the Attribute Table of COBIT, which is composed of six attributes: Awareness and Communication; Policies, Plans and Procedures; Tools and Automation, Skills and Expertise, Responsibility and Accountability and Goal Setting and Measurement.

This research was carried out due to the low incidence of academic studies (thesis, articles and books) that deal with both IT Governance and Strategic Planning in public organizations, as well as the repeated interventions of internal and external control agencies. The research in the Court of Audit, specially, pointed out the weaknesses on IT Governance in the agencies and entities of the Brazilian Federal Public Administration. The huge financial resources that have been invested by the public sector in activities related to information technology were also considered. In the last ten years, for example, 12.5 billion dollars have been spent on IT resources, according to the Court of Audit.

The proposed method, called COMPLAN-GTI, allows linking the guidelines of an IT strategic planning to COBIT processes. In this study, the version 4.1 of the COBIT framework was used.

Initially, it was carried out an evaluation of the relation of the IT strategic planning established by the National Judicial Council for the Judiciary concerning the COBIT processes. The same analysis was done with the PETI of the High Courts and the Supreme Court, making it possible to determine the degree of alignment between the various strategic plans. The Courts are, on average, 68% aligned with the guidelines and actions established by the National Council of Justice for the Judiciary.

The application of the method permitted to check if the IT governance and management practices are consistent with the strategic plan of the organization. It was observed on the survey carried out in the Courts that the average convergence between PETI and IT governance and management practices lies at 70%, therefore concluding that the strategic plans have influenced the action plans in these organizations.

The results obtained will allow the Federal Public Administration agencies, in particular the Brazilian Supreme Courts, to conduct benchmarking aiming to identify the strengths and weaknesses and, with the support of those who implemented best practices in the Courts, to contribute to the improvement of the Brazilian public sector. It is also possible to perform an analysis to identify the position of the Court in relation to other Courts, in order to enable the search for creative solutions to solve common problems.

It is worth mentioning that the proposed method can, in principle, be applied to public or private organizations, as a general tool for the analysis of IT governance management practices.

As for the limitations of this research, it can be mentioned that the method requires minimum skills for the assessor, such as knowledge of the maturity measurement model based on attributes of the COBIT 4.1, knowledge of the actions of IT governance and management practiced on the agency, and ability to relate the actions taken by the Court and the related COBIT processes. In addition, as the survey did not have the characteristics of an audit, there was no evidence of responses, what requires caution on the analysis of the results. Finally, it is important to point out that this research has not undergone a validation process, given the difficulty of reproducing the conditions necessary for its implementation, such as the existence of an overall strategic plan of the sector, a strategic plan for each agency evaluated and a recent IT Governance maturity evaluation for each one of them. Nowadays, this situation is found only in the Judiciary, particularly in the CNJ and the High Courts, being unique on the Federal Public Administration.

It is suggested, as a future work, to undertake a focus group meeting with managers of the Federal Public Administration for model validation. In this focus group meeting the principles, guidelines and procedures of the COMPLAN - GTI method will be presented and the perceptions of the managers about the proposed model will be collected through semi-structured interviews. The contributions of these experts will be included in a new version of the COMPLAN-GTI method. Moreover, the proposed model can be enhanced to implement its guidelines on the new COBIT 5 framework, published by ISACA in April 2012. The evolution of the current model 4.1 to the version 5 model will bring benefits due to the separation of the governance practices from the management practices, simplifying the application of the method. Overall, this work may serve as a reference for other research studies related to the same general themes: IT governance, strategic planning, and IT management in public organizations

REFERENCES

Brasil. Conselho Nacional de Justiça. Resolução nº 99, de 24 de novembro de 2009. Planejamento Estratégico de TI do Poder Judiciário. http://www.cnj.jus.br/images/gestao-planejamento-poder-judiciario/petic_nacional.pdf

Henderson, John; Venkatraman, N. Strategic alignment: Leveraging information technology for transforming organizations. IBM Systems Journal, Vol. 32, No. 1, 1993.

IBGC. Código das melhores práticas de governança corporativa. 4ª Edição. São Paulo: IBGC, 2009.

ITGI (Information Technology Governance Institute). Cobit 4.1. USA: 2007. <http://www.isaca.org/Knowledge-Center/cobit/Documents/cobit41-portuguese.pdf>.

_____. Global Status Report on the Governance of Enterprise IT. USA, 2011. <http://www.isaca.org/Knowledge-Center>.

_____. IT Governance and Process Maturity. USA, 2008.

Rezende, Denis Alcides. Planejamento de Sistemas de Informação e Informática. Guia Prático para Planejar a Tecnologia da Informação Integrada ao Planejamento Estratégico das Organizações. 4º Edição. São Paulo: Editora Atlas, 2011.

Weill, Peter e ROSS, Jeanne. W. Governança de Tecnologia da Informação. São Paulo: M. Books do Brasil Editora Ltda., 2006.

Xavier, M. B. G. Mensuração da Governança de TI na Administração Direta Federal Brasileira. 2010. 123p. Dissertação de Mestrado. Universidade Católica de Brasília, Brasília, 2010. http://www.bdtd.ucb.br/tede/tde_busca/arquivo.php?codArquivo=1333&PHPSESSID= 21faebff671d65448560a0b967731d20

8

IT MANAGEMENT MODEL FOR FINANCIAL REPORT ISSUANCE AND REGULATORY AND LEGAL COMPLIANCE

José Rogério Poggio Moreira
Universidade Salvador (UNIFACS) – Salvador, Bahia, Brazil
Paulo Caetano da Silva
Universidade Salvador (UNIFACS) - Salvador, Bahia, Brazil

ABSTRACT

The development of information systems for financial report issuance must be adherent to the demands of the law and regulations that regulate the financial market. In order to perform this task, organizations need to implement control in the Information Technology (IT) area to maintain their systems´ conformity to laws and regulations. In the development of this work, it was found, through a state-of-art study, that there are no proposals contemplating the solution of this problem in its totality. In order to achieve this goal, in this paper it is presented a model for Information Technology management constituted by COBIT, ITIL and BPM management good practices, together with SOA and XBRL Technologies. This model is composed by 03 layers that aim at structuring the organization IT and business processes, besides defining a process for implementing SOA and integrating its Web services with XBRL language. One can expect this work to contribute to companies to decrease the negative impact coming from the lack of conformity with laws and regulations, through the creation of a corporative and IT environment that is flexible and more adaptable to changes, which may occur in legal demands, as well as improving the quality and reliability of financial report issuance.

Keywords: BPM, COBIT, IT, ITIL, SOA, XBRL Governance.

Address for correspondence / Endereço para correspondência

José Rogério Poggio Moreira é graduado em Sistemas de Informação pelo Centro Universitário Jorge Amado (2009). Pós graduado em Qualidade e Governança de TI pela Faculdade Ruy Barbosa. Atualmente é mestrando em Sistemas e Computação, pela Universidade Salvador (UNIFACS) e trabalha como analista de sistemas no Ministério Público. Possui experiência na área de Engenharia de Software, Qualidade e Governança de TI e Gerência de Projetos, atuando com os temas: COBIT, ITIL, BPM, SOX, SOA E XBRL.

Paulo Caetano da Silva is graduated in Chemical Engineering by Bahia Federal University (1985). Master in Computer Networks by Salvador University - UNIFACS (2003). Doctor in Computer Sciences (2010) by Pernambuco Federal University. Currently is a professor at Salvador University (UNIFACS) at Master's program in Systems and Computing, as well as an analyst at Central Bank of Brazil. He holds experience in the area of computer sciences, focused in Software Engineering, Database, SOA and XML, acting mainly in XBRL, OLAP for XML, information systems, Web and financial information.

1. INTRODUCTION

This work development was performed based on research regarding management and governance good practices in the area of information technology, as well as on the identification and analysis of XBRL language and service oriented architecture technical features for applying only concepts that are necessary to the context of the problem in question. It was also performed bibliographic research consisting in the reading of academic texts and papers and study of COBIT, ITIL and BPM technical specifications. In this phase of the work, non-existences and limitations of elements defined in proposals similar to this work were found.

The solution presented in this article aimed at contemplating theses deficiencies through the proposition of a model of management and governance for creating and releasing financial reports in the organizations that must be in conformity with specific laws and regulations for this purpose. The proposed model development was performed in parts, being divided in layers, so its implementation in the organizations may be performed iteratively and independently, allowing that the layers that attend the organization needs are implemented independently. However, a case study was not performed due to the proposal complexity, which would make its practical application unviable in a well-timed occasion.

The evolution in the area of Information Technology (IT) has taken place through diverse factors; one of them occurs due to the legislations that the organizations must follow. Sarbanes-Oxley law – SOX (ITGI, 2006) was one of the laws that significantly impacted the IT area, increasing its relevance in the organizations that must be in conformity with this law (Guerra, 2007). In this context, the organizations performed more investments in IT and valued the bond that the IT area maintains with the organization strategic goals, making the development in the IT area a critical factor for organizational success, as well as a competitive differention in the market. To help with the conformity with legal demands, according to Guerra (2007), companies´ IT areas have started to adopt *Control Objectives for Information and Related Technology* (COBIT) (ITGI, 2007a), because COBIT defines what the goals that IT controls must conform with are, in order to satisfy SOX (ITGI, 2006).

COBIT is a good management practice, independently of the technological platform, which helps IT governance to structure a monitoring process to check and measure processes. Through COBIT, the companies are able to assure that IT will be aligned to businesses goals, which involve laws, and, therefore, obtain competitive advantages for the organizations businesses (ITGI, 2007a).

Another good IT management practice, which combined with COBIT helps organizations to be conformed to laws and regulations, is ITIL. ITIL is a set of good practices regarding life cycle management of IT infrastructure services focused on business. With COBIT, the organization determines control criteria and goals to be reached by IT processes and, through the use of ITIL, these IT processes are structured and defined.

Organizations´ business processes, not only IT processes, also need to be well controlled and defined so the company may establish the control points required by laws and regulations. A good practice for managing processes that conform to this need is *Business Process Management* (BPM) (BPMN, 2006). With BPM it is possible not only to select and align business critical processes to the organization strategy, but also to create a mechanism for structuring, evaluating, measuring and controlling the business processes.

Although COBIT, ITIL and BPM enable the creation of an IT and corporative environment that contributes to the conformity required by laws and regulations, companies must deal with issues related to the diversity of data format that contributes to the creation of financial reports. It increases significantly: (i) the time of financial report issuance, due to the efforts towards data transformation; (ii) the costs coming from these efforts performance and; (iii) the risks of errors occurrence, decreasing, furthermore, report reliability and generating, consequently, negative impacts on the business.

The usage of two technologies together, SOA (Erl, 2009) and XBRL (Silva, 2003, 2002), may contribute to the improvement of problems related to the format diversity of financial data and provide a better adaptation capacity of the information systems for changes in business processes. The *Extensible Business Reporting Language* (XBRL) is an international standard adopted by companies of public and private areas, which contributes to solving the problem related to the diversification of financial information data format (Silva, 2003). XBRL provides a structure that enables data and financial information interchange and consequently data integration, which are found in different formats and in different information systems. The Service Oriented Technology (Erl, 2009) or SOA (acronym for *Service Oriented Architecture*) that has as its main goal, in the context of this paper, to facilitate services creation (SOA applications) that will automatize the business processes related to the organization´s financial and accounting areas. SOA allows the construction of more flexible and adaptable applications to the changes in business processes.

Through the analysis of the good practices and technologies discussed in this section and the lack of a model of IT management that attend the needs that the organization have, in order to conform its IT and corporative environment to the laws and regulations, it is seen the necessity of proposing a structured model for IT management that integrate these good practices and technologies (COBIT, ITIL, BPM, SOA and XBRL) in order to contribute to issue financial reports and improve the organizations´ adherence to laws and regulations.

The rest of this article is organized as follows. Section 02 presents correlate works that were analyzed and subsidies the construction of the model. Section 03 details the structure of the model of IT management. Finally, in Section 04 the conclusions and final considerations of this article are made.

Correlative Works

In this section, it is performed an analysis of the works related to the IT management structured model proposed in this paper.

(Biancolino & Critofoli, 2008) performed an analysis of SOA and XBRL technologies, which constitute an important resource that may be used by controllers, in order to provide an IT solution that would provide a link between the business demands and regulatory departments. Through the analysis performed, the authors concluded that SOA is a facilitator for corporative information systems as modulator of business services that can be easily integrated and reused, creating a flexible and adaptable IT infrastructure. The analysis performed for XBRL technology, however, has highlighted the importance this language holds in the financial area, due to the facility offered in sharing and searching financial information in the context of organizational information systems. Nevertheless, although other authors highlight the importance of these technologies, for the accountant area and for the issuance of financial reports, in order to successfully develop information systems through SOA and XBRL, they do not discuss business processes structuring. (Gluchowski & Pastwa, 2006) have proposed to investigate reliable and fast ways of performing financial and business data interchange through SOA, with *Web Services* and XBRL technologies, in order to eliminate problems related to the issuance of financial reports and making the business processes more flexible. The authors presented a proposal of how to develop financial information systems, through SOA with *Web Services* and XBRL, and discussed the benefits that the services would bring to financial report issuance. However, the business processes organization was not discussed.

The work of (Waldman, 2009) aimed at describing a script for performing the SOA implementation in medium and large size corporations. In order to do that, the author suggests that the implementation be done in phases, starting, firstly, with a single system that is small and simple. From the success of the first implementation, according to (Waldman, 2009), the same process should be repeated in other systems, until it is performed in the whole organization. If the evaluation of the first implementation is not satisfactory, new attempts must be made until the organization is familiarized and confident with the new concept (SOA) and, thus, it may advance to other systems. However, this work does not fill the gap regarding the alignment of SOA applications with business processes, and it does not discuss deeply the phases of SOA implementation and the relation of SOA with IT governance.

The work of (Baldam, Valle, Pereira, Hilst, Abreu and Sobral, 2010) aimed at describing BPM good practices, contributes to its implementation in a corporative environment. The authors then created a life cycle model for implementing and maintaining processes management, using BPM in the companies. According to the authors, the benefits generated by the model proposed are: (i) creating improvement goals; (ii) eliminating reworks; (iii) aligning the activities to the company strategies; (iv) standardizing tasks and; (v) improving information for the information systems present in the companies. Nevertheless, this work has not discussed the relation of the good practices of management processes, using BPM, with the SOA application, nor has treated the aspects related to IT processes that will support the SOA services.

(Moreira, 2009) proposed a methodology that integrates COBIT with ITIL, in order to implement IT governance in the organizations that need to be in conformity with Sarbanes-Oxley Law. Through the phases and files proposed in the methodology, the organizations might be able to have their IT processes well defined and controlled, which contribute to better attending the needs of the information systems, besides providing an improvement in the company business processes. With the integration of these good practices, according to (Moreira, 2009), the company that implements IT management will get the possibility, through the usage of COBIT, of: (i) strategically aligning IT with the business; (ii) selecting the organization critical processes and that have a bad performance, so they may be improved; (iii) identifying the company risk profile and evaluating the risks related to the services that are being delivered; (iv) evaluating the maturity of the more critical processes for the business and aligning them to a level of ideal maturity in an efficient way, through the improvement projects. Through the ITIL good practices, however, the work of (Moraes, 2009) aims at structuring IT processes in an efficient way so that these processes may reach their control goals defined by COBIT, making them better projected, controlled and enabling them to generate more benefits for the business, as well as attending the demands of Sarbanes-Okley Law. Although providing well defined and controlled IT processes, through the proposed methodology, the author does not discuss business processes management.

2. IT MANAGEMENT STRUCTURED MODEL

The IT management structured model proposed, in this work, is based on good management practices such as BPM, COBIT and ITIL and on SOA and XBRL technologies. Its architecture was developed from the problems discussed in Section 01 and the analysis of good practices and technologies discussed in Section 02. This section is organized in the following way: Section 3.1 presents the IT management model together with the elements that compose its structure, after that, in Section 3.2, the aspects related to the business process layer of the IT management model are discussed, Section 3.3 describes the layer related to the model IT processes and Section 3.4 presents the layer related to SOA and XBRL technologies.

2.1   Model Structure

The proposed model goal is to provide subsides of management and governance so that companies may be more adherent to the laws and regulations by which they abide, and so that they can improve the quality and reliability of the financial report issuance.

In order to provide a better understanding, visualization and grouping of the involved practices and technologies, the proposed model is divided into three layers, as it can be seen in Figure 3.1. Each layer has management associated good practices or technologies to allow them to reach their goals. The model is organized in phases, which have activities that may be subdivides into tasks.

It is important to emphasize that the sequence of the model layers execution, as it can be seen in Figure 3.1, was defined with the assumption that the company needs to have, before developing SOA services, business processes which are defined and aligned to the organization strategy and IT processes which are structured and aligned to the business goals, towards IT.

The layers execution order is justified, because the business processes will originate the functionalities and information, which will be automatized and stored through the SOA services. If the processes do not work, due to their loss of structure, lack of maturity or inefficiency, there is no point for a company, with these processes, in adopting SOA architecture for developing and maintaining information systems. SOA architecture will not improve the performance of non-structured business processes, once they originate the flows and information for SOA services. Another aspect that justifies the sequence of execution established for the management model proposed regards services construction. In order to do that, it is necessary that the company has an IT process structure that maintains the development and the evolution of the services, in a way that they generate the expected results for the company.

Although the proposed model establishes an execution order for the layers, these may be executed independently from one another. This is important because not all the companies have the need of implementing all the layers, due to, for example, the fact that they already have their IT or business processes management structure. Thus, the companies that are in this context may use the model layers as a reference to maturate their practices and develop new initiatives.

The main goals of the three layers that compose the proposed model are:

(i) **Business Processes Layer:** In this layer, the aspects related to such organization business processes as controlling, optimizing, evaluation, selection, identification and planning are discussed, based on the company strategic priorities. The model is then based on BPM good practices. In this layer, it is discussed the whole life cycle adopted so that the organization business processes can evolve and become mature over time. This layer contributes to the creation of IT and corporative environment, through BPM good practices;

(ii) **IT Processes Layer:** In this layer, the aspects of IT processes management that enable the organizations to implement IT governance are discussed. In this layer, COBIT and ITIL good practices are used to identify business and IT goals, selecting the IT processes, perform analysis and diagnoses and implement the processes and improvements projected for them. This layer, like the Business Processes layer, also contributes to the creation of a more adherent IT and corporative environment to laws and regulations;

(iii) **SOA and XBRL Layer:** In this layer, the aspects related to SOA implementation and risk control and identification, coming from this implementation, are treated. Another aspect is SOA integration, through the *Web Services*, with XBRL, enabling, this way, information systems that are more flexible, connectable and aligned to the business processes, besides improving the quality and reliability if integrated with financial reports issuance.

The following subsections discuss each one of the model architecture layers.

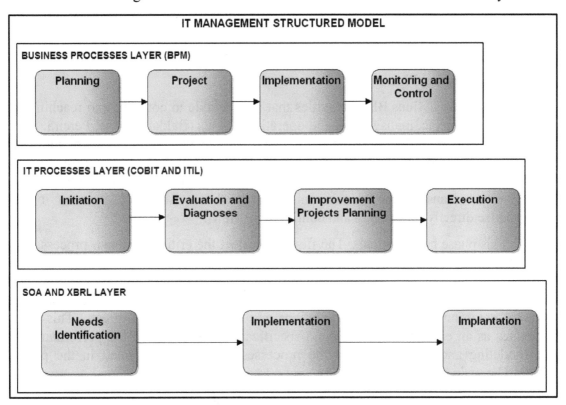

Figure 3.1. IT Management Structured Model.

2.2   Business Processes Layer

This layer treats the aspects related to business processes management, using BPM good practices. This layer application is performed through some tools, techniques, and reference business process management maturity models. This layer, through the business process management structure provided by BPM good practices, contributes to the creation of a technological and corporative environment which is more adherent to laws and regulations and more suitable to the efficient generation of financial reports.

The BPM life cycle model proposed in this paper, as it can be seen in Figure 3.2, is based on that proposed by (Baldam, Valle, Pereira, Hilst, Abreu and Sobral, 2010), being composed by 04 phases that will be discussed in the following subsections.

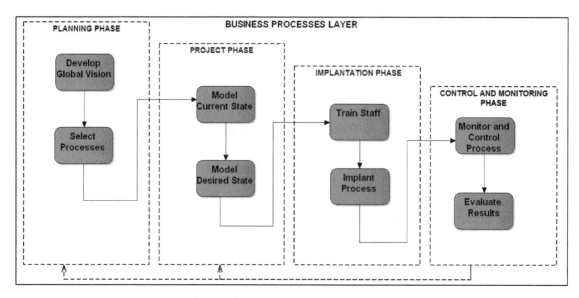

Figure 3.2. Business Layer Life Cycle.

2.2.1   Planning Phase

This phase defines BPM activities that will be able to contribute to reaching the organization strategic, management and operational goals (Baldam, Valle, Pereira, Hilst, Abreu and Sobral, 2010). It is relevant to emphasize that administrative initiatives involve organization internal processes, implicating, most of the times, interest conflicts and lack of comprehension of the goals. Because of that, it is very important the support from the top management of companies that wish to use BPM, because it may compromise directly the success and continuity of BPM.

This phase has two goals. The first is to select the critical business processes for the company. The second is to provide a holistic view and the business processes alignment to the organization strategy, through the development of a global vision of the processes. In this phase, the entrances are obtained through the strategic planning, external environment, laws and regulations and opportunities and threats. This phase generates as an exit, the guidelines and specifications necessary to the performance of the modeling and optimization of the processes, which is performed in the project phase. The main activities in this phase are:

(i)   Develop a global vision of the processes, allowing the company to have a general vision of relationships among processes and starting an alignment of the processes with the company strategy. This activity is relevant for the company to have a better understanding of the functioning and the relationship between the processes, from the strategic level to the operational level. A better understanding of how the processes relate to each other is expected, improving, thus, the model projects and isolated process studies. The development of a global vision of processes must be performed before initiating a project of BPM practices inclusion;

(ii) Select the company key processes, defining in which of processes (strategic, management or operational) the organization is stronger, weaker, which the weak spots are, which threats and opportunities are presented, which indicators were defined. It is important to observe that some processes, not necessarily processes with quality, cost and deadline problems, may be optimized so the company obtains a better cost and deadline reduction, even if the process is perfectly working. It must be performed a classification by order of priority of the organization business processes, giving attention to the processes that need immediate solutions.

2.2.2 Project Phase

This life cycle phase aims at performing the study of the current situation of the organization processes and proposes a better future situation for each one of the selected processes. This phase goals are: (i) documenting the processes; (ii) employing methodologies to optimize the processes; (iii) redrawing and innovate the processes; (iv) performing BPM *benchmarking* (technique that allows defining, understanding and develop processes through the study of how other organizations perform the same activities) (Baldam, Valle, Pereira, Hilst, Abreu and Sobral, 2010) and; (v) performing simulations. This phase is formed by two large activities: (i) modeling the process current state and; (ii) modeling the process desired state.

Before starting the modeling project, it is necessary to analyze specifications and guidelines that were generated in the planning phase. It also important to analyze the global vision of the processes so that the company can define the number of subprocesses related to the process that will be modeled and, thus, estimate the effort and the resources necessary to perform the modeling.

a) Current State Modeling

This activity, in the Project phase, aims at understanding the existing process and identifying its failures so that the errors previously made are not repeated. The current state modeling involves the following tasks: (i) planning the modeling; (ii) collecting information about the process, identifying possible improvement points; (iii) modeling the process; (iv) validating the process and adjusting, if necessary, the discrepancies between the model of the process modeled in this activity and the process that is in execution. This is necessary for confirming if the process that was modeled, in this activity and based on the process that is in execution, does not have any inconsistent data and if the data is precisely represented.

b) Desired State Modeling

The desired state modeling provides improvements in the process under analyses. To do so, this activity involves tasks: (i) selecting improvement techniques; (ii) model process and; (iii) simulating and validating processes. Among the techniques that may be used, are (Baldam, Valle, Pereira, Hilst, Abreu and Sobral, 2010):

(i) **Continuous Improvement:** that seeks to continuously establish goals and identifies improvement opportunities through critical analysis performed regarding process data, audit reports and other sources.

(ii) **FAST** (*Fast Analyses Solution Technique*): allows the rapid improvement of a process, giving immediate returns to the organization (Harrington, Esseling and Nimwegen, 1997);

(iii) ***Benchmarking***: allows defining, understanding and creatively developing the processes through the study of how other organizations perform the same activity.

(iv) **Redrawing:** aims at refining the current process. This technique is applicable to processes that are not good and;

(v) **Innovation:** consists in a more severe approach of process improvement, providing a totally new vision of the current process.

Each one of the presented techniques results in improvements and cost reduction, time and margin of error for the process. The definition of which technique or techniques combination must be used will depend a lot on the organization needs and importance of the process for the business. This way, each organization must choose and perform the necessary techniques association to achieve the desired result., from the analyses performed in the process, based on its importance for the business and factors such as execution time and process cost, as well as competitiveness that the business demands.

2.2.3 Implantation Phase

This phase is responsible for the optimized process implantation. Among the activities that compose this phase, are: (i) training and empowering users and; (ii) implementing the process. This phase puts in practice what was defined in the project phase. It is a critical phase, because it is at this moment that the process will start to be executed by the users and the negative and positive impacts of the changes performed in the process will be actually put in practice.

Baldam, Valle, Pereira, Hilst, Abreu and Sobral (2010) assert that the process implantation be treated as a specific project, being able to be managed through the good practices of *Project Management Institute* (PMI) (PMI, 2008). The processes implantation may demand the creation of subprojects for configuration, customization or even creation of specific information systems for the process being discussed, although the process execution does not necessarily demand these systems.

2.2.4 Control and Monitoring Phase

This phase performs the monitoring and control of the processes in execution, aiming at maintaining them inside the planned goals. The monitoring and control provide the decision makers with information regarding the process behavior, allowing one to analyze if the processes are in conformity with what is expected and if they attend the needs of organization´s strategies (Baldam, Valle, Pereira, Hilst, Abreu e Sobral, 2010). This phase provides the necessary feedback to the planning and BPM life cycle project phases. Among the activities that compose this phase are: (i) monitor and control the process and; (ii) evaluate the results.

2.3 IT Processes Layer

This layer treats the aspects related to the IT process management and the implementation of an IT governance program, enabling the creation of a more efficient and manageable corporative and technological environment, which is adherent to laws and regulations. In order to that, the IT management model proposed uses COBIT and ITIL good practices.

This layer is divided into four sequential phases that have activities directed to achieve each phase goals. The phases that compose this layer are:

(i) Initiation: this phase mainly aims at identifyingIT needs and selecting the processes that must be reorganized inside the organization based on the business priorities and IT risks in the company.

(ii) Evaluation and Diagnoses: this phase mainly aims at providing the solution for the IT area needs, based on the critical processes selected through the IT goals and the business goals;

(iii) Planning Improvement Projects: this phase mainly aims at organizing and defining the projects that must be aligned with the organization business for implementing IT governance based on improvements proposed by the evaluation and diagnoses phase;

(iv) Execution: this phase mainly aims at executing the improvement projects that were created in the previous phase.

Initially, in order to achieve the goals of the two first phases, the IT management model uses COBIT. ITIL will be, initially, used in the GAP analyses activity (that will be explained in section 3.3.2) that belongs to the evaluation and diagnoses phase. Thereafter, in the planning and execution phases, ITIL will be used to perform the definitions of the improvement projects and to implement these processes. However, in the planning and execution phases, COBIT also may be used as a reference to clarify issues related to the goals and practices of control associated to the IT processes that are part of the improvement projects. A detailed view of the structure of this layer may be seen in Figure 3.3.

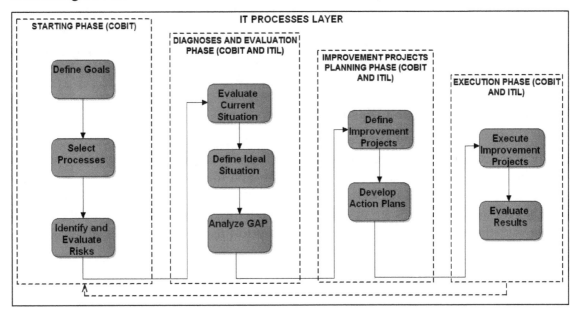

Figure 3.3. IT Layer Life Cycle.

2.3.1 Starting Phase

This phase is responsible for identifying IT area goals and business goals towards IT, obtained through the analysis of the company´s strategic planning together with other documents such as, for example, *Balance Scored Card* (BSC) (Kaplan and Norton, 1997). It is relevant to emphasize that activities related to obtaining strategic planning and the company BSC are out of the scope of the model proposed in this work.

In this phase IT process selection takes place, based on IT goals, taking into account the company operating area and identification and evaluation of IT risks that are related to the organization. This phase is composed of 03 activities:

(i)   **Identifying Goals:** this activity comprehend the identification of business goals towards IT area and IT goals. IT goals are selected from the business goals that satisfy the company´s corporative strategy. Thus, the IT goals selected are part of an IT area strategy that is aligned to the corporative strategy to satisfy the company business goals. COBIT is used in this activity to perform the mapping between the organization corporative goals and the business goals towards IT (ITGI, 2007a).

(ii)   **Selecting Processes:** this activity aims at selecting IT processes that are critical for the organization business. After identifying the IT goals, it is possible to identify associated processes, which will assure that the IT goal is satisfied.

(iii)   **Identifying and Evaluating Risks:** this activity mainly aims at identifying IT risks related to the company that may affect the IT governance implementation program. In order to do so, according to ITGI (2007b), it is necessary to understand how the company administration treats the issues regarding risks, so it is possible to identify the company risk treatment profile. Once the profile is identified, risks related to business goals and IT goals and processes need to be identified. One must analyze and document all the relevant threats and vulnerabilities, as well as their respective impacts over the services that are currently delivered by the company IT area and that are related to the business goals and to the IT goals and processes that were selected (ITGI, 2007b). After identifying the risks related to the services delivered by the company IT area, one must identify and relate the risks concerning IT governance implementation, in what regards new developments and activities executed by the IT governance program. Once the risks are identified, one must define how they will be treated.

2.3.2   Evaluation and Diagnoses Phase

This phase mainly aims at evaluating and diagnosing IT area needs based on critical processes that were selected through IT goals and business goals. This possible solution is suggested based on the analysis and diagnoses performed in critical processes, in a way that the current situation and which future goals the organization wishes for these processes are understood, considering the distance between the current state and the wished state and the business priorities. This phase is divided in 03 activities:

(i)   **Evaluating current situation:** this activity mainly aims at evaluating the current maturity of the processes that were selected in the initiation phase. This activity is responsible for the understanding of how the processes, which were selected, are being executed and managed inside the company. COBIT is used in this activity through its maturity model, which is based on the CMM maturity model (ITGI, 2007a). Through this model it is possible to measure the selected processes current stage and to establish an improvement goal for these processes.

(ii)   **Defining Ideal Situation:** this activity mainly aims at establishing the ideal maturity level for the critical processes that were selected in this first phase layer. This definition, the ideal maturity level definition, must be done by taking into account the IT process importance for the company business and IT area and the entries and exits obtained and generated by the analyzed process. One can also perform a *benchmarking* to analyze similar processes at the current maturity levels in the companies, which operate in the same market segment, so the company has an external comparison for analysis and decision making purposes.

(iii) **Analyzing GAP:** this activity mainly aims at analyzing the selected processes at thecurrent maturity level together with the ideal maturity level, translating into improvement opportunities for the process. In order to do so, one must determine, for each one of the analyzed processes, the cause of problems, the existing risks, the common related issues and the good practices and standards that may help to eliminate the gap between the current maturity level and the ideal one for a determined IT process.

2.3.3 Improvement Project Planning Phase

This phase mainly aims at planning the improvement projects based on improvements proposed by the GAP analysis activity, performed in the evaluation and diagnoses phase, in Section 3.3.2. These improvements are projected and executed through ITIL good practices, taking into account COBIT control practices. This phase is composed of 02 activities:

(i) **Defining Improvement Projects:** this activity mainly aims at transforming the improvements proposed in the evaluation and diagnoses phase into projects that will be later added to the IT governance implantation program. These improvements are the ITIL set of control goals, control practices and best practices that were related in the evaluation and diagnoses to achieve the established maturity level. For each project, the organization must establish a priority that might be based on the analysis performed in the aspects related to the project cost, deadline, importance for the business and benefits that will be generated. After this analysis, the approved projects will move to the next activity.

(ii) **Developing Action Plan:** this activity basically sums up in defining the sequence in which the approved projects will be executed. This sequence may be defined taking into account the priority that each project had in the previous activity. It is relevant that the company have an efficient change control, in order to guarantee that all activities that are necessary and included in the projectes are controlled, and so that any change is documented, analyzed and approved, assuring that only the approved changes are implemented, avoiding, thus, losses. This change control may be performed by the usage of *Project Management Institute* (PMI) project management good practices (PMI, 2008).

2.3.4 Execution Phase

This phase mainly aims at performing the improvement project implementation, using the ITIL good practices and COBIT control practices considerations. In this phase, it is also important to use PMI project management good practices to assure that the results desired for the business are obtained, through the improvement projects execution. This phase has 02 activities:

(i) **Executing Improvement Projects:** this activity consists in executing all of the improvement projects, which were approved in this layer planning phase, according to the sequence defined by project prioritization. The whole improvement project implementation must use ITIL good practices, so that the processes that are being improved or implanted are reorganized or structured in an efficient way. This activity is also responsible for acquiring, developing, testing and executing the solutions that better satisfy the projects´ goals, so, in the end, the IT governance implementation program goals are achieved (ITGI, 2007b).

(ii) **Evaluating Results:** this activity aims at evaluating experiences and results obtained from the IT governance implementation program, registering and sharing the lessons learned. This activity allows the organization to evaluate what IT governance implementation program is delivered, comparing the expectations of the involved ones. This may be obtained through the comparison of original information criteria in relation to the ones obtained and combining it to a program implantation staff evaluation, together with the evaluation of the ones involved in the program. This evaluation may be performed through workshops, satisfaction surveys and interviews. It is also relevant to register and share the lessons learned, because they contain relevant information that may be used not only by the program staff, but also in future projects of process improvement. This way, the steps for concluding this activity are: (i) combining the satisfaction survey evaluation, interviews and workshops; (ii) comparing and reporting the obtained results in relation to what was initially proposed by the performed project and; (iii) promoting brainstorming with all the ones involved in the program to register the lessons learned.

2.4   SOA and XBRL Layer

This layer treats the aspects related to SOA implementation, including risks management and SOA integration, through web services, with XBRL, enabling, thus, financial reports emission. In order to do that, an SOA implementation model is proposed. The model, through SOA services, aims at providing information systems which are more flexible, interoperable and aligned to business processes, providing more flexibility to the changes that happen in the organization business, due to the need of adequacy of the information systems to the changes that take place in legal requirements.

This model contributes, through XBRL usage, for: (i) decreasing the need for financial data format transformation, due to XBRL being a technology used as a standard for data integration; (ii) decreasing the cost of data extraction, due to the usage of XBRL and; (iii) decreasing the error risk and, consequently, increasing the reliability of financial information, since it is not necessary to perform huge efforts to transform and extract data from different formats anymore (Silva, 2003).

SOA implementation model considers the following aspects: (i) start SOA implementation through a single system, preferably a system that provides a good migration process. It is also important that the system is small and simple; (ii) repeat the same process for other systems, until it is performed for the whole organization and; (iii) perform services compositions for developing new information systems.

Figure 3.4 presents SOA and XBRL layers, together with the model phases and the activities that compose them. As it is possible to observe, through Figure 3.4, SOA and XBRL layer implementation model lead the companies to the process of SOA adoption and integration of web services with XBRL language. The phases, together with the activities that are part of this layer and that compose the SOA implementation model, will be described in the following subsections.

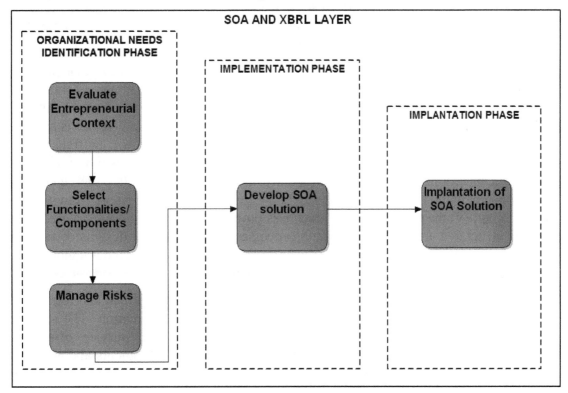

Figure 3.4. SOA and XBRL Life Cycle Layer.

2.4.1   Organizational Needs Identification Phase

This phase aims at evaluating the organization current context, besides identifying the elements that will be transformed into SOA services, providing risk management. To do that, this phase contains the following activities:

(i)   Evaluate Entrepreneurial Context

This activity aims at evaluating de company current scenario analyzing the following elements: (a) the business processes that should be already structured, defined and efficient; (b) the information systems, which automatize the business processes and from which the legacy components will be extracted to be transformed into services and; (c) governance structure or program necessary to structure and control IT processes, which will allow the adequate use of resources for developing and maintaining service oriented solutions.

(ii)   Select Functionalities/Components

This activity concentrates in the selection of components or functionalities of the legacy systems that will be transformed into services.

(iii)   Manage Risks

This activity aims at performing the risk management in SOA implementation. This activity is divided into two tasks: (a) identify and evaluate risks in SOA implementation and; (b) control risks in SOA implementation. These tasks are detailed below:

a)   Identify and Evaluate Risks in SOA Implementation

This task identifies and evaluates the risks that are associated to SOA implementation. The SOA adoption process is susceptible to some occurrences that may be decisive to its conception and must be identified, because they might make SOA implementation in the organization not viable or suspend it. In this activity, some risks common to SOA implementations are also approached.

Once the company risk treatment profile has already been defined in the phase of IT processes layer starting, Section 3.3.1, the risks related to SOA implementation must be identified. The risk identification in SOA implementation process must evaluate: (i) if the company technical staff understands what service oriented architecture is and if it has the capacity for its adoption; (ii) the legacy components that will be transformed into services and chosen in the SOA implementation planning activity; (iii) the company capacity in perform the changes that are necessary to realize the benefits of SOA implementation; (iv) the existence of IT governance and support from the top management; (v) the methodology of business processes management used and if there are well structured and efficient business processes; (vi) the budget designated to SOA adoption; (vii) the adequacy of risk management practices and methodologies. Once identified the risks, one must define how they will be treated.

One must document how the risk management will be performed and register all the risks identified during this activity and along SOA implementation. The steps to successfully perform this task are: (i) identify the risks related to the services offered by the company; (ii) identify the risks that are related to new developments and activities that will be performed in SOA implantation and; (iii) define the treatment that will be given to find risks.

b)   Control Risks in SOA Implementation

This task aims at providing the necessary support for the company to perform risk control in SOA implementation, through the IT management good practices that have been used to create the IT and corporative environment. The implementation of IT governance, through the usage of COBIT and ITIL good practices, and through a good business processes management, through the usage of BPM good practices, helps understanding, structuring, maintaining and evolving the process (IT and business ones) and guaranteeing a commitment from the top management. The usage of these good management practices contributes to controlling risks and threats that may appear in SOA implementation.

The companies that want to avoid and control diverse factors (organizational or technical) that generate risks to the SOA implementation process must have a unique understanding about their IT and business processes and must guarantee full support from the top management, assuring, thus, the support from all the departments that are involved in the initiative.

2.4.2   Implementation Phase

This phase´s main goal is to develop the SOA solution that will attend the organization needs. In order to do so, this phase contains the following activity:

(i)   Develop SOA Solution

This activity regards the survey of requirements, analysis and project, implementation and services test. It is relevant to emphasize that, in the analysis and project, one must consider the aspects related to the reuse and integration of the services that will compose the business solution. Normally, in order to perform the decomposition of business processes into IT services, a top-down (Marzullo, 2009) approach is adopted, as it is shown in Figure 3.5. According to this approach, a business process may be decomposed in several subprocesses, which may be unfolded into activities that, in the end, are divided into tasks. These tasks are automatized and consequently transformed into web services, which are grouped into modules that, once integrated, form the information system that automatizes the whole business process. In this activity, the integration of web services with XBRL language still happens.

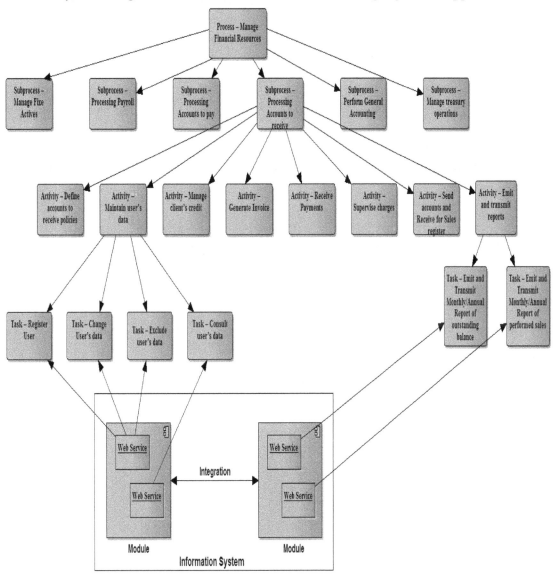

Figure 3.5. Business process decomposition into IT services. Adapted from (Marzullo, 2009)

The following subsection describes the task responsible for performing the integration between web services and XBRL.

a) Integrate *Web Services* with **XBRL**

The *Web Services* represent a way of implementing services in a service oriented architecture and provide an infrastructure independent from the platform, also making different technology integration and development easier. This task aims at integrating the *Web Services* with the XBRL language. In order to do so, illustrating architectural model and scenario were created, respectively, in addition to the integration architecture and process.

The integration architectural model may be seen in Figure 3.6, which shows, through a layer division, how the integration between XBRL and the *Web Services* may happen. It is possible to observe in the model that *Web Services* usage is useful both to format XBRL data and to consolidate them in financial reports. However, initially, it is necessary to transform the legacy systems components into web services, responsible for the financial information, or to create web services for the legacy systems functionalities that relate them directly to the financial information that will be present in the financial reports to be issued. This is necessary so that the *Web Services* are able to extract the data from the legacy systems, put them in the XBRL format and later, through these data consolidation, create a financial report, performing, thus, the integration between the two technologies. An issue to be considered, in this architectural model, is that the business processes are the architectural model elements that direct, through regulations and laws by which they are linked, the needs of the XBRL documents that will be constructed by the organization through their *Web Services*.

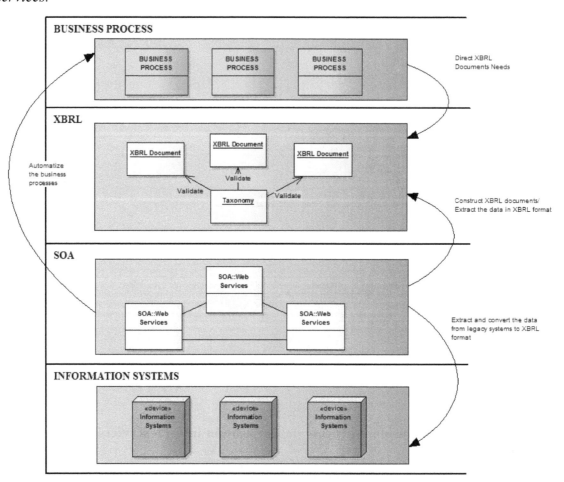

Figure 3.6. SOA and XBRL Integration Architecture.

An example of integration between SOA and XBRL may be visualized in Figure 3.7, which presents a situation where a multinational and open capital company that has 03 branches with distinct data systems and base send their financial information in XBRL format, through *Web Services,* to their main office, which consolidates this information in an integrated financial report to, later, send them to regulatory departments. In this context, the integration between XBRL and *Web Services* may happen in two distinct moments. The first moment happens in the XBRL file creation, when the *Web Services* will access the heterogenic data base to extract the data, converting them into XBRL format. The second moment happens in two situations: (i) when the company branches provide the *Web Services* that send the XBRL files to their main offices that represent the financial report for a certain month or year, so that they can be integrated in a single report and; (ii) when the organizations make *Web Services* available to send the XBRL file, which represent the integrated financial report for a certain month or year to the regulatory departments.

The integration between XBRL and *Web Services* happens when the XBRL instance file is packed inside the SOAP message that will be transmitted. This way, right after the XBRL taxonomy definition or selection and the posterior XBRL file creation, it is possible to start the XBRL file packing inside the SOAP message so that it can be transmitted. It is important to emphasize that the defined taxonomy must be useful as a standard, because the XBRL file must be validated during its creation and after the SOAP message unpacking and, consequently, reception of the XBRL file for processing and for the financial report issuance.

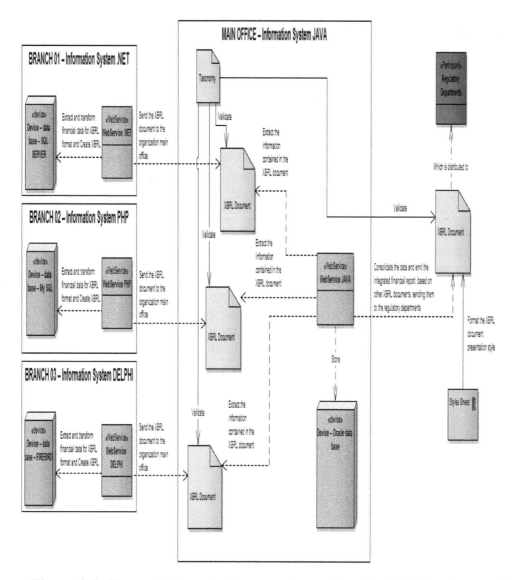

Figure 3.7. Financial Reports Issuance Scenario with Web Services and XBRL.

2.4.3 Implantation Phase

This phase aims at implanting an SOA solution. This phase contains the activity that implant an SOA solution, which is responsible for putting in operation the services developed in the previous phase.

If the first initiative of an SOA implementation does not turn out to be effective, the company must perform a detailed analysis of the reasons that make the initiative unsuccessful, so that the committed errors or risks, which occurred during the implantation attempt, may be duly corrected or eliminated. Later, when the organization becomes more familiarized with and confident about the new concept (SOA), new attempts may be performed. After the implantation success, the organization may advance towards the implantation in other systems. However, until the end of an SOA implantation, the legacy systems and SOA applications will exist in a concomitant way. During an SOA adoption process, the governance polices must be totally implanted, if they do not exist.

With the organization advance and maturation, in what concerns the use of SOA, one expects that the new projects will become faster, cheaper and with fewer implantation problems, because, the higher the level of reuse, the lower the effort for development will be and problems are likely to occur. When all the systems are service oriented, the organization must have a stabilized scenario and all the services must be in the company´s services repository and the presence of duplicated services inexistent. In this context, it is important that any new service follows the development process and the organizational policies directed to SOA. The usage of services, made available by the company, must also be made through the services repository and with a formal contract of services rendering (Waldman, 2009).

2.4.4 Final Considerations Regarding the Model

The model proposed in this work uses information technology governance good practices accepted by the market and the academia, besides new technologies for develping financial reports and information systems. Figure 3.8 shows the relation between IT processes (structured and defined through good COBIT and ITIL practices), SOA applications (developed through *Web Services* and XBRL) and the Business Processes (structured and maintained through BPM good practices) for the accomplishment of entrepreneurial strategies.

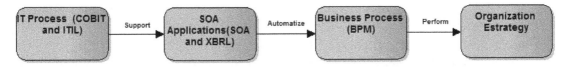

Figure 3.8. Relation among the IT processes, the SOA applications and the Business processes.

BPM helps defining, structuring and managing the business processes present in the organization. COBIT and ITIL, together, structure and improve IT processes that support the information systems (SOA applications), which automatize the company business processes, in order to achieve its strategy. The change management IT process is an example of support given by IT processes to SOA applications. Once it is structured and defined, through COBIT and ITIL practices, the change management process must support SOA applications, in what regards the changes and modifications in legal requirements imposed by laws and regulations by which the organizations abide.

With the use of BPM good practices, the organization is able to manage with more efficiency the business processes, mitigating or eliminating risks related to the lack of these process mapping, which, in this case, may generate the decrease of advantages that will be obtained from an SOA implementation, due to the complexity of the business processes and the fact that they involve diverse departments in the organization.

The COBIT that acts as an IT governance model and, thus, embodies SOA governance helps to intensify the control over the processes that support the development and provision of service oriented applications, as it is the case of processes of service level management, changes, configuration, acquisition and maintenance of systems. In this way, COBIT contributes tothe mitigation or elimination of the risks related to the lack of governance and support from the company´s top management(both described in the previous section).

ITIL contributes to managing the service level, the services that will be used or offered by the organization, minimizing the risk of not accomplishing what was previously agreed (OGC, 2007). ITIL also provides a contribution, through changes and configuration management, to the services that are already in production, because, through this management, it is possible to establish a higher control over the changes that may occur in the services, avoiding, thus, risks and problems coming from non-authorized changes and/or performed in some service that is being rendered (OGC, 2007).

3.   CONCLUSION

This paper presented an IT management model for financial reports issuance. The model is divided into 03 layers and provides the creation of a corporative and IT environment which is more adherent to laws and regulations and more favorable to financial reports generation.

The business processes layer aims at planning, evaluating, optimizing and controlling the organization business processes, through the usage of BPM good practices.

In the IT processes layer, the IT area governance is implemented, based on business priorities and IT risks, using COBIT and ITIL good practices. In this layer, techniques are used to select, analyze and implement an organization IT process. The business layer and the IT layer contribute to the creation of a corporative environment and to the IT area. COBIT, as an IT governance model, allows measuring, controlling, and evaluating all the IT processes that, in turn, supports the organization business processes, contributing to achieving the company strategy. ITIL, however, contributes, through its practices, to projecting and structuring projects in a suitable way, making them more efficient and controlled inside the organization. This way, one may observe the good effects that IT governance implementation brings to the organization.

SOA and XBRL implementation layer deals with aspects related to risk identifications and control in the service oriented architecture implementation. In this context, the execution of this layer of the proposed model enables risk reduction and a controllable SOA implementation, through the usage of good practices, such as the ones from COBIT, ITIL and BPM, since these practices improve the SOA implementation control, security and risk reduction. In the SOA/XBRL layer, it is presented a model for implementing this architecture integrated with XBRL, through *Web Services*, enabling the provision of information systems that are more flexible, connectable and aligned to the business processes, besides improving the reliability and quality in financial reports issuace.

The structured management model proposed presents the benefit of creating an IT and corporative environment which is more adherent to laws and regulations and more favorable to financial reports generation. This model also contributes to decreasing the needs for financial data format transformation and for decreasing the extraction costs due to XBRL usage. Error risksand, consequently, increase of financial information reliability are also reduced, since there is no need to perform big efforts to transform and extract data in a different format anymore. With the SOA usage, the model is able to provide information systems that are more flexible, interoperable and aligned to the business processes, providing more flexibility to the changes that occur in the organization business.

With the intention of performing a comparison between correlate works and the IT management structured model proposed in this paper, it was performed an analysis between the works described in Section 03 and the proposed model, discussing the deficiencies and benefits identified in the works. Table 4.1 presents a comparison between these works.

Table 4.1. Comparasion between the works and the IT management model.

WORKS	USE OF GOOD PRACTICES AND TECHNOLOGIES				
	COBIT	ITIL	BPM	SOA	XBRL
IT Management Model	YES	YES	YES	YES	YES
(Biancolino & Critofoli, 2008)	-	-	-	YES	YES
(Gluchowski & Pastwa, 2006)	-	-	-	YES	YES
(Waldman, 2009)	-	-	-	YES	-
(Baldam, Valle, Pereira, Hilst, Abreu and Sobral, 2010)	-	-	YES	-	-
(Moreira, 2009)	YES	YES	-	-	-

Through the comparison, it is possible to observe that only the IT management structure model proposal contemplates all the good practices of technology management described in this paper. This is important, because with the collaborative usage of these management practices and technologies treated in this paper, it becomes possible to solve the problems related to IT management and to financial reports issuance, in a context of continuous change in the laws and regulations that govern them.

It becomes evident, through the analysis of Table 4.1, that it was not found, in the literature researched for this work development, a similar proposal, emphasizing, thus, the need to create an IT management model that would make the corporative and IT environment more favorable for financial reports issuance and more adherent to laws and regulations.

REFERENCES

Baldam, Roquemar de Lima; VALLE, Rogerio de Aragão Bastos do; PEREIRA, Humberto Rubens Maciel; HILST, Sérgio de Mattos; ABREU, Mauricio Pereira de; SOBRAL, Valmir Santos. (2010). Gerenciamento de Processos de Negócios BPM – Business Process Management. Erica.

BPMN. (2006). Business Process Modeling Notation Specification. Needram.

Erl, T. (2009). Service-Oriented Architecture (SOA): Concepts, Technology, and Design, Edited by Prentice Hall, 9ª Edition.

Guerra, Márcia R. (2007). Governança de TI com COBIT. São Paulo: TIEXAMES. Disponível em: http://www.tiexames.com.br/ensino/home.php. Acessado em: 20/08/2008.

Harrington, H. J.; Esseling, E.K.C.; Nimwegen, H. V. (1997). Business Process Improvement. New York: McGraw-Hill.

ITGI. (2007a). COBIT 4.1. USA: IT Governance Institute. Disponível em: http://www.isaca.org/Template.cfm?Section=Downloads3&Template=/MembersOnly.c fm&ContentID=49581. Acessado em 20/08/2008.

ITGI. (2007b). IT Governance Implementation Guide. USA: ITGI. Disponível em:http://www.isaca.org/Template.cfm?Section=Downloads3&Template=/MembersOn ly.cfm&ContentID=49582. Acessado em: 20/03/2009.

ITGI. (2006). IT Control Objectives for Sarbanes-Oxley. USA: ITGI. Disponível em: http://www.cobitonline4.info/Pages/Public/Browse/PdfDownload.aspx. Acessado em: 20/03/2009.

Josuttis, N. M. (2007). SOA in Practice: The Art of Distributed System Design (Theory in Practice), Edited by OReally Media.

Kaplan, Robert S.. Norton, David P. (1997). A Estratégia em Ação. Rio de Janeiro: Campus.

Leal, M.A.M. (2006). A Organização e Arquitetura de Processos na Telemar. In: segundo Seminário Brasileiro de Gestão de Processos, Rio de Janeiro. Volume único. CD-ROM.

Marzullo, Fabio Perez. (2009). SOA na Prática Inovando o seu negócio por meio de soluções orientadas a serviço, Editado por Novatec.

Moreira, José Rogério Poggio. (2009). Governança de ti: metodologia para integração do COBIT e ITIL em empresas que buscam conformidade com a lei Sarbanes-Oxley. UNIJORGE, Salvador.

OGC. (2007). The Official Introduction to the ITIL Service Lifecycle. UK: TSO.

Paim, R., Caulliraux, H., Cardoso, V. e Clemente, R. (2009). Gestão de Processos: pensar, agir e aprender. Bookman.

PMI. (2008). Um Guia do Conhecimento em Gerenciamento de Projetos (Guia PMBOK). Pensilvania, EUA: PMI.

Silva, P. C. (2003). Explorando linguagens de marcação para representação de relatórios financeiros. Dissertação de Mestrado. UNIFACS, Salvador.

Silva, P. C., Teixeira, C. C. (2003) A Gestão da Informação Financeira do Banco Central do Brasil Apoiada por XBRL In: I Workshop de Tecnologia da Informação e gerência do Conhecimento, 2003, Fortaleza.

Silva, P. C., Teixeira, C. C. (2002) Informações Financeiras como Hiperdocumentos na Web In: VIII Brazilian Symposium on Multimedia and Hypermedia Systems - SBMIDIA 2002, 2002, Fortaleza. SBC, p.356 – 364.

Siqueira, L. G. P. (2006). Modelo de Governo de Processos da Área Internacional da Petrobras. In: Segundo Seminário Brasileiro de Gestão de Processos, Rio de Janeiro, Anais. Volume único. CD-ROM.

Waldman, Daniel. (2009). Cenários e Etapas para Implantação SOA. Disponível em: <http://www.aqueleblogdesoa.com.br/2009/05/cenarios-e-etapas-para-implantacao-soa/>. Acessado em: 18/12/2010.

OASIS. UDDI. (2004). Disponível em: http://uddi.org/pubs/uddi-v3.0.2-20041019.pdf. Acessado em 20/12/2011.

Shuja, Ahmad K; Krebs, Jochen. (2008). Unified Process Reference and Certification Guide. IBM Press.

W3C. HTTP. (2009). Disponível em: http://www.w3.org/standards/techs/http#w3c_all. Acessado em 20/12/2011.

W3C. SOAP. (2007a). Disponível em:
http://www.w3.org/standards/techs/soap#w3c_all. Acessado em 20/12/2011.

W3C. WSDL. (2007b). Disponível em:
http://www.w3.org/standards/techs/wsdl#w3c_all. Acessado em 20/12/2011.

W3C. XML. (2008). Disponível em: http://www.w3.org/standards/techs/xml#w3c_all. Acessado em 20/12/2011.

9

A FUZZY MULTICRITERIA APPROACH FOR IT GOVERNANCE EVALUATION

Angel Cobo
University of Cantabria, Santander, Spain
Adolfo Alberto Vanti
Universidade do Vale do Rio dos Sinos, Brasil
Rocío Rocha
University of Cantabria, Santander, Spain

ABSTRACT

This work seeks to provide a new multi-criteria approach to assess IT Governance (ITG) in the area of Strategic Alignment. The complete methodological development process is described. The evaluation model uses Fuzzy Analytic Hierarchy Process (FAHP) and it is targeted to IT processes, more specifically to the COBIT© IT maturity levels, domains and processes, thus providing a differentiated analysis of importance for each item. Its relevance is related to addressing isolated and individual evaluation criteria that are normally practiced in audits of processes. The model allows generating information that extends the guarantees of compliance and corporate governance from different organizations. This research demonstrates that the combined use of multi-criteria decision methodologies and soft computing proves to be particularly suitable for Strategic Alignment such as the focal area of COBIT. The model was applied in a big retail Brazilian company.

Keywords: Corporate Governance, IT Governance, Strategic Alignment, COBIT, FAHP.

Address for correspondence / Endereço para correspondência

Angel Cobo, Doctor's Degree in Applied Mathematics, University of Cantabria. Avda. Los Castros s/n 39005 Santander (Spain).

Adolfo Alberto Vanti, Doctor's Degree in Business Administration. Universidade do Vale do Rio dos Sinos. Escola de Gestão de Negócios. Av. UNISINOS, 950, Cristo Rei, 93022000 - São Leopoldo, RS - Brasil.

Rocío Rocha, Doctor's Degree in Business Administration, University of Cantabria. Avda. Los Castros s/n 39005 Santander (Spain).

1.   INTRODUCTION

The multidisciplinary process of Corporate Governance (CG) and of IT Governance (ITG) (Weill & Ross, 2004; Van Grembergen & Haes, 2004) reduce agency conflicts in aspects such as informational asymmetry and help to reach fundamental principles related to disclosure, compliance, fairness, accountability and transparency (Jensen & Meckling, 1976). These principles are supported by good governance codes aligned with the Information Systems that support business processes, as the codes established by the Cadbury Report (1992), OECD (2011) and IBGC (2012).

Information Systems (IS) develop operational and managerial activities in internal control, increasing the guarantee of CG mainly related to the measurement requirement of confidentiality, integrity, availability and compliance. These aspects are present in different evaluation frameworks related to information security processes (Kwok & Longley, 1999; Taylor & Fitzgerald, 2007) and COBIT (ITGI, 2013). This paper focuses specifically on the analysis of the strategic alignment focal area, using the COBIT framework and seeking to reduce the problems between business and IT.

The lack of a strategic alignment between IT and business causes competitiveness losses as established by (Hirschheim & Sabherwal, 2001; Weiss & Thorogood, 2011) and also a limited improvement in strategic information systems (SIS) planning (Lederer & Sethi, 1992) that supports the achievement of the organizational objectives (Zviran, 1990), as well as the impacts and performance of the organization (Lederer & Mendelow, 1989; Chen, 2010; Li & Tan, 2013; Tiwana & Konsynski, 2010). These studies emphasize that alignment and IT Governance (ITG) must be studied together, because they are strongly related and complementary concepts. ITG guides the use of IT in the company in strategic control and adds value to business, improving decision-making processes (Van Grembergen & De Haes, 2010; Zarvi´c, Stolze, & Thomas, 2012).

In this direction of alignment between business and IT through the ITG, we propose a COBIT based model for assessing IT processes, integrating business and fuzzy aspects that will reduce the limitation detailed above.

In Marnewick & Labuschagne (2011) it became obvious that CG fails in the decision of IT projects in organizations. The study considered ITG models such as COBIT, ISO 35000, PRICE2 and PMBoK[©]. In the case of IT Governance using the COBIT, the companies in the study stated that they did not meet the requirements, postponing goals.

Strategic alignment problems between IT and business may arise from critical IT management processes with low levels of maturity. These problems can lead to wrong decisions and not reach the desired compliance, leading to problems of governance and conflicts between owners and agents or executives. Different works evidence problems related to the use of technology during decision making processes (Merali *et al*, 2012; Benítez *et al* 2012)

In this context, this paper aims to contribute to the improvement of ITG by applying a methodology for fuzzy multi-criteria evaluation, namely FAHP (Chang, 1996), and focuses on assessing the level of strategic alignment according to the COBIT 4.1 framework. This FAHP application expands the traditional IT audit process in which the valuation is produced using maturity levels in a pre-established scale (0 to 5 coming from CMMI©). The inclusion of FAHP methodology in the proposed model provides greater robustness in qualitative and subjective aspects or even fuzzy or unclear results in the pair to pair evaluation of the audited processes.

2.   A FRAMEWORK FOR IT GOVERNANCE: COBIT

COBIT (Control Objectives for Information and related Technology) is a framework created by the ISACA (Information Systems Audit and Control Association) for information technology management and IT Governance itself (ISACA, 2012), it includes an ontological metamodel of IT Governance framework (Neto & Neto, 2013). The ISACA published the current version, COBIT 5, in 2012. In (De Haes *et al*, 2013) research questions for future research on enterprise governance of IT and COBIT 5 are proposed and discussed. COBIT 5 reveals new conceptual ideas compared to the previous COBIT 4.1 version (Preittigun *et al*, 2012), however, in this work COBIT 4.1 was used. This version of COBIT defines a process model that subdivides IT into four domains and 34 processes. It provides best practices across a domain and process-based framework and presents activities in a manageable and logical structure. The business orientation of COBIT consists of linking business goals to IT goals, providing metrics and maturity models to measure their achievement, and identifying the associated responsibilities of business and IT process owners.

COBIT focuses strongly more on control and less on execution, and is contextualized in Information Technology Governance (ITG). According to Simonson, Johnson and Ekstedt (2010), it is defined as a technology managed and structured in an organization, providing mechanisms that also contribute to the strategic and IT planning of the organization.

COBIT supports IT governance by providing a framework to ensure that IT is aligned with the business, IT resources used responsibly, and IT risks managed appropriately. Finally, performance measurement is an essential aspect for IT governance. In short, IT governance (ITG) is structured around 5 major focus areas that are defined by COBIT. These areas describe the topics that executive managers need to address in order to govern IT within their organizations. According to COBIT's executive overview (ITGI, 2013), the five focus areas are: *Strategic alignment,* focused on ensuring the linkage of business and IT plans; *Value delivery*, about executing the value proposition; *Resource management*, engaged in optimal investment; *Risk management*, focused on risk awareness; and, finally, *Performance measurement,* tracks and monitors strategy implementation.

COBIT 4.1 subdivides IT into 4 domains and 34 processes in line with the responsibility areas of planning, building, running and monitoring, providing an end-to-end view of IT. COBIT is a tool for managing IT processes that includes concepts of management, mainly through the business requirements for information:

confidentiality, availability and integrity in four domains and their interrelations. These domains are briefly described below.

Plan and Organize (PO) includes strategies and tactics with the intention of identifying the best way on how IT can contribute to the achievement of the business objectives. *Acquire and Implement* (AI) is a domain that analyzes the IT solutions that need to be identified, developed or acquired, implemented and integrated into the business process. *Deliver and Support* (DS) refers to the delivery of the services requested, which includes service delivery, safety and continuity of management, support services for users and data management and operational resources. Finally, *Monitor and Evaluate* (ME) domain establishes the regular assessment processes to ensure adherence to quality and control requirements. This domain addresses performance management, monitoring of internal control, regulatory compliance and governance.

Each domain has a different number of processes involved; in fact, PO has 10 processes; AI has 7; DS has 13; and ME has 4. The complete list of 34 processes is included in the annex. It is important to note that this division into domains and processes allows to infer a hierarchy of criteria that can be used later in the AHP (Analytic Hierarchical Process) methodology applied to this work. In short, the hierarchy that will be used is shown in Figure 1.

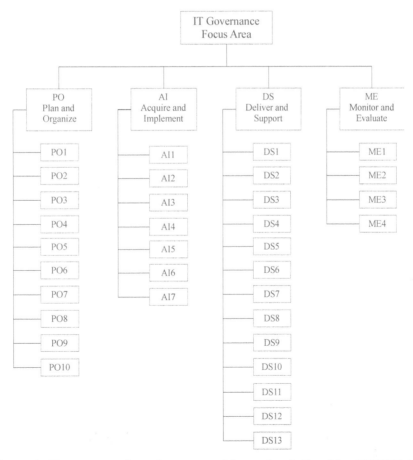

Figure 1. Focus area-domain-process hierarchy defined by COBIT 4.1.

COBIT 4.1 also includes an assessment framework of processes that defines maturity levels for each process. The model is based on the Capability Maturity Model Integration (CMMI©). This assessment framework defines a 0-5 scale with an alphanumeric description of each numeric value as it is briefly shown in Table 1. This scale allows an assessment of the degree of development of each process in an organization and the evaluation model provides guidelines for assigning maturity levels.

Value	Name	Description
0	None	There is no recognition of the need for internal control.
1	Initial	There is some recognition of the need for internal control.
2	Repeatable	Controls are in place but are not documented.
3	Defined	Controls are in place and are adequately documented. However, the evaluation process is not documented and employees are aware of their responsibilities for control.
4	Managed and measurable	There is an effective internal control and a risk management environment with a formal and documented evaluation of controls, which occurs frequently. A limited, tactical use of technology is applied to automate controls.
5	Optimized	Control evaluation is continuous, based on self-assessments and gap and root cause analyses. Employees are proactively involved in control improvements.

Table 1. Maturity levels (ITGI, 2013).

3.   METHODOLOGY

Our aim is to construct a model that allows the assessment of IT governance in an organization based on the maturity levels of COBIT's processes. To achieve this objective we have used a fuzzy multi-criteria decision methodology: FAHP.

The proposed approach is a fuzzy extension of the classical Analytic Hierarchy Process (AHP) multi-criteria technique. This technique is especially useful for obtaining a single assessment value based on different previously selected indicators or criteria (levels of maturity of processes). Furthermore, it also allows us to incorporate subjective appreciations or opinions from the IT manager on the processes that may prove more significant when it comes to measuring this assessment of IT governance. In the AHP, each element in the hierarchy of criteria is considered to be independent of all the others. When there is interdependence among criteria, and extension of AHP known as Analytic Network Process (ANP) would be used.

This approach to IT evaluation via COBIT 4.1 is very important because it is normally evaluated in an individually and isolated way, without taking into consideration subjective and fuzzy aspects. It means that the maturity levels are evaluated by choosing grades in the CMMI© (from 0 to 5) scale, ignoring that each evaluated process (34 all) has a strong influence and is influenced.

3.1. Fuzzy numbers

(Zadeh, 1965) introduced the theory of fuzzy sets in 1965 to model the concept of vagueness, characteristic of human thought. Fuzzy numbers allow to face problems in which the criteria are not precisely defined. In fuzzy logic, a statement can not only be true or false, as in classical logic, but also, and moreover, it provides a range of intermediate values between absolute certainty and absolute falsehood. In this context, a fuzzy set is determined by a membership function which determines the degree of certainty with which an element x belongs to the set.

A triangular fuzzy number is a special type of fuzzy number whose membership is defined by three real numbers, expressed as (l, m, u), where l is the lower limit, m the most promising and u the upper limit value. The membership function of M=(l,m,u) is given by:

$$\mu(x) = \begin{cases} \dfrac{x-l}{m-l} & if\ l \leq x \leq m \\ \dfrac{u-x}{u-m} & if\ m \leq x \leq u \\ 0 & if\ \ x < l\ or\ x > u \end{cases}$$

The graphical representation of this function can be seen in Figure 2.

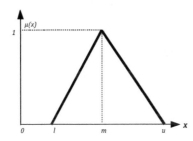

Figure 2. Membership function defining the triangular fuzzy number $M=(a,b,c)$.

The assumption of triangular fuzzy numbers is a simplification, which can be frequently found in the literature and which facilitates fuzzy arithmetic calculations (Meixner, 2009). It is possible to use the operation laws following Zadeh's extension principle via this simplification which makes calculations much easier. Given the triangular fuzzy numbers $A=(a_1,a_2,a_3)$ and $B=(b_1,b_2,b_3)$, the basic arithmetic operations are defined as follows:

$$A+B = (a_1+b_1,\ a_2+b_2,\ a_3+b_3)$$
$$A*B = (a_1b_1,\ a_2b_2,\ a_3b_3)$$
$$nA = (na_1,na_2,na_3)\ for\ all\ n>0$$

It is also possible to define the concepts of opposite $-A=(-a_3,-a_2,-a_1)$ and inverse $1/A=(1/a_3,1/a_2,1/a_1)$ fuzzy triangular numbers.

3.2. Fuzzy Analytic Hierarchy Process (FAHP)

Analytic Hierarchy Process (AHP) is a multi-criteria decision technique proposed by Saaty (1980) to solve problems of planning needs and management of scarce resources that, in time, has become one of the most widely used techniques in decision making processes on multiple criteria (Chang, 1992). In general, this technique can be applied to problem solving that requires an evaluation and measuring in which different and very often opposed criteria intervene. The main advantages of AHP are the relative ease with which it handles multiple criteria, as well as the fact that it is easy to understand and can effectively handle both qualitative and quantitative data (Markaki, Charilas, & Askounis, 2010).

The AHP technique is developed through six key stages:

• Definition of the problem and establish clear objectives and expected results.

• Deconstruction of a complex problem in a hierarchical structure with elements of decision. At a high level of hierarchy, general objectives and criteria are divided into particular objectives or subcriteria for reaching the lowest level in which the alternatives are located.

• Carrying out of pair comparisons between decision elements, forming comparison matrices based on the establishment of the relative importance between the factors of each hierarchical level.

• Checking of the consistency properties of the matrices in order to guarantee that the judgments issued by the decision makers are coherent and consistent.

• Estimation based on previous matrices of the relative weights of the decision elements for achieving the general objective.

• Making of an evaluation of the alternatives based on the weights of the decision elements.

The relative importance of the decision elements in AHP is assessed indirectly through a series of pairwise comparisons, in which the decider provides preferences by comparing all criteria and subcriteria with respect to upper level decision elements. AHP uses a 1-9 numeric scale in order to establish priority values a_{ij} for each pair of criteria. If the element E_i is preferred to E_j then $a_{ij}>1$. At each level of the criteria hierarchy we obtain an n-dimensional squared matrix, where n is the number of elements or criteria of the level. The reciprocal property $a_{ij}=1/a_{ji}$ and $a_{ii}=1$ and $a_{ij} >0$ always remains the same. In order to calculate the weights that the AHP model will assign to each criterion there are different alternatives. One of the most common methods, though computationally more complicated, is the calculation of an eigenvector associated to the dominant eigenvalue of the comparison matrix. This value must be proximate to n and is also used to define the consistency index (CI) and the consistency ratio (CR), which allows us to value the appreciation carried out by the decider on coherence when estimating the relative importance of the elements.

Among the advantages of the AHP method, we can cite the facility for incorporating multiple criteria, the possibility of using linguistic variables, as well as the need to carry out an exhaustive analysis of the definition of the values of comparison, which leads to a greater understanding of the problem tackled. However, for complex problems or those with many options, excessive computational effort may be required and a high level of pairwise comparisons. In spite of its popularity, the AHP method is often criticized for its inability to adequately handle the inherent uncertainty and imprecision associated with the mapping of a decision-maker's perception to crisp numbers. A natural way to cope with uncertainty in judgments is to express the comparison ratios as fuzzy sets or fuzzy numbers, which incorporate the vagueness of the human thinking. Therefore, fuzzy AHP (FAHP), a fuzzy extension of AHP, can be used to solve hierarchical fuzzy problems (Van Laarhoven & Pedrycz, 1983; Mikhailov & Tsvetinov, 2004). FAHP applications can be found in diverse areas such as selection of operating systems (Balli & Korukoglu, 2009), recruitment of staff, (Chen, 2009), risk assessment projects in information technology (Iranmanesh *et al*, 2008), selection of ERP systems (Lien and Chan, 2007).

Using the concept of triangular fuzzy numbers, one can obtain a "fuzzy" or diffuse version of the classical AHP. When comparing two elements E_i and E_j, the exact value ratio a_{ij} can be approximated with a fuzzy ratio which is represented by a fuzzy triangular number. The construction of a hierarchical model in FAHP is exactly equal to the original AHP.

The fuzzy numbers required to form the decision matrix may be determined directly according to the decision maker or may derive from linguistic variables in a verbal scale, which can be then converted into fuzzy numbers using a suitable conversion as shown in Table 2 and Figure 3. In order to construct a positive reciprocal matrix of pairwise comparisons, a full set of n(n-1)/2 comparison judgments are required. The pairwise comparison matrix is constructed as

$$\tilde{A} = \begin{pmatrix} \tilde{1} & \tilde{a}_{12} & \cdots & \tilde{a}_{12} \\ \tilde{a}_{21} & \tilde{1} & \cdots & \tilde{a}_{2n} \\ \vdots & \vdots & \ddots & \vdots \\ \tilde{a}_{n1} & \tilde{a}_{n2} & \cdots & \tilde{1} \end{pmatrix}$$

where $\tilde{a}_{ij} = (l_{ij}, m_{ij}, u_{ij})$; $\tilde{1} = (1,1,2)$ and $\tilde{a}_{ji} = 1/\tilde{a}_{ij}$

Intensity of Importance of one criterion over another	*AHP: Crisp number*	*FAHP: Fuzzy number*
Equal	1	(1,1,2)
Weak: moderately more important	3	(2,3,4)
Strong: significantly more important	5	(4,5,6)
Very strong: strongly more important	7	(6,7,8)
Absolute: extremely more important	9	(8,9,9)
Intermediate values	2,4,6,8	(1,2,3) (3,4,5) (5,6,7) (7,8,9)

Table 2. Triangular fuzzy numbers to construct the pairwise comparison matrices (equivalence between the AHP and FAHP approaches).

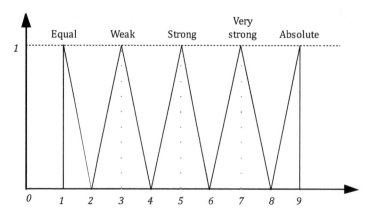

Figure 3. Fuzzy pairwise comparison scale.

The final weights of the decision elements can be calculated using different methods that have been proposed in the literature. One of the most popular methods is the Fuzzy Extent Analysis, proposed by Chang (1996). The steps of Chang's extent analysis can be summarized as follows:

First step: computing the normalized value of row sums by fuzzy arithmetic operations:

$$\tilde{S}_i = \sum_{j=1}^{n} \tilde{a}_{ij} * \left(\sum_{k=1}^{n} \sum_{j=1}^{n} \tilde{a}_{kj} \right)^{-1}$$

Second step: computing the degree of possibility of $\tilde{S}_i \geq \tilde{S}_j$ defined as

$$V(\tilde{S}_i \geq \tilde{S}_j) = sup_{y \geq x}\left[\min(\tilde{S}_j(x), \tilde{S}_i(y))\right]$$

x and y being the values on the axis of the membership function of each criterion. This expression is equivalently expressed as

$$V(\tilde{S}_i \geq \tilde{S}_j) = \begin{cases} 1 & if\ m_i \geq m_j \\ \dfrac{u_i - l_j}{(u_i - m_i) + (m_j - l_j)} & if\ l_j \geq u_i \\ 0 & otherwise \end{cases}$$

where $\tilde{S}_i = (l_i, m_i, u_i)$ and $\tilde{S}_j = (l_j, m_j, u_j)$. Using these expressions the degree of possibility of $\tilde{S}$ to be greater than all the convex fuzzy numbers $\tilde{S}_j$ is computed as follows:

$$V(\tilde{S} \geq \tilde{S}_1, \tilde{S}_2, ..., \tilde{S}_n) = \min_k V(\tilde{S} \geq \tilde{S}_k)$$

Third step: defining the priority normalized vector of the fuzzy comparison matrix as:

$$w_i = \frac{V(\tilde{S}_i \geq \tilde{S}_1, \tilde{S}_2, ..., \tilde{S}_n)}{\sum_{k=1}^{n} V(\tilde{S}_k \geq \tilde{S}_1, \tilde{S}_2, ..., \tilde{S}_n)}; \quad i = 1, 2, ..., n$$

Observe that the final normalization weight vector W is a real non-fuzzy vector that can be used to perform an evaluation of the alternatives based on the weights of the decision elements in each hierarchy level. The local priorities represent the relative weights of criteria within a group with respect to their parent in the hierarchy. The global priorities are obtained by multiplying the local priorities of the siblings by their parent's local priorities.

4. A FAHP MODEL BASED ON COBIT FOR IT GOVERNANCE EVALUATION

With the aim of constructing a model that allows us to measure the governance of TI according to the focus areas defined by COBIT 4.1 and taking as reference the basic stages of the methodology described before, we proceeded to carry out the actions illustrated in Figure 4. Each of the stages will be explained in detail below.

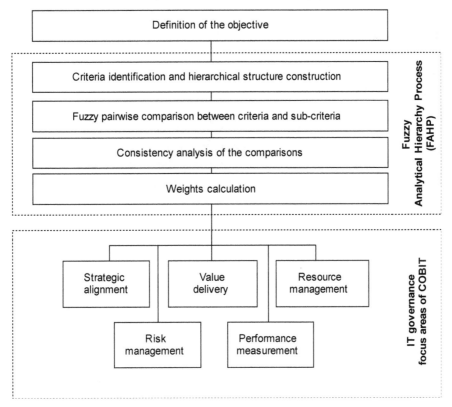

Figure 4. Stages for the construction of a model for evaluating IT governance.

4.1. Definition of objectives

The model we have developed aims to achieve a double objective. Firstly, to evaluate the level of performance of the IT governance using maturity levels in COBIT processes, and to use it to try to identify critical aspects in the governance model within organizations in five focus areas. With the aim of checking the effectiveness of the model, we sought its practical application in a Brazilian firm that operates in Rio Grande do Sul State.

4.2. Identification of criteria hierarchy

In order to achieve the proposed objectives, we decided to select the 34 processes defined by COBIT 4.1. These processes are hierarchically organized as shown in Figure 1. In the first level of the criteria hierarchy we consider the four main domains D_i $(i=1,2,3,4)$. Specifically, D_1 corresponds to "Plan and Organize", D_2 is "Acquire and Implement", D_3 is "Deliver and Support" and D_4 is "Monitor and Evaluate".

COBIT 4.1 also defines a set of processes associated with each main domain; we will use the following notation to refer to the processes involved in D_i: $P_{i,j}$ with i in $\{1,2,3,4\}$ and j in $\{1,2,...,n_i\}$, where i indicates the associated domain and j the number of process in the domain. Each domain has a different number of processes involved, in fact $n_1=10$, $n_2=7$, $n_3=13$, and $n_4=4$. The complete list of 34 processes is shown in the Annex. The processes define the second level in the criteria hierarchy.

4.3. Pairwise comparison between criteria

COBIT 4.1 defines significance levels for each process, and priority levels associated with each process and focus area. With this information, we proceed to the construction of pairwise comparisons matrices between areas and between the processes associated with the same domain. The building process is described as follows.

In accordance with the significance level defined by COBIT for each process, we define the following function:

$$I(P_{i,j}) = \begin{cases} 1 & \text{if the importance is defined by COBIT as LOW} \\ 2 & \text{if the importance is defined by COBIT as MEDIUM} \\ 3 & \text{if the importance is defined by COBIT as HIGH} \end{cases}$$

These importance levels are defined in the mapping of IT processes for IT governance focus areas (Appendix II of COBIT 4.1)

COBIT also associates a primary or secondary priority for each process in each focus area. According to this information we define:

$$Pr_{i,j,k} = \begin{cases} 1 & \text{if process } P_{i,j} \text{ is primary in area } k \\ 0.5 & \text{if process } P_{i,j} \text{ is secundary in area } k \\ 0 & \text{otherwise} \end{cases}$$

Firstly, we proceed to define the fuzzy pairwise comparisons between domains with respect to a particular focus area. For D_a and D_b domains, we need to compare both of them using the fuzzy preference scale defined in Table 2, which assigns fuzzy triangular numbers to different levels of preference with respect to the focus area selected (FA_p).

In order to define the importance levels the following process we compute:

$$ratio(D_a, D_b) = \frac{\sum_{j=1}^{n_a} I(P_{a,j})PR_{a,j,p}}{\sum_{j=1}^{n_b} I(P_{b,j})PR_{b,j,p}}$$

and

$$Pref\_Domains(D_a, D_b) = \begin{cases} ceil\big(ratio(D_a, D_b)\big) & if \ ratio(D_a, D_b) \geq 1 \\ \dfrac{1}{ceil(\frac{1}{ratio(D_r, D_s)})} & if \ ratio(D_a, D_b) < 1 \end{cases}$$

where $ceil()$ is the function that maps a real number to the smallest following integer. After this process the fuzzification comprises the process of transforming the crisp value into a triangular fuzzy number using the correspondence defined in Table 2.

In this work we focus on the evaluation of strategic alignment. According to the previous expressions the fuzzy pairwise comparison matrix for this focus area is shown in Table 3.

	D_1	D_2	D_3	D_4
D_1	(1,1,2)	(3,4,5)	(4,5,6)	(2,3,4)
D_2	(1/5,1/4,1/3)	(1,1,2)	(1,2,3)	(1/3,1/2,1)
D_3	(1/6,1/5,1/4)	(1/3,1/2,1)	(1,1,2)	(1/3,1/2,1)
D_4	(1/4,1/3,1/2)	(1,2,3)	(1,2,3)	(1,1,2)

Table 3. Pairwise domains comparison matrix in "Strategic Alignment" focus area.

These numbers maintain the fuzzyfication from the priority of each process in each focus area of COBIT and the importance levels, defined in the same technological process evaluation framework.

Once the comparisons at the first hierarchical level were made, the same process was made comparing the different criteria that stem from the general criteria in the hierarchy. For D_a a domain, we need to compare the processes associated to D_a using the fuzzy scale. In this case we proceed as follows:

For $P_{a,i}$ and $P_{a,j}$ processes in the domain D_a, we define

$$Pref\_Proc(P_{a,i}, P_{b,j}) = \begin{cases} 1 & if \ I(P_{a,i})PR_{a,i,p} = I(P_{a,j})PR_{a,j,p} \\ 9 & if \ I(P_{a,j})PR_{a,j,p} = 0 \\ 1/9 & if \ I(P_{a,i})PR_{a,i,p} = 0 \\ ceil\left(\dfrac{I(P_{a,i})PR_{a,i,p}}{I(P_{a,j})PR_{a,j,p}}\right) & if \ I(P_{a,i})PR_{a,i,p} > I(P_{a,j})PR_{a,j,p} \\ 1/ceil\left(\dfrac{I(P_{a,j})PR_{a,j,p}}{I(P_{a,i})PR_{a,i,p}}\right) & if \ I(P_{a,i})PR_{a,i,p} < I(P_{a,j})PR_{a,j,p} \end{cases}$$

Again the fuzzification process is performed using defined in Table 2.

This expression allows constructing the pairwise comparisons matrices for the specific domains. The Tables 4, 5, 6 and 7 show the matrices associated to the 4 domains in the strategic alignment focus area.

	$P_{1,1}$	$P_{1,2}$	$P_{1,3}$	$P_{1,4}$	$P_{1,5}$	$P_{1,6}$	$P_{1,7}$	$P_{1,8}$	$P_{1,9}$	$P_{1,10}$
$P_{1,1}$	(1,1,2)	(2,3,4)	(2,3,4)	(5,6,7)	(2,3,4)	(1,2,3)	(2,3,4)	(1,2,3)	(1,1,2)	(1,1,2)
$P_{1,2}$	(1/4,1/3,1/2)	(1,1,2)	(1,1,2)	(1,2,3)	(1,1,2)	(1/3,1/2,1)	(1,1,2)	(1/3,1/2,1)	(1/4,1/3,1/2)	(1/4,1/3,1/2)
$P_{1,3}$	(1/4,1/3,1/2)	(1,1,2)	(1,1,2)	(1,2,3)	(1,1,2)	(1/3,1/2,1)	(1,1,2)	(1/3,1/2,1)	(1/4,1/3,1/2)	(1/4,1/3,1/2)
$P_{1,4}$	(1/7,1/6,1/5)	(1/3,1/2,1)	(1/3,1/2,1)	(1,1,2)	(1/3,1/2,1)	(1/5,1/4,1/3)	(1/3,1/2,1)	(1/5,1/4,1/3)	(1/7,1/6,1/5)	(1/7,1/6,1/5)
$P_{1,5}$	(1/4,1/3,1/2)	(1,1,2)	(1,1,2)	(1,2,3)	(1,1,2)	(1/3,1/2,1)	(1,1,2)	(1/3,1/2,1)	(1/4,1/3,1/2)	(1/4,1/3,1/2)
$P_{1,6}$	(1/3,1/2,1)	(1,2,3)	(1,2,3)	(3,4,5)	(1,2,3)	(1,1,2)	(1,2,3)	(1,1,2)	(1/3,1/2,1)	(1/3,1/2,1)
$P_{1,7}$	(1/4,1/3,1/2)	(1,1,2)	(1,1,2)	(1,2,3)	(1,1,2)	(1/3,1/2,1)	(1,1,2)	(1/3,1/2,1)	(1/4,1/3,1/2)	(1/4,1/3,1/2)
$P_{1,8}$	(1/3,1/2,1)	(1,2,3)	(1,2,3)	(3,4,5)	(1,2,3)	(1,1,2)	(1,2,3)	(1,1,2)	(1/3,1/2,1)	(1/3,1/2,1)
$P_{1,9}$	(1,1,2)	(2,3,4)	(2,3,4)	(5,6,7)	(2,3,4)	(1,2,3)	(2,3,4)	(1,2,3)	(1,1,2)	(1,1,2)
$P_{1,10}$	(1,1,2)	(2,3,4)	(2,3,4)	(5,6,7)	(2,3,4)	(1,2,3)	(2,3,4)	(1,2,3)	(1,1,2)	(1,1,2)

Table 4. Pairwise processes comparison matrix in domain D1.

	$P_{2,1}$	$P_{2,2}$	$P_{2,3}$	$P_{2,4}$	$P_{2,5}$	$P_{2,6}$	$P_{2,7}$
$P_{2,1}$	(1,1,2)	(1,1,2)	(8,9,9)	(3,4,5)	(8,9,9)	(8,9,9)	(1,2,3)
$P_{2,2}$	(1,1,2)	(1,1,2)	(8,9,9)	(3,4,5)	(8,9,9)	(8,9,9)	(1,2,3)
$P_{2,3}$	(1/9,1/9,1/8)	(1/9,1/9,1/8)	(1,1,2)	(1/9,1/9,1/8)	(1,1,2)	(1,1,2)	(1/9,1/9,1/8)
$P_{2,4}$	(1/5,1/4,1/3)	(1/5,1/4,1/3)	(8,9,9)	(1,1,2)	(8,9,9)	(8,9,9)	(1/3,1/2,1)
$P_{2,5}$	(1/9,1/9,1/8)	(1/9,1/9,1/8)	(1,1,2)	(1/9,1/9,1/8)	(1,1,2)	(1,1,2)	(1/9,1/9,1/8)
$P_{2,6}$	(1/9,1/9,1/8)	(1/9,1/9,1/8)	(1,1,2)	(1/9,1/9,1/8)	(1,1,2)	(1,1,2)	(1/9,1/9,1/8)
$P_{2,7}$	(1/3,1/2,1)	(1/3,1/2,1)	(8,9,9)	(1,2,3)	(8,9,9)	(8,9,9)	(1,1,2)

Table 5. Pairwise processes comparison matrix in domain D2.

	$P_{3,1}$	$P_{3,2}$	$P_{3,3}$	$P_{3,4}$	$P_{3,5}$	$P_{3,6}$	$P_{3,7}$	$P_{3,8}$	$P_{3,9}$	$P_{3,10}$	$P_{3,11}$	$P_{3,12}$	$P_{3,13}$
$P_{3,1}$	(1,1,2)	(8,9,9)	(3,4,5)	(1,2,3)	(8,9,9)	(8,9,9)	(3,4,5)	(8,9,9)	(8,9,9)	(8,9,9)	(8,9,9)	(8,9,9)	(1/9,1/9,1/8)
$P_{3,2}$	(1/9,1/9,1/8)	(1,1,2)	(1/9,1/9,1/8)	(1/9,1/9,1/8)	(1,1,2)	(1,1,2)	(1/9,1/9,1/8)	(1,1,2)	(1,1,2)	(1,1,2)	(1,1,2)	(1,1,2)	(1,1,2)
$P_{3,3}$	(1/5,1/4,1/3)	(8,9,9)	(1,1,2)	(1/3,1/2,1)	(8,9,9)	(8,9,9)	(1,1,2)	(8,9,9)	(8,9,9)	(8,9,9)	(8,9,9)	(8,9,9)	(1/9,1/9,1/8)
$P_{3,4}$	(1/3,1/2,1)	(8,9,9)	(1,2,3)	(1,1,2)	(8,9,9)	(8,9,9)	(1,2,3)	(8,9,9)	(8,9,9)	(8,9,9)	(8,9,9)	(8,9,9)	(1/9,1/9,1/8)
$P_{3,5}$	(1/9,1/9,1/8)	(1,1,2)	(1/9,1/9,1/8)	(1/9,1/9,1/8)	(1,1,2)	(1,1,2)	(1/9,1/9,1/8)	(1,1,2)	(1,1,2)	(1,1,2)	(1,1,2)	(1,1,2)	(1,1,2)
$P_{3,6}$	(1/9,1/9,1/8)	(1,1,2)	(1/9,1/9,1/8)	(1/9,1/9,1/8)	(1,1,2)	(1,1,2)	(1/9,1/9,1/8)	(1,1,2)	(1,1,2)	(1,1,2)	(1,1,2)	(1,1,2)	(1,1,2)
$P_{3,7}$	(1/5,1/4,1/3)	(8,9,9)	(1,1,2)	(1/3,1/2,1)	(8,9,9)	(8,9,9)	(1,1,2)	(8,9,9)	(8,9,9)	(8,9,9)	(8,9,9)	(8,9,9)	(1/9,1/9,1/8)
$P_{3,8}$	(1/9,1/9,1/8)	(1,1,2)	(1/9,1/9,1/8)	(1/9,1/9,1/8)	(1,1,2)	(1,1,2)	(1/9,1/9,1/8)	(1,1,2)	(1,1,2)	(1,1,2)	(1,1,2)	(1,1,2)	(1,1,2)
$P_{3,9}$	(1/9,1/9,1/8)	(1,1,2)	(1/9,1/9,1/8)	(1/9,1/9,1/8)	(1,1,2)	(1,1,2)	(1/9,1/9,1/8)	(1,1,2)	(1,1,2)	(1,1,2)	(1,1,2)	(1,1,2)	(1,1,2)
$P_{3,10}$	(1/9,1/9,1/8)	(1,1,2)	(1/9,1/9,1/8)	(1/9,1/9,1/8)	(1,1,2)	(1,1,2)	(1/9,1/9,1/8)	(1,1,2)	(1,1,2)	(1,1,2)	(1,1,2)	(1,1,2)	(1,1,2)
$P_{3,11}$	(1/9,1/9,1/8)	(1,1,2)	(1/9,1/9,1/8)	(1/9,1/9,1/8)	(1,1,2)	(1,1,2)	(1/9,1/9,1/8)	(1,1,2)	(1,1,2)	(1,1,2)	(1,1,2)	(1,1,2)	(1,1,2)
$P_{3,12}$	(1/9,1/9,1/8)	(1,1,2)	(1/9,1/9,1/8)	(1/9,1/9,1/8)	(1,1,2)	(1,1,2)	(1/9,1/9,1/8)	(1,1,2)	(1,1,2)	(1,1,2)	(1,1,2)	(1,1,2)	(1,1,2)
$P_{3,13}$	(1/9,1/9,1/8)	(1,1,2)	(1/9,1/9,1/8)	(1/9,1/9,1/8)	(1,1,2)	(1,1,2)	(1/9,1/9,1/8)	(1,1,2)	(1,1,2)	(1,1,2)	(1,1,2)	(1,1,2)	(1,1,2)

Table 6. Pairwise processes comparison matrix in domain D3.

	$P_{4,1}$	$P_{4,2}$	$P_{4,3}$	$P_{4,4}$
$P_{4,1}$	(1,1,2)	(8,9,9)	(1/3,1/2,1)	(1/3,1/2,1)
$P_{4,2}$	(1/9,1/9,1/8)	(1,1,2)	(1/9,1/9,1/8)	(1/9,1/9,1/8)
$P_{4,3}$	(1,2,3)	(8,9,9)	(1,1,2)	(1,1,2)
$P_{4,4}$	(1,2,3)	(8,9,9)	(1,1,2)	(1,1,2)

Table 7. Pairwise processes comparison matrix in domain D4.

4.4. Consistency analysis of comparison judgments

Seeking to contrast the consistency of comparative judgments between the criteria made by COBIT, the AHP model proposes the calculation of a ratio of consistency. In this sense Saaty (1980) recommends a radius of consistency of 0.1 or lower so that pairwise comparisons undertaken by the decision maker can be considered as acceptable. In the case proposed, we used the crisp numbers associated to the fuzzy triangular comparison values to obtain the radius of consistency of the crisp pairwise matrices; the values obtained were as follows:

- For first level comparisons we obtained a radius of consistency of 0.02.

- For second level comparisons we obtained radii of consistency of 0.00, 0.04, 0.02, and 0.02 respectively.

All ratios of consistency were, therefore, perfectly admissible.

4.5. Calculation of the relative weights of each criterion

Once the pairwise comparison has been performed, the FAHP methodology allows us to calculate weights for each criterion which will influence their importance in achieving the final goal. We applied the methodology proposed by Chang (1996) in order to calculate these weights in Local (L) and Global (G), considering the strategic alignment focus area. The computation of these weights was performed using an ad hoc implemented application in Java programming language. Table 8 shows the final values obtained for the weights in the two levels of the hierarchy.

Focus Area: Strategic Alignment					
	L	G		L	G
Plan and Organize		**0,678**	**Deliver and Support**		**0**
PO1	0,1853	0,1256	DS1	0,2937	0
PO2	0,0599	0,0406	DS2	0	0
PO3	0,0517	0,0351	DS3	0,2283	0
PO4	0	0	DS4	0,2519	0
PO5	0,0425	0,0288	DS5	0	0
PO6	0,1305	0,0885	DS6	0	0
PO7	0,0318	0,0216	DS7	0,2262	0
PO8	0,1278	0,0866	DS8	0	0
PO9	0,1853	0,1256	DS9	0	0
PO10	0,1853	0,1256	DS10	0	0
Acquire and Implement		**0,072**	DS11	0	0
AI1	0,3006	0,0216	DS12	0	0
AI2	0,3006	0,0216	DS13	0	0
AI3	0	0	**Monitor and Evaluate**		**0,25**
AI4	0,1729	0,0124	ME1	0,2691	0,0673
AI5	0	0	ME2	0	0
AI6	0	0	ME3	0,3655	0,0914
AI7	0,226	0,0163	ME4	0,3655	0,0914

Table 8. Priority weights for criteria

Table 8 prioritizes specifically strategic alignment COBIT focal area, proposed in this paper. In future works it will be applied in other focal areas as Value Delivery, Risk Management, Resource Management and Performance Measurement, using the same methodological procedure. As can be observed the model identifies only 16 key processes in making an assessment of the focal area strategic alignment. Specifically, these processes are those with non-null global weights in Table 8. As can be observed, some processes in domains closely related with strategic alignment have null weights assigned by the model. For instance, despite of PO4 is of secondary influence like other process in domain "Plan and Organize", as PO3, in the mapping of IT processes to IT governance focus areas, COBIT 4.1 declares PO4 with a low importance and the weighting scheme assigns to it a null weight.

In order to measure the maturity levels of the different processes defined by COBIT, it is possible to request independent evaluations by an expert group and to collect multiple crisp data sets reflecting different opinions and then form the fuzzy maturity level (FML) of a process as the triangular fuzzy number (*min,mean,max*) deriving from the specific data sets.

To evaluate the applicability of the proposed model, we performed an assessment from the point of view of IT governance in a Brazilian company that operates in three states of Rio Grande do Sul. Individual interviews were conducted with the IT manager and supervisor, asking each of them independently conduct an assessment on the scale 0-5 the degree of maturity of each of the processes of COBIT 4.1. With the responses generated the FML values shown in Table 9 were obtained. As shown in this preliminary assessment most processes are in repeatable and defined states, especially those who have more weight in measuring the level of strategic alignment of IT in the organization according to the FAHP model developed. None of the processes can be considered optimized.

Process	FML	Process	FML	Process	FML	Process	FML
PO1	(3; 3,5; 4)	AI1	(3; 3,5; 4)	DS1	(3; 4; 5)	ME1	(3; 3,5; 4)
PO2	(2; 2; 2)	AI2	(3; 3,5; 4)	DS2	(3; 3,5; 4)	ME2	(2; 2,5; 3)
PO3	(2; 2; 2)	AI3	(2; 2,5; 3)	DS3	(2; 3; 4)	ME3	(1; 1,5; 2)
PO4	(2; 2,5; 3)	AI4	(2; 2,5; 3)	DS4	(2; 3; 4)	ME4	(2; 2,5; 3)
PO5	(1; 2; 3)	AI5	(1; 2,5; 4)	DS5	(2; 2,5; 3)		
PO6	(3; 3; 3)	AI6	(4; 4; 4)	DS6	(3; 3,5; 4)		
PO7	(1; 1; 1)	AI7	(4; 4; 4)	DS7	(1; 1; 1)		
PO8	(2; 2; 2)			DS8	(3; 4; 5)		
PO9	(2; 2,5; 3)			DS9	(2; 2,5; 3)		
PO10	(3; 3,5; 4)			DS10	(2; 3; 4)		
				DS11	(2; 2,5; 3)		
				DS12	(3; 3; 3)		
				DS13	(4; 4; 4)		

Table 9. Fuzzy maturity levels (FML).

The global weights calculated with the FAHP model and shown in Table 8, allow to obtain an overall strategic alignment assessment of IT governance in the studied company. The overall assessment is obtained by performing a weighted average of the levels of maturity of each of the 16 processes with non-null weight. In the studied case the global evaluation of the "strategic alignment" focus area is (2,341; 2,711; 3,082). It means that the maturity level comprehends a larger interval of compliance in the company, when the IT processes are evaluated. This way, there is more alignment between IT and Business.

Analyzing the results in the company, it could be said that the level of strategic alignment of IT in the organization is not properly managed. An improvement in several processes is required, especially in those that received a lower evaluation of maturity and have a greater impact on achieving an optimal level of alignment; in this case, the processes that have to be improve are PO8 and PO9 in the "plan and organize" domain, and processes ME3 and ME4 in the "monitor and evaluate" domain.

5.   CONCLUSIONS

This work provided a new multi-criteria approach to assess IT Governance (ITG) for strategic alignment between IT and Business using Fuzzy Analytical Hierarchy Process (FAHP) in the COBIT framework, more specifically to the maturity levels, domains and processes, thus providing a differentiated analysis of importance for each item.

This research demonstrated that the combined use of multi-criteria decision methodologies and soft computing proves to be particularly suitable for the evaluation of IT strategic alignment. The model generated improvements the classic focus of the individual and isolated of process that are audited. This way, it is possible to better consider the choices in intervals that correspond to more qualitative, subjective or fuzzy analysis.

This model has been applied to a big retail enterprise, located in the south of Brazil, through individual interviews to generate Fuzzy maturity levels (FML). For future studies, the authors will direct efforts to increase the model in other focal areas of COBIT as CMMI$^©$ (Capability Maturity Model Integration) which means the best practices to the development and maintenance activities for new projects.

Furthermore, in future works we will try to adapt the multi-criteria model to the latest version of COBIT, version 5.0 includes a new domain and reorganizes some of the processes. With the corresponding adjustments to the hierarchy of processes, the methodology can be generalized to integrate the latest changes of framework COBIT in the evaluation model. We also propose as future work the integration of an Analytical Network Process (ANP) model to define more complex interrelationships between processes to evaluate.

REFERENCES

Balli, S. & Korukoglu, S. (2009). Operating System Selection Using Fuzzy AHP and TOPSIS. *Mathematical and Computational Applications,* 14(2), 119-130.

Benítez, J., Delgado-Galván, X., Izquierdo, J. & Pérez-García, R. (2012). An approach to AHP decision in a dynamic context. *Decision Support Systems*, 53, 499-506.

Cadbury Committee (2011). *Report of the Committee on the Financial Aspects of Corporate Governance.* London, 1992. Retrieved March 8, 2014, from http://www.jbs.cam.ac.uk/cadbury/report/index.html

Chang, D. (1992). Extent analysis and synthetic decision. *Optimization techniques and applications, World Scientific,* Singapore, 1, 352.

Chang, D. (1996). Applications of the extent analysis method on fuzzy AHP. *European Journal of Operational Research,* 95, 649–655.

Chen, P.C. (2009). A Fuzzy Multiple Criteria Decision Making Model in Employee Recruitment. *International Journal of Computer Science and Network Security,* 9(7), 113-117.

Chen, L. (2010). Business–IT alignment maturity of companies in China. *Information & Management,* 47, 9–16.

De Haes, S., Van Grembergen, W. & Debreceny, R. (2013). COBIT 5 and Enterprise Governance of Information Technology: Building Blocks and Research Opportunities. *Journal of Information Systems,* 27(1), 307.

Hirschheim, R., & Sabherwal, R. (2001). Detours in the path toward strategic information systems alignment. *California Management Review*, 44 (1), 87-108.

IBGC (2012). *Código das melhores práticas de governança corporativa.* 4ª ed., São Paulo, Instituto Brasileiro de Governança Corporativa (IBGC). Retrieved March 8, 2014, from http://www.ibgc.org.br/CodigoMelhoresPraticas.aspx

Iranmanesh, H., Shirkouhi, S.N. & Skandari, M.R. (2008). Risk Evaluation of Information Technology Projects Based on Fuzzy Analytic Hierarchal Process. *World Academy of Science, Engineering and Technology,* 40, 351-357.

ISACA, Information Systems Audit and Control Association (2012). *COBIT Five: A Business Framework for the Governance and Management of Enterprise IT.* Rolling Meadows, IL: ISACA.

ITGI (2013). *COBIT 4.1:* Framework, Control Objectives, Management Guidelines, Maturity Models. Information Technology Governance Institute. Retrieved March 8, 2014, from http://www.isaca.org

Jensen, M. & Meckling, W. (1976). Theory of the firm: managerial behavior, agency costs and capital structure. *Journal of Financial Economics*, 3, 305-360.

Kwok, L. & Longley, D. (1999). Information security management and modeling, *Information Management & Computer Security*, 7(1), 30-40.

Lederer, A. L. & Mendelow, A. L. (1989). Coordination of information systems plans with business plans. *Journal of Management Information Systems*, 6 (2), 5-19.

Lederer, A. L. & Sethi, V. (1992). Root Causes of Strategic Information System Planning Implementation Problems. *Journal of Management Information Systems*, 9 (1), 25-45.

Li, Y. & Tan, C.H. (2013). Matching business strategy and CIO characteristics: The impact on organizational performance. *Journal of Business Research*, 66(2), 248–259.

Lien, C.T. & Chan, H.L. (2007). A Selection Model for ERP System by Applying Fuzzy AHP Approach. *International Journal of the Computer, the Internet and Management*, 15(3), 58-72.

Markaki, O., Charilas, D. & Askounis, D. (2010). Application of Fuzzy Analytic Hierarchy Process to Evaluate the Quality of E-Government Web Sites. *DESE-10 Proceedings of the 2010 Developments in E-systems Engineering*, 219-224.

Marnewick, C. & Labuschagne, L. (2011). An investigation into the governance of information technology projects in South Africa. *International Journal of Project Management*, 29, 661–670.

Meixner, O. (2009). Fuzzy AHP Group Decision Analysis and its Application for the Evaluation of Energy Sources. *Proceedings of the 10th International Symposium on the Analytic Hierarchy/Network Process Multi-criteria Decision Making.* University of Pittsburgh, USA.

Merali, Y., Papadopoulos, T. & Nadkarni, T. (2012). Information systems strategy: Past, present, future? *Journal of Strategic Information Systems*, 21, 125-153.

Mikhailov, L. & Tsvetinov, P. (2004). Evaluation of services using a fuzzy analytic hierarchy process. *Applied Soft Computing*, 5(1), 23–33.

Neto, J.S., Neto, A.N.F. (2013). Metamodel of the IT governance framework COBIT. *Journal of Information Systems and Technology Management*, 10(3), 521-540.

Preittigun, A., Chantatub, W. & Vatanasakdakul, S. (2012). A Comparison between IT Governance Research and Concepts in COBIT 5. *International Journal of Research in Management & Technology*, 2(6), 581-590.

Saaty, T. (1980). *The Analytical Hierarchy Process: Planning, Priority Setting, Resource Allocation.* New York: Mc Graw-Hill.

Simonson, M., Johnson, P. & Ekstedt, M. (2010). The Effect of IT Maturity on IT Governance Performance. *Information Systems Management*, 27, 10-24.

Taylor, F. & Fitzgerald, T. (2007). Clarifying the Roles of Information Security: 13 Questions the CEO, CIO, and CISO Must Ask Each Other. *Information Systems Security*, 16(5), 257-263.

Tiwana, A. & Konsynski, B. (2010). Complementarities between organizational IT architecture and governance structure. *Information Systems Research*, 21(2), 288–304.

Van Laarhoven, P. & Pedrycz, W. (1983). A Fuzzy Extension of Saaty's Priority Theory. *Fuzzy Sets and Systems*, 11, 229-241.

Van Grembergen, W. V. & Haes, S. D. (2004). IT Governance and Its Mechanisms, *Information Systems Control Journal*, 1, 27-33.

Van Grembergen, W., & De Haes, S. (2009*). Enterprise Governance of Information Technology: Achieving Strategic Alignment and Value*. New York: Springer, 233.

Wajeeh, I.A. & Muneeza, A. (2012). Strategic corporate governance for sustainable mutual development. *International Journal of Law and Management*, 54(3), 197-208.

Weill, P. & Ross, J.W. (2004). *IT Governance - How Top Performers Manage IT Decision Rights for Superior Results*. Boston. Massachusetts: Harvard Business School Press.

Weiss, J. & Thorogood, A. (2011). Information Technology (IT)/Business Alignment as a Strategic Weapon: A Diagnostic Tool. *Engineering Management Journal*, 23(2), 30-41.

Zadeh, L.A. (1965). Fuzzy Sets. *Information and Control*, 8, 338-353.

Zarvi´c, N., Stolze, C., Boehm, M. & Thomas, O. (2012). Dependency-based IT Governance practices in inter-organisational collaborations: A graph-driven elaboration. *International Journal of Information Management*, 32(6), 541–549.

Zviran, M. (1990). Relationships between Organizational and Information Systems Objectives: Some Empirical Evidence. *Journal of Management Information Systems*, 7(1), 66-84.

ANNEX: 34 PROCESSES DEFINED IN COBIT 4.1

Planning and Organization
- PO1 Define a Strategic IT Plan
- PO2 Define the Information Architecture
- PO3 Determine Technological Direction
- PO4 Define the IT Processes, Organization and Relationships
- PO5 Manage the IT Investment
- PO6 Communication Management Aims and Direction
- PO7 Manage IT Human Resources
- PO8 Manage Quality
- P09 Assess and Manage IT Risks
- P10 Manage Projects

Acquisition & Implementation
- AI1 Identify Automated Solutions
- AI2 Acquire and Maintain Application Software
- AI3 Acquire and Maintain Technology Infrastructure
- AI4 Enable Operation and Use
- AI5 Procure IT Resources
- AI6 Manage Changes
- AI5 Install and Accredit Solution and Changes

Delivery and Support
- DS1 Define and Manage Service Levels
- DS2 Manage Third Party Services
- DS3 Manage Performance and Capacity
- DS4 Ensure Continuous Service
- DS5 Ensure Systems Security
- DS6 Indentify and Allocate Costs
- DS7 Educate and Train Users
- DS8 Manage Service Desk and Incidents
- DS9 Manage the Configuration
- DS10 Manage Problems
- DS11 Manage Data
- DS12 Manage the Physical Environment
- DS13 Manage Operations

Monitor and Evaluate
- ME1 Monitor and Evaluate IT Performance
- ME2 Monitor and Evaluate Internal Control
- ME3 Ensure Compliance with External Requirements
- ME4 Provide IT Governance

10

THE IMPACT OF IT GOVERNANCE ON IT PROJECTS -THE CASE OF THE GHANA RURAL BANK COMPUTERIZATION AND INTER-CONNECTIVITY PROJECT

William Allassani
University of Professional Studies, Legon-Accra, Ghana

ABSTRACT

This research seeks to analyse the root causes of the massive failures of IT Projects especially in government establishments. This study shows that the successful implementation of IT projects does not lie only Project in Management principles. It answers the question 'why are IT projects failing despite the application of tried and tested Project Management principles ? The paper also concludes that Project Management principles per se do not guarantee the successful implementation of IT projects, but have to be brought within the principle of IT Governance. Conclusions are drawn from the Ghana Rural Bank Computerization and Inter-connectivity Project, an activity under the Millennium Challenge Account of the Millennium Development Authority to show that IT Governance needs to be inculcated into IT Projects to make its implementation successful.

Keywords: IT Governance, Project Management, IT Projects

1. INTRODUCTION

The concept of IT governance emerged in the late 1990's when Brown (1997), Sambamurthy and Zmud (1999) wrote about "IT Governance arrangement and Framework". They said that IT Governance represents an organization's IT related authority patterns. However, IT Governance was not treated as a field until 2004 when 2 researchers, Weill and Ross (2004) consolidated existing research about how IT is managed in 250 organizations, including 400 direct case studies and hundreds of interviews with managers. The result of the study was the realization that IT governance is a key component of realizing value from IT investment, ensuring that IT is aligned with and supports organizational goals. Their research showed that firms with superior IT governance have more than 25% higher profits than firms with poor governance

Address for correspondence / Endereço para correspondência

William Allassani, lecturer in E-Commerce at the Department of Information Technology of the University of Professional Studies, in Accra, Ghana Contact Address is: P.O.Box CT 289, Accra. E-mail: wallass123@yahoo.com given the same strategic objectives. These top performers have custom designed IT governance for their strategies. They argued that just as corporate governance aims to ensure quality decisions about all corporate assets, IT governance links IT decisions with company objectives and monitors performance and accountability. Based on the study of 250 enterprises worldwide, IT Governance shows how to design and implement a system of decision rights that will transform IT from an expense to a profitable investment.

IT governance objectives are to define structures, processes, mechanisms that will influence decision making rights and responsibilities about main IT issues, control and monitor the effectiveness of such issues and mitigate IT related risks in order to achieve organizational objectives.

IT Governance in Ghana

There is presently no published work on IT Governance in Ghana although research has been undertaken in areas like Local Governance and decentralization. Ghana's decentralization system and local government system are intended to give ordinary people the opportunity to participate in decisions that affect their lives (section 35, Clause 5d of Ghana's 1992 constitution). Gender equity and gender sensitivity have been regarded as prerequisite of a sustainable development, Ofei-Aboagye (2004).

It is not surprising therefore that the absence of any research on IT Governance both in the public and private sector of Ghana has led to all manners of challenges facing a national IT project like the National Identification System (NIS), which is being implemented by the National Identification Authority.

The NIS is supposed to be a computerised registry that will keep information on all Ghanaian citizens and, legally and permanently resident foreigners. Out of the registry, an identity document that uniquely identifies the Ghanaian citizen (resident or living abroad) or the legally resident foreigner will be produced. Other aims of the project was to

- Help with crime prevention, healthcare, welfare services, disaster management;

- Assist in the delivery of public services to targeted populations, banking services;

- Create a credible voters register, social security;

- Check the application and acquisition of passports and drivers' licences and aid with increased revenue collection, Multi-Sectoral Technical Committee Report (2002)

National identity cards were first issued to citizens in the border regions of Ghana including Volta, Northern, Upper (East and West), Brong Ahafo, and parts of the Western Region in 1973. The project was however discontinued three years later due to problems with logistics and lack of financial support. This was the first time the idea of national identification systems arose.

Again, in 1987, the Government of the Provisional National Defence Council (PNDC) through the National Commission for Democracy (NCD), revisited the national identity card concept by establishing several committees including a Technical Implementation Committee. Due to economic difficulties, the issue was not pursued.

Once again, in 2001, when the National Economic Dialogue was convened, the National Identification System (NIS) was seen as a major policy concern. As a result, a multi-sectoral Technical Committee consisting of stakeholder organisations was established to resurrect the project. Consequently in 2003, the National identification Secretariat was set up by the government to implement and manage the National Identification System (NIS). The Act establishing the National Identification Authority was passed in 2006

A pilot mass registration exercise was held to test the forms and equipment deployed for the exercise as well as the registration process as outlined by the Authority. This pilot registration exercise took place in two communities, Abokobi and Sege, both located in the Greater Accra Region, for ten (10) days from July 27, 2007 to August 4, 2009. The testing selection and training of staff for the Central and Western Regions were also executed successfully, with mass registration taking off in the Central Region on July 1, 2008.

However as it 2009 the project was still not completed,dogged with problems mainly due to lack of funds. This situation seriously threatened the successful completion of the project. The NIA commenced the distribution of the identity documents in 2011 but it had to stop the distribution due to lack of funds, History of National Identification Authority ((2010)

This paper seeks to prove that applying IT governance principles to Project management principles would ensure the successful implementation of IT projects. The paper uses the case study of the Ghana Rural Bank Computerization and Inter-connectivity Project to prove the hypothesis that Project management principles per se do not guarantee the successful implementation of IT projects.

2.   LITERATURE REVIEW

The emerging e-marketplace has changed the face of business for thousands of business organizations. The result of being thrust into the technological market place has resulted in a massive rise in IT project failures, with failures running as high as 80%, (Johnson, 1994).

In information systems and organization theory research, the alignment or fit between information technology (IT) and organizational structure has long been hypothesised to be the sine qua non for success. Raymond, Paré and Bergeron (1995) argued that taking organizational size and environmental uncertainty into account, it was found that IT sophistication is positively related to structural sophistication, and also IT usage is positively related to organizational performance, and the relationship between IT management and structural sophistication is stronger among the better-performing firms than among the worst-performing firms.

Huang, Zmud, and Price (2010) also postulated that Information technology (IT) governance practices involved efforts by an organization's leadership to influence IT-related decisions through the location of decision rights and the structure of decision processes. They contended that governance practices such as Steering Committees and governance related communication policies had positive effects on IT related decisions.

Using the Telecentres project as the focus of her research, Madon (2005) argues that the long term survival of a project depends on how interactions are managed between a host of players including the government, private entrepreneurs, international donors, telecommunications suppliers, local companies, civil society organisations and individual community members. She proposes sociology of governance approach in managing these relationships.

Using the corporate governance of IT standard, i.e. ISO/IEC 38500:2008, Wilkin, Campbell and Moore (2012) analysed how Information Technology Governance (ITG) was practised in the deployment of a large IT project in an inter-organisational public/private sector context. Their findings demonstrated that ITG strategies related to human agency's contribution to the realisation of value for participating stakeholders, particularly through pre-emptive stakeholder participation in evaluating IT functionality of the old system and iteratively in the deployment of the new system. Further, their research showed that ISO/IEC 38500:2008 has merit as an analytical framework to objectively evaluate corporate governance of IT, although there is need for some enhancement. LeCardinal and Marle (2006) proposed a definition process of a project structure which should be constructed in order to reach the objectives of the project and to deliver the final results.

Failed Projects

In the US, the American Reinvestment and Recovery Act of 2009 also known as the HiTec Act for the National Health Service. The project which is expected to cost £11 billion has the initial aim amongst others to establish (a) an electronic transfer of prescription service, (b) an electronic booking service (c) a detailed electronic patient record to be viewed by local organizations and an authorized summary worth$787 billion in tax cuts and spending by the government to stimulate the economy, The Recovery Act (2009). Of this amount nearly 10% ($75.8 billion) was invested in technology projects which included a $1.2 billion increase in IT operating and projects budget of the Departments of Veterans Affairs, and $200 million for improvements to the Department of Homeland Security's Technology infrastructure, Kauffman (2009). However, as in 2008 68% of IT projects were shown to be either partial or total failures, Schwalbe (2009). Some of the Projects that failed include the FBI's Virtual Case File System Project, which the agency scrapped in 2005 after sinking $170 million into it; the $8 billion system modernization of the Inland Revenue Service launched nearly 10 years ago; and the U.S. Citizenship and Immigration Services' $190 million automation effort. Bishop (2008)

In the UK, the unpleasant story of the Electronic Patient Record Project readily comes to mind with regards to project failures. In 1998 the UK government launched the National Health Service Information strategy dubbed 'Information for Health'. The strategy was intended to run until 2005. The goals of the strategy included the creation of an Electronic Health Record containing 'life long core' clinical information for each patient by 2005 developed initially by linking local primary health systems. However this project was superseded in 2002 by the 10-year National Programme for Information Technology Project (NPfIF) which had as its theme, 'Delivering 21st Century IT Support record available nationally'.

However, in 2011, 9 years after its launch, the UK parliamentary Public Accounts Committee report said parts of the $16 billion national programme for IT had proved to be unworkable, Public Accounts Report (2011). Donabedian (1988) and Batalden and Buchanan (1989) suggested 3 steps by which an ERP could be made more relevant. They are, identifying the customers, understanding the system requirements, and translating those requirements into functional characteristics of the system. The

Committee was of the view that the intention of creating electronic records was a "worthwhile aim" but one "that has proved beyond the capacity of the Department of Health to deliver. The report went on further to say that the "Implementation of alternative up-to-date IT systems has fallen significantly behind schedule and costs have escalated. The Department of Health could have avoided some of the pitfalls and waste if they had consulted at the start of the process with health professionals." This is a clear case of lack of an effective governance structure. This confirms the argument that the key challenge of governance is at the operational level where governance hinges on individual and organizational integrity and ability to translate strategies and legal frameworks into institutional effectiveness and efficiency, Alabi and Alabi (2011). The Report also said officials were "unable to show what has been achieved for the £2.7bn spent to date on care records systems", adding that taxpayers were "clearly overpaying BT", one of the project's consultants said. The company was receiving £9m for every NHS site, yet the same systems had been sold for just £2m to other hospitals". The report also criticised the Department of Health's "weak programme management" It also noted thatthe massive scale of the project had caused companies to walk away, leaving just two groups holding the contract.

3.   BACKGROUND OF THE GHANA RURAL BANK COMPUTERIZATION AND INTER-CONNECTIVITY PROJECT(GRBCIP)

The Millennium Challenge Corporation (MCC) signed a five-year, approximately $547 million Compact with the Republic of Ghana on August 1, 2006. The Millennium Challenge Account (MCA) is viewed as an opportunity to address fundamental structural problems in the local economy, as well as to help improve the economic, political and social stability of the sub-region. Ghana's principal economic goal is to improve the standard of living for its citizens, and to achieve middle-income status within a decade, driven by private sector led growth. The Compact program was intended to advance these goals by enhancing economic growth through poverty reduction. The Millennium Development Authority (MiDA) was charged with the responsibility for managing the Ghana Millennium Challenge Account (MCA) Compact.

The goal of the MCA Ghana Program was to accelerate the reduction of poverty through economic growth led by agricultural transformation. This was to be accomplished through the transformation of agricultural practices in identified locations in Ghana and involved promoting a commercial orientation to the production, post-harvest storage, transportation, processing and marketing of high-value cash and staple food crops. The support was targeted at improving resources and removing infrastructural constraints in the agricultural value chain from production through processing and marketing.

Specifically, the MCA Ghana Program sought to achieve the identified goal by deploying the following projects:

- **Agriculture Project**: This project set out to transform agricultural practices through the introduction of capacity-building interventions to improve crop-husbandry and business management skills of\ operators of the agriculture value-chain. It provides resources in terms of infrastructure (irrigation, post-harvest equipment and feeder roads) and credit as well as land security.

- **Transportation Project**: This intervention addressed highways, trunk roads, feeder roads and ferries to improve access to domestic and international markets for agricultural produce.

- **Rural Development Project**: This was designed to strengthen rural institutions that provide services complementary to, and supportive of, agricultural and agri-business development. It includes support for the development of professionals, provision of basic services (electrification, educational facilities and water and sanitation) and strengthening of rural financial services ("Financial Services Activity"). The Ghana Rural Bank Computerization and Inter-connectivity Project was under the Financial Services Activity of the Ghana Compact.

Rural Financial Services in Ghana

Rural and community banks are the primary formal financial service institutions in Ghana. Rural banks operate as commercial banks under the Banking Law of Ghana, except that they cannot undertake foreign exchange operations, and their minimum capital requirement is significantly lower than that required of commercial banks. Rural banks operate as unit banks owned largely by members of the rural community through purchase of shares and are licensed to provide financial intermediation. They were first initiated in 1976 to expand savings mobilization and credit services in rural areas not served by commercial and development banks. As at the time of the project, there were 121 rural banks in Ghana, spread across the 10 regions of Ghana, with 534 agencies and branches. About twenty of these rural banks are ranked among Ghana's top 100 businesses. Ghana Club 100 (2010)

Since 1976, when they were first established, rural banks have improved their overall performance. The need to enhance this desirable trend led to the establishment of ARB Apex Bank Limited which started operations in July 2002 as the Apex Body for Rural banks in Ghana. The apex body seeks to provide rural bank capacity building programs and some supervisory role to further develop the performance and the image of the rural banks in the financial services industry in Ghana. Rural banks finance their activities mainly through deposits from clients' borrowings from banks, equity and concessionary loans from government microfinance programs.

Project Rationale

The Ghana Rural Bank Computerization and Interconnectivity Project (GRBCIP) represented an important aspect of strengthening and improving the capacity of the rural banks to deliver financial services. It was also to allow the rural banks to offer and support new banking services, credit services and financial instruments. The project concentrated on building a technical infrastructure intended to open the door for a broad range of new financial services and capabilities that will directly benefit not only the small rural farmers but also most of the people of Ghana.

The project was intended to draw a large number of people currently not served or underserved into the financial system by automating and inter connecting private and community owned rural banks. 121 rural banks with 534 branches were expected to be inter-connected through a Wide Area Network (WAN) and this was completed. The WAN was focused on moving cash electronically domestically and internally and making the rural banks part of the country's payment system. Simultaneous to the rolling out of the WAN, the project was expected to support the computerization and automation of the rural banks. This involved providing computers and accessories such as printers and UPS, banking software and training for all operational and technical staff of the all the rural banks:

Project Description

The objectives of the GRBCIP were threefold:

(i)   Continue and complete the computerization of rural banks in Ghana which was started under the Rural Financial Services Project

(ii)   Install a based V-SAT based Wide Area Network (WAN) to link all rural bank HQs and branches.

(iii)   Provide a reliable network for implementing electronic payments/funds transfer capabilities among the rural banks.

The GRBCIP had three (3) main components.

a) The first component was the computerization and standardization of the banking operations in the rural banks. This component was expected to: (i) strengthen the competency of rural bank staff through change management, consistent and standardized procedures, automated banking operations and computer literacy training; (ii) installation of computer server hardware at the Data Centre located at Apex Bank and install computer workstations hardware and local area network (LAN) equipment in all the rural banks; (iii) install consistent and reliable banking software that supports electronic payments/transfer capabilities; and (iv) strengthen the technical skills of the Apex Bank technical team to enable them to manage and support the infrastructure.

b) The second component dealt with the design and implementation of a wide area network (WAN) that inter-connected the rural banks. The network technology (VSAT) also provided voice communications and internet connectivity to the rural banks.

c) The third component installed reliable secondary power source through standalone generators to each branch of all the rural banks.

Details of Various Project Tasks

a) Strengthening the Competency of Rural Bank Staff.

This task focused on the change management/mindset required to transform the current manual operations of the rural banks into a consistent and automated process. It involved data analysis and data conversion, computer literacy training and training in the use of computerized banking software.

b) Installation of Computer Hardware.

This task planned the design and construction of a state of the art Data Centre and a Disaster Recovery site, installation of servers, redundant storage, tape backup facility and corresponding uninterruptible power supplies which are all located at Apex Bank headquarters that run the standardized banking software. It also configured and installed the Local Area Network, workstations and printers at the rural banks.

c) Installation of Banking Software.

This task configured and installed the banking software on a central server and at the rural banks. It will also migrate the bank's data into eMerge. The installation and migration will be coordinated for a specific rural bank HQ and all of its branches/agencies.

d) Strengthening the Technical Skills of the Apex Bank Technical Team.

This task strengthened the technical skills required by the Apex Bank Technical Team through a training program. This training program was needed to build up institutional knowledge and expertise in the eMerge banking software in order to make up for the scarcity and high cost of the requisite technical expertise to implement and support the deployment of the software.

e) Design and Implementation of a Wide Area Network (WAN).

This component designed and implemented a wide area network that interconnected the rural banks with the Data Centre at Apex Bank and the branches of the rural banks. The telecom method recommended was pure VSAT (very small aperture terminal) satellite network utilizing KU band and the recommended network topology was the star topology. The VSAT network also provided voice communication interface to the rural banks.

f) Installation of a Reliable Secondary Power Source (Generator Sets).

This component installed standalone generators, if necessary, and based on the reliability and availability of electrical power in each rural bank. The capacity of the generators provided to each rural bank was scaled to the power requirements of the new computerized environment.

The key questions to be answered were:

- Did the project increase the interconnectedness of the rural banks?
- Did the project increase efficiency and reduce transaction cost for rural banks?
- Did the project draw additional people into the financial system?

4.   METHODOLOGY

This paper uses the case study approach to explore the Governance structure that complemented the project management principles that ensured the successful implementation of the Ghana Rural Bank Computerization and Inter-Connectivity Project. It then makes a comparative analysis of the methods used in the above projects that were either abandoned or stalled.

As a qualitative research, the paper examines the governance principles adopted in the GRBCIP and relates it to the other projects that failed and shows that the governance principle that complemented the project management principle in the GRBCIP ; if it had been adopted in the other projects, it could have saved those projects. The hypotheses that this paper seeks to test are the project management principles per se. They would not guarantee the successful implementation of IT projects if they were not combined with solid governance principles

Data Collection

In evaluating the effectiveness of the governance principles adopted in the GRBCIP, the following documents and reports were reviewed:

a.   The Implementing Entity Agreement signed between the Millennium Development Authority (MiDA) and the ARB Apex Bank. Being the apex body with supervisory role over the Rural banks, MiDA selected Apex Bank as the entity to supervise and coordinate the project

b.   Monthly reports of the Steering Committee of the project, including the monthly reports of the Project Management Supports Consultants i.e. KPMG who were the main project managers, quarterly reports of MiDA's Monitoring and Evaluation department, reports of the Technical Committee of the project, monthly reports of the Data Centre manager, monthly and quarterly reports of various contractors and consultants who undertook the actual implementation.

c.   Interviews with Branch managers of selected banks including selected customers. 20 branch managers were selected at random. However, it was restricted to 2 managers per region. The interview was either face to face or via telephone. It also included first hand observations of live banking hall transactions before and after the project.

d.   Report on projects that either failed, or stalled including the National Identification Project of Ghana, and the Electronic Patient Records Project of the UK National Health Service.

Data Analysis

The data that was gathered was used to analyse the governance structure of the Project Implementation Team including the reporting structure, the decision making process within the project team. The structure was compared with the structure found in the above mentioned projects. The Monitoring and Evaluation (M&E) reports of MiDA was also used to ascertain whether the project objective of was fulfilled through the quarterly tracking of pre-determined indicators such the total number of inter-bank of cheques and total value of deposits within the rural banking system as well as the monthly total number of customers and customer transactions. The responses given by the branch managers in the interviews were tabulated and inferences and conclusions drawn.

5.   RESULTS AND DISCUSSION

Governance Structure of the Project Implementation Team (PIT)

a) Project Steering Committee

The project had a well defined structure with clear reporting lines. At the helm of affairs was the Project Steering Committee (PSC) which had as its core mandate the development of policy guidelines. All major policy decisions were mademade at the PSC which had as its chairman, the managing director of ARB Apex Bank. The committee met once a month or when the occasion demands for an emergency meeting and submitted monthly reports to the project sponsors MiDA. The deputy managing director of ARB Apex Bank was the alternate chairman of the committee. Other members of the committee were:

i.   Head of Finance of ARB Apex Bank

ii.   Head of ICT of ARP Apex Bank

iii.   Two Representatives of the Association of Rural Banks

iv.   Representative of Bank of Ghana (Until his appointment, the current second deputy Governor of Bank of Ghana was the central bank's representative on the committee. He was then Head of Payment Systems)

v.   The Project Manager of the Project Management Support Consultants (PMSC) i.e. KPMG who were the Project Managers

There were 3 ex-officio members of the committee i.e. the Project Manager of MiDA in charge of the GRBCIP and his deputy and then the Project Director for the Project Management Support Consultants, the managers of the project.

b) Technical Sub-Committee of the Steering Committee

Next on the project team structure was the Technical Sub-committee of the Steering committee. Their core mandate was to advise the Steering Committee on all technical issues. The committee was responsible for the technical design of the project including the specifications for the construction of the Data centre, Wide Area Network and Local Area Network, specifications for PCs and accessories and the electric generators. Its chairman was the Head of Finance of Apex Bank, and the other members were the Head of IT of Apex Bank and his deputy, the Head of Banking Operations of Apex Bank, the Project Manager of PMSC and his deputy. The Project Manager for MiDA in charge of the GRBCIP and his deputy were ex-officio members. The Technical committee met at least twice in a month or when the occasion necessitated the holding of an emergency meeting. The project managers of the various consultants on the projects were invited at regular intervals to attend the meetings of the committee to clarify issues where necessary. The chairman of the committee presented a monthly report to the Steering Committee.

c) Role of Other Committees

There were 2 other committees that reported to the Technical Committee. They were the Technical Infrastructure Committee whose membership was the Project Manager of Data Centre, Wide Area Network, Local Area Network consultants, Computer Hardware and Generator sets suppliers. The Project Manager of the PMSC chaired that committee. The other committee was the Applications Committee comprising Project Managers for the banking software consultants and suppliers of other third party software such as Anti-Virus, and Server applications. This committee was chaired by the deputy Project Manager of the PMSC.

d) Role of the Project Management Support Consultants (PMSC)

Apart from being members of the Steering committee and other sub-committee, the core mandate of the PMSC was to advise MiDA on all technical and operational issues and most importantly, sign-off on all deliverables by the various consultant and contractors. Consequently they coordinated all the field work involving all the various consultants, ensuring that all supplies and installations of equipment and software at Rural bank all sites including the Data Centre were according to specifications. MiDA only paid consultants for deliverables after the PMSC had certified that the work had been actually completed satisfactorily and according to specifications. This is a far cry from the Electronic Patient Record Project of the UK, where the parliamentary selected committee on health report stated that officials were "unable to show what has been achieved for the £2.7bn spent to date on care records systems", adding that taxpayers were "clearly overpaying BT, one of the project consultants said. The PMSC also liaised with Apex Bank and coordinated all technical and operational training and Change management programmes for the Rural banks.

Benefits of the PIT Structure

From the structure it is very clear and apparent that the project was bound to succeed. The PIT was structured and aligned to the strategic vision of the project. One advantage of the structure was that it made it possible for decision to be made quickly. The information loop was such that information flowed throughout the project team very easily despite the massive nature of the project. Risks identified were quickly dealt with. With the Project Manager of MiDA and his deputy being ex-officio members of both the Steering Committee and the Technical sub-committee, information flow to the Project sponsors was instant despite the monthly reports of the Steering Committee

The structure allowed for the Rural Banks to be part of all decisions made on the project because they had reps on the Steering committee. What is more, the Technical Committee and the PMSC made presentations at all Rural bank managers conference and workshops on the project progress and took feedback and suggestions. Representatives of the rural banks ably assisted by Apex Bank staff were the main participants in the User Requirement Analysis for the customization of the banking software and also the User Acceptance Test and coordinated by the PMSC. This is contrary to what happened in the UK Electronic Patient Record Project where the Parliamentary sub-committee report stated that officials of the Department for Health did not consult with health professionals at the start of the project. Direct providers of care (physicians, nurses, dentists and other health care professionals) will remain the users of the highest priority in design consideration. This is because by designing any system, direct users need to be involved (Dick and Steen 1991). The same goes for the National Identification Project in Ghana where there was no Requirement Analysis and User Acceptance Test involving the citizenry.

So it can be said that the governance structure of the GRBCIP allowed for an all inclusive and holistic approach to the project. All stakeholders from the sponsors MiDA, to partners such as Apex Bank and Bank of Ghana, and the beneficiary community were all involved at every stage of the project and were all kept in the information loop.

Organizational Chart of the Project Implementation Team

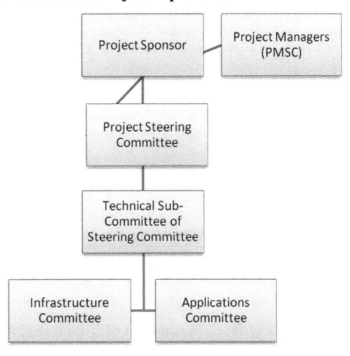

Source: PMSC Inception Report

Achieving the Objectives of the Projects

The successful completion of a project is not an end in itself. What is more important are the benefits that would accrue from the completed projects to the intended beneficiaries. Some of the benefits can be gleaned from the MiDA Monitoring and Evaluation quarterly reports which tracked the following indicators:

a) **The total number of inter-bank transactions**. This is defined as the number of cheques received by rural banks plus number of remittances received by these banks. The financial services intervention is at two levels i.e. Bank of Ghana (for all clearing banks in the country, that is, mainly commercial banks and the Apex Bank acting as a clearing bank for all the rural banks), and Rural Banks (nationwide). Inter-bank transaction is a record of business conducted among banks on behalf of their customers as well as on their own behalf. The classification of the inter-bank transactions are as follows: (i) Total number of cheques received from clearing (ii) Total number of cheques sent to clearing (iii) Total number Apex Link Transfer transactions. This is a money transfer system between Apex Bank and the Rural banks (iv) Others are a total number of money transfer transactions such as Western Union which runs on the back of the internet services provided by the project. This indicator shows the importance of the wide Area network. Through the network, the rural banks are now able to clear customers' cheques through the

Cheque Codeline Clearing system which is managed by the Ghana Inter Payment and Settlement Systems (GhIPSS) within 3 working days. This certainly would bring joy to their customers. Hitherto, clearing of cheques by rural banks could take up to 21 working days.

Table 1 shows that the end of the compact target of inter-bank transactions of 1,106,925 was achieved and it represents an increase of 114% of the baseline figure of 516,565.

b) **Amount of Account Deposits in the Rural Banks**. This is defined as the amount of total deposits in Rural Banks nationwide. The deposits are classified as (i) Fixed Deposits (ii) Savings Account (iii) Current Account (iv) Susu Account. This indicator is expected to improve with the introduction of the automation of the banks because their customer base is expected to increase due to improved services.

Table 1 shows that the end of the compact target of US$1,117,776,372 was achieved representing a whopping 294% increase from the baseline figure of US$283, 421932. The Year 3 figure of US$745,184,248 also shows a 163% increase, while the Year 4 figure of US$931,480,310 shows an increase of 228%.

c) **Number of Banks Connected to the WAN**. This is defined as the number banks connected to the WAN by way of installation of indoor and outdoor VSAT equipment and activating the connection to the central hub and to the Data Centre. The baseline figure was zero. However, by Year 3, 21 banks had been connected, representing 17.3% of the baseline. By Year 4 the number of banks connected to the WAN had increased to 91 representing 71.2% of the baseline figure. The end of the compact figure of 121 was achieved.

d) **Number of Banks Automated with Banking Software**: This is defined as the number of banks that are connected to the banking software which is located on the central server at the Data Centre. The baseline and annual targets were the same as that of the number of banks connected to the WAN

Other Achievements

In an interview with selected branch managers of the rural banks, it was revealed that the turnaround time for processing a cheque for payment by a teller reduced from an average of between 10-15 minutes on a very busy day to between 2-5 minutes. This has led to new customers walking through the doors of the banks to open new accounts and transact business with rural banks. Again problems associated with manual computation of bank transactions were eliminated because all processes are now automated.

Comparative Analysis of the GRBCIP and other Failed Projects

From the above, it can be seen that all targets set by the GRBCIP were achieved. This means that the project objectives were met and thus was successfully implemented. This can be attributed in part to the IT governance principles that were very evident throughout the duration of the project.

This is in sharp contrast to projects like the Ghana National Identification Project which is yet to be completed after more than 10 years of implementation. In effect the project is yet to achieve its objectives as compared to the GRBCIP. The same can be said of UK's Electronic Patient Record Project which is also behind schedule, with a massive cost overrun. What is more, there is no end in sight for the 2 projects.

Table 1: MiDA M&E Indicator Tracking

Indicator	Indi-cator Level	Indi-cator Type	Unit of Measure	Base-line	Year1 Feb 07-Mar 08	Year 2 Apr08-Mar 09	Year 3 Apr 09-Mar 10	Year 4 Apr10-Mar 11	Year 5 Mar 11-Feb 12	End of eCompact Target Year 1-
								Annual Targets		**End of eCompact Target**
Amount of AccountDeposit in Rural Banks	Outcome	Level	US$	283,421,932			745,184,248	931,480,310	1,117,776,372	1,117,7
Number of Inter-bank transactions	Output	Cumulative	Number	516,565				983,993	1,106,925	1,106,92
Number of Banks Connected to the WAN	Output	Cumulative	Number	0			21	91	121	121
Number of Banks Automated with Banking Software	Output	Cumulative	Number	0			21	91	121	121

6.   CONCLUSION AND RECOMMENDATIONS

This study shows that for an IT project to be completed on schedule, within budget and according to specification, there should be a strong presence of an effective governance structure. Merely applying project management principles would not accomplish the task. For example a PRINCE2 principle recommends the development of a Project Charter which is a statement of the scope, objectives and participants in a project. And it provides a preliminary delineation of roles and responsibilities, outlines the project objectives, identifies the main stakeholders, and defines the authority of the project manager. However, if the governance structure is not right, information flow within the team would be very limited. Whether there is a change of personnel of a project team or a change of government, a solid presence of a governance structure would definitely see the successful completion of a project.

A clear governance structure, with well defined responsibilities and reporting lines is a pre-requisite for the successful implementation of a project. One important fact that must be noted is that individual members of project teams should be removed from their normal schedules and attached permanently to teams. However this situation can be circumvented only if a proper governance structure ensures that the individual or group of individuals allocate a specific time frame to the project as it happened to staff of ARB Apex Bank who were drafted into the project team. The allocation of specific time frame can be adhered to if the executive is fully involved in the process and approves this arrangement. Without executive involvement and approval it would be impossible to achieve this feat.

Finally, without the executive being fully involved in every aspect of a project, challenges are bound to exist especially with regards to funding. MiDA being the sponsors of the GRBCIP were fully involved in every aspect of the project and were therefore prepared to release extra funding where it was needed. Ghana's National Identification Project consistently failed since its inception in 1973 mainly due to funding. Perhaps, lack of executive support and commitment to the project could be the cause.

It must, however, be noted that there are similarities between the IT Governance methodologies that were applied in the case of the Ghana Rural Bank Computerization Project and methodologies applied in other countries. The methodology applied in the GRBCIP should not be seen as been peculiar to only Ghana, as it can be successfully applied in different enterprises either public or private as well as in other countries worldwide.

7.   LIMITATIONS OF STUDY

One limitation of the study was the inability to interview members of the Steering Committee of the Project as well as officials of the Millennium Development Authority to obtain their views on the impact of the structure and design of the project team. Any future research should consider interviews with these officials.

There is however scope for future research. This has to do with any role of IT Corporate Governance on Post Project Implementation.

REFERENCES

Alabi J, Alabi G. (2011). Institutional Evaluation Program (IEP) as Governance Tool in Public Higher Education Institutions in Ghana: A case of the Institute of Professional Studies (IPS). Journal of Business Research, 5(1), 19-37.

Batalden P.B, Buchanan E.D. (1989). Providing Quality Care: The Challenge to Clinicians. American College of Physicians pp 133-159

Bishop M, (2008) Federal IT Projects Failures Proposed Legislation Aim to Stop the Insanity.http://www.cio.com/article/469928/FederalITProjectFailuresProposedLegislati onAimstoStoptheInsanity. Retrieved on 7 September, 2012

Brown C.V, (1997). Examining the Emergence of Hybrid IS Governance Solution: Evidence from a   Single Case Site. Information Systems Research. 8(1), 69-94

Dick R.S, Steen E.B. (1991). The Computer-based Patient Record. An Essential Technology for Healthcare. Washington DC National Academy Press

Donaldbedian A. (1998). The Quality of Care. How can It be Accessed? Journal of the American Medical Association 260, 1743-1748.

The Ghana Club 100 (2010)

History of National Identification Authority (2010)

Huang R, Zmud R.W., Price R.L., (2010). Influencing the Effectiveness of IT Governance Practices Through Steering Committees and Communication Policies. European Journal of Information Systems, 19, 288-302.

Johnson J.H,, (1994) Micro Projects Cause Constant Change. The Standish Group International, Inc. http://cf.agilealliance.org/articles/system/article/file/1053/file.pdf. Retrieved 4 September, 2012

Kaufman T. (2009) 7% Increase Planned for IT Projects. Federal Times, 18 May PP1-3

Madon S. (2005). Governance lessons from the experience of telecentres in Kerala. European Journal of Information Systems.14, 401–416

Multisectoral Technical Committee Report (2002) government/agencies-commissions/national-identification-authority. Retrieved on 4 September, 2012

Ofei-Aboagye E, (2004). Promoting Gender Sensitivity in Local Governance in Ghana. Development in Practice. 14(6), 753-760.

Recovery Act (2009) http://www.whitehouse.gov/the_press_office/arra_public_review Retrieved on 4 September, 2012

Raymond L, Paré G, Bergeron F. (1995). Matching Information Technology and Organizational Structure: An empirical Study with Implications for Performance. European Journal of Information Systems, 4, 3–16.

Sambamurthy V, Zemud R.W, (1999). Arrangements for Information Technology Governance: A Theory of Multiple Contingencies. MIS Quarterly, 23(2) 261-290

Schwalby Kathy. (2011). Information Technology Project Management. Sixth Edition (Revised), Cengage Learning.

 Stal-Le Cardinal J, Marle F. (2005). Project: The Just Necessary Structure to Reach Your Goals. International Journal of Project Management 24(3), 226-233.

UK Parliamentary Public Accounts Committee (2011). The National Programme for IT in the NHS: an Update on the Delivery of Detailed Care Records Systems: 45th Report. http://www.publications.parliament.uk/pa/cm201012/cmselect/cmpubacc/1070/107004.htm

Weil P, Ross J.W. (2004). IT Governance: How IT Top Performers Manage IT Decisions Rights for Superior Results. Harvard Business School Press

Wilkin C. L., Campbell J, Moore S, (2012). Creating Value Through Governing IT Deployment in a Public/Private-sector Inter-Organisational Context: A Human Agency Perspective. European Journal of Information Systems Advance Online Publication 19 June 2012;

11

THE EVALUATION AND IMPROVEMENT OF IT GOVERNANCE

Patricia Pérez Lorences
Lourdes Francisca García Ávila
Central University "Marta Abreu" from Las Villas, Santa Clara, Cuba

ABSTRACT

The present article aims to propose a general procedure to evaluate and improve the Information Technology (IT) Governance in an organization, considering the Business–IT alignment and risk management. The procedure integrates management tools such as business processes management, risk management, strategic alignment and the balanced scorecard. Additionally, to assess the IT Governance level we proposed an indicator based on the process maturity. The concepts and ideas presented here had been applied in four case studies, verifying their implementation feasibility. The results indicate a low level of IT governance and the existence of several problems primarily in the Plan and Organize and Monitor and Evaluate domains.

Keywords: IT Governance, IT Management, IT Strategic Alignment, IT Risk Management, IT Governance Assess, IT Governance Improvement

1 INTRODUCTION

Information technologies (IT) have revolutionized the business world irrevocably and in the context of the information age companies increase their IT investments, becoming a major competitive component for companies (Dehning, Dow, & Stratopoulos, 2004). Specific studies have shown empirically: the positive relationship between corporate profitability and the use of IT in business processes (Piñeiro Sánchez, 2006); the elevation of the productivity (Neirotti & Paolucci, 2007), the improvement in the performance of processes inducing elevation enterprise performance (Prasad & Heales, 2010), and the improvement in the performance of services (Roberto Giao, Mendes Borini, & Oliveira Júnior, 2010).

The implementation of these resources is not enough to obtain the expected uses of IT. These resources only offer a potential that the company should develop and adapt

Address for correspondence / Endereço para correspondência

Patricia Pérez Lorences, Industrial Engineer, Master in Business Informatics (MBI) Assistant professor of Business Informatics Group. Industrial Engineering Department Central University "Marta Abreu" from Las Villas, Santa Clara, Cuba.

Lourdes Francisca García Ávila, Industrial Engineer, PhD in Technical Sciences, Consultant professor of Business Informatics Group. Industrial Engineering Department , Central University "Marta Abreu" from Las Villas, Santa Clara, Cuba.

to their specific business context, using management skills. Neirotti and Paolucci prove with their study (Neirotti & Paolucci, 2007) that companies show a successful return on IT investment, have better IT management practices that allow them to adapt their organizational routines to meet business needs. Similarly, a study of more than 400 Brazilian companies showed that companies that adopt IT governance mechanisms have an improvement in their financial performance, primarily in relation to profitability (Lunardi, Becker, & Macada, 2012). Other research (Kobelsky, Hunter, & Richardson, 2008) y (Yao, Liu, & Chan, 2010) shows that the influence of IT on the future profits of the company depends on various contextual factors such as quality of management and strategic alignment. It is essential to have a clear strategic vision of the role of IT in business (Laurindo, Shimizu, Caravalho, & Rabechini Junior, 2001). There is empirical evidence (Bulchand-Gidumal & Melián-González, 2011) that the planning and management of IT influence the allocation of human resources and IT, which have positive effects on organizational performance. Management efforts to sustain high levels of IT capability translate into sustainable competitive advantages (Huan, Ou, Chen, & Lin, 2006), (Bharadwaj, 2000), (Masli, Richardson, Sanchez, & Smith, 2011).

The evaluation and improvement of IT governance is extremely important because it allows companies to control if they are really making effective management of their IT, to ensure maximum benefits and management of the associated risks.

Investigations in hundreds of companies around the world have revealed a trend toward the increased maturity level in the area of IT in organizations; however, there is a lot left for improvement. In 2008 (ITGI, 2009) and 2010 (ITGI, 2011) the IT Governance Institute implemented a comprehensive study in organizations of various sectors in 23 countries representing all continents. Based on the results of the study, it is a fact that the vast majority (92%) of respondents are aware of the problems with the use of these resources and the need to take action in this regard. The research reflects the importance of how IT continues to grow and has significantly increased interest in adoption and implementation of best practices, but there are still many incidents. While security and compliance are important elements mentioned, people are the most critical problem. 58% of respondents considered insufficient the number of IT people in their organizations, which is the main problem presented. The second problem, reflected by 48%, refers to the incidents relating to the provision of services. Then 38% of the respondents said the lack of IT staff skills is another problem. Moreover, it was found that communication between IT and users is improving, but slowly. Although the gap is significant for improving the alignment with the business strategy, 36% of the respondents indicated that the alignment between IT strategy and corporate is bad or very bad.

These results confirm the relevance and importance of having tools to improve governance of these resources. Hence, enterprises need help to raise the level of IT governance, under the conditions and requirements imposed by today's business environment and prospects. The objective of the study reported in this paper was to develop a general procedure to assess and improve IT Governance in an organization, considering the Business–IT alignment and risk management.

In this paper, some concepts of IT governance are recapitulated in section 2 and the propose procedure is presented in Section 3. The main results of the case studies are analyzed in section 4, and conclusions are described in section 5.

2   LITERATURE REVIEW

Information technology (IT) has become pervasive in current dynamic and often turbulent business environments. While in the past, business executives could delegate, ignore or avoid IT decisions, this is now impossible in most sectors and industries. This major IT dependency implies a huge vulnerability that is inherently present in IT environments. IT of course has the potential not only to support existing business strategies, but also to shape new strategies. In this mindset, IT becomes not only a success factor for survival and prosperity, but also an opportunity to differentiate and to achieve competitive advantage. (Wim Van Grembergen & De Haes, 2009).

IT governance specifies the decision rights and accountability framework to encourage desirable behavior in the use of IT (Peter & J, 2004). This behavior relates to the form of the leadership, and organizational structures and processes that ensure that the organization's IT sustains and extends the organization's strategies and objectives (ITGI, 2009). The scope of IT governance are not single decisions themselves but the determination which decisions need to be made, who can contribute to the decision-making processes and who is eventually eligible to make the decision. In this sense, every company has IT governance, but only an explicitly designed one is able to align IT effectively and efficiently to the goals of the company.

IT governance addresses the definition and implementation of processes, structures and relational mechanisms in the organization that enable both business and IT people to execute their responsibilities in support of business/IT alignment and the creation of business value from IT-enabled business investments (Wim Van Grembergen & De Haes, 2009). Multiple researchers share the same view of IT Governance (e.g. (Peterson, 2004); (Wim Van Grembergen, De Haes, & Guldentops, 2004); (Van Bon, 2008))

IT governance essentially places structure around how organizations´ IT strategy aligns with business strategy. This IT-business alignment will ensure that organizations continue to achieve their strategies and goals, and implement ways to evaluate its performance. One special aspect of IT governance is that it considers the interests of all stakeholders and ensures that processes provide measurable results. This situation is possible with lateral IT governance structures, with the involvement of all levels of management (Prasad, Heales, & P, 2010).

In recent years, standards, frameworks, and best practices addressing different aspects of IT management and governance have emerged and matured. Among these, the most mentioned are: ITIL (Commerce, 2011) and ISO/IEC20000 (ISO, 2011) which address IT service management. The ISO/IEC 38500:2008, corporate governance of information technology, provides a framework for effective governance of IT to assist those at the highest level of the organizations (Standardization, 2008). The standard assists top management to understand their legal, regulatory, and ethical obligations in respect of their organizations' use of IT. ISO27000 (ISO, 2012) referred to information security and IT BSC (W. Van Grembergen, 2000) as an adaptation of the BSC to the IT environment. The Control Objectives for Information and related Technology (COBIT) is an approach to standardize good information technology security and control practices. COBIT provides tools to assess and measure the performance of 34 IT processes of an organization (ITGI, 2007). COBIT framework has an integration nature, responding adequately to the governance of IT and its alignment with business objectives.

Searching the literature, organizations can follow a few supporting mechanisms to guide their implementation of IT governance, integrating all the IT governance´s aspects with a strategic approach, and they could be used as a support for its assessment and improvement. Therefore, it was necessary to develop a method.

3 PROCEDURE TO EVALUATE AND IMPROVE THE IT GOVERNANCE

The proposed procedure was divided into four phases as shown in figure 1 to ensure the cycle of continuous improvement for IT governance.

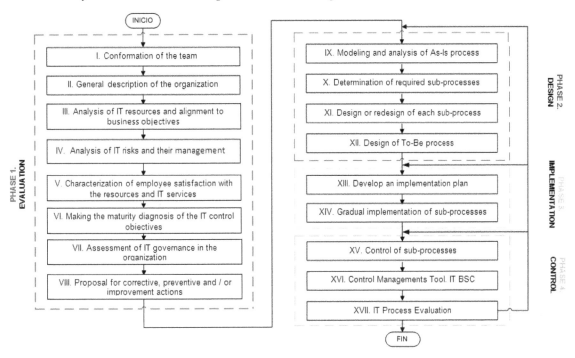

Fig. 1. Procedure to evaluate and improve the IT governance

The first phase is dedicated to the **Evaluation** of the current state of IT governance in the organization. It begins with the conformation of the team and the second stage proceeds with the general characterization of the organization. The third stage is dedicated to analyzing the alignment of IT resources to the business objectives of the organization, proposing a set of tools to carry out this assessment. In the fourth stage we propose a specific procedure to analyze IT risk management, whcih let you get an assessment of risks in the organization. Because of its importance as a reflection of the actions of IT management,   stage five is characterized by employee level of satisfaction with IT services and resources. The maturity diagnosis takes place at the sixth stage and the calculation of a comprehensive indicator of IT governance that characterizes the current state of the organization take place in stage 7. This phase of the procedure culminates with the proposal of improvement actions, depending on the assessment (stage 8).

In the second phase, the **Design** of the IT governance process is carried out, defined under the BPM approach. It begins with modeling and analysis of the As-Is process in stage 9, which allows the identification of opportunities for improvement in the process, from the results of the previous phase. Stages 10 and 11 describe in detail the selection and design of the sub-processes. This phase ends with the design of the To-Be process, including its modeling and the approval of the suggestion. Already in the third phase, **Implementation**, we proceed to execute the process designed. The general procedure ends with a **Control** phase which is the "engine" of continuous improvement, because depending on the results, it might involve a return to earlier stages. We propose the calculation of indicators to monitor the sub-processes implemented and we designed a generic scorecard as a tool management control of IT, based on the principles of IT BSC, and it must be redefined by the organization. To monitor the achievement of the procedure objectives a final stage dedicated to the recalculation of the proposed indicator is included, which also includes situation analysis and ends with the proposal of improvement measures.

3.1 Phase 1: IT Governance Evaluation

Stage 1: Conformation of the team

The first stage is aimed at the conformation of the team, which will feature the full implementation of the procedure. It includes: Definition of the team structure, determination of members quantity and selection of the personnel, assignment of responsibilities and tasks, and the training of staff.

Stage 2: General description of the organization

This second stage corresponds to the general characterization of the organization under study, which should,in particular, appreciate the value of information technology to achieve their business objectives. It includes: Description of the organization general data, and identification of the objectives and business processes.

Stage 3: Analysis of IT resources and alignment to business objectives

At this stage we will analyze the impact of IT in achieving business goals and current conditions of the company to meet these requirements. It includes the following steps:

I. Carry out an inventory of IT resources of the organization

The folowing should be identified: the applications, infrastructure and staff; which are required to plan, organize, acquire, implement, deliver, support, monitor and evaluate the systems and information services. We propose an inventory model that is a format table useful to organize the information for categories and its impact classification.

II. Classify the IT resources in terms of their impact on business

From the inventory of IT resources in the organization we proceed to classify them individually, according to their impact on the business, into: Strong, Medium or Weak. To do that, we design an algorithm as shown in Figure 2, considering the current and potential importance of IT resources, and its ease of replacement.

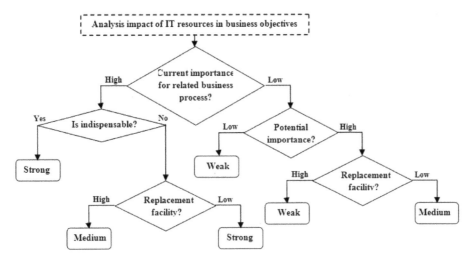

Fig. 2. Algorithm to classify the IT resources in terms of its impact on business

Once each one is classified, we proposed a set of indices useful to determine the impact of each type of IT resource (applications, infrastructure and staff)on the business and the global impact of all resources.

III. Evaluate business processes according to their degree of dependence on IT

The literature offers few precedents where it is allowed to establish the dependence on IT from a business process to be classified into one scale. Little (Little, 1981) establishes one scale to assess the technological position in an enterprise and (Brito Viñas, 2000) modify that propose, but in both cases it is a breadth scale, which is not specific for IT. (Jiménez Quintana, 2002) defines a set of measures that assess: the business process degree of automation, the support degree of information systems and the support degree of information systems on-line. We used these bases and our empirical experience to define a qualitative scale for the degree of dependence on IT in three levels: Strong, Medium or Weak.

IV. Analyze the correlation between IT resources and requirements of the organization based on business objectives

Once there is the classification of IT resources according to their impact on the business and evaluation of business processes according to their degree of dependence on IT, in this step we analyze the alignment between the two aspects. To support this analysis the matrix shown in Figure 3 was developed. The proposed matrix is useful to analyze the alignment and possible strategies to follow. It is based primarily on the following elements: Strategic Alignment Model (Luftman, 2004), the IT strategic grid to examine the strategic role of IT McFarlan and McKenney (MacFarlan & macKenney, 1983) and Matrix Technology Management (Edwards & Bytheway, 1991).

Impact of IT resources on business objectives

<table>
<tr><th rowspan="9">Dependence on IT of business process</th><th></th><th>STRONG</th><th>MEDIUM</th><th>WEAK</th></tr>
<tr><th rowspan="2">STRONG</th><td>**Alignment**</td><td>**Misalignment**</td><td>**Non-Alignment**</td></tr>
<tr><td>*Maintain / Improve IT Governance*</td><td>*Assess Investment projects / Cost-Benefit analysis*</td><td>*Execute Investment projects / Cost-Benefit analysis*</td></tr>
<tr><th rowspan="2">MEDIUM</th><td>**Misalignment**</td><td>**Alignment**</td><td>**Non-Alignment**</td></tr>
<tr><td>*Innovation in IT / Identify opportunities offered by IT resources for business*</td><td>*Maintain / Improve IT Governance*</td><td>*Assess Investment projects / Cost-Benefit analysis*</td></tr>
<tr><th rowspan="2">WEAK</th><td>**Non-Alignment**</td><td>**Non-Alignment**</td><td>**Alignment**</td></tr>
<tr><td>*Identify process improvements*</td><td>*Assess process improvements / Use IT potentialities*</td><td>*Improve process / Identify opportunities offered by IT resources for business*</td></tr>
</table>

Fig. 3. Matrix (dependence on business processes / impact of IT resources), alignment analysis

Stage 4: Analysis of IT risks and their management

At this stage we analyze the management of IT risks in the enterprise. For this, we propose a specific procedure, structured in nine steps as shown:

1. Establish the strategic context of risk

• Are critical IT resources identified?

2. Identify threats

• Are threats identified?

3. Identify vulnerabilities

• Are vulnerabilities identified?

4. Analyze controls

• Which controls are implemented?

5. Determine probability level

• Is the likelihood of a threat to act on a determined vulnerability, considering existing controls?

6. Analyze impact

• Have you analyzed the impacts of a threat to act on vulnerability?

7. Determine risk level

• Have you determined the risk levels?

8. Recommend controls

9. Document results

The content and tools of each step, guidance for the implementation of the diagnonis to obtain the risks, and on the other hand, provide the necessary elements to answer the question proposed, enabling the analysis of IT risk management.

Stage 5: Characterization of employee satisfaction with the resources and IT services

The special importance of employee satisfaction with IT resources and services motivated the inclusion of this stage in the diagnostic procedure. A survey was designed to characterize employee satisfaction with infrastructure, applications, IT staff and services.

Stage 6: Making the maturity diagnosis of the IT control objectives

The first step of this stage is to define the domains and control objectives to diagnose. A general proposal was made starting from COBIT 4.1 framework, which must be adapted by the team considering elements to be added or removed depending on the characteristics of the organization. Then we proceed with the collection, verification and analysis of information to determine the maturity level of each control objective according to the maturity models defined by COBIT.

Stage 7: Assessment of IT governance in the organization

At this stage we assess IT governance in the organization, for which we propose an indicator to evaluate the level of IT Governance (I_{GTI}). The equations and model evaluation were developed by the authors considering the maturity level of each control objective and the assumption that these control objectives do not have the same importance in the enterprise. The steps to develop this stage are:

I. Determination of the relative importance of domains and control objectives
II. Assessment of the domains and control objectives

We propose the assessment of each control objective through the following expression:

$$EOC_{dg} = \frac{W_{dg}.xNM_{dg}}{5} \tag{1}$$

EOC_{dg}: Assessment of the control objective "d" of the domain "g"

W_{dg}: Weight (relative importance) of the control objective "d" of the domain "g"

NM_{dg}: Maturity level of the control objective "d" of the domain "g"

The sum of the assessments of the control objectives gives the domain result

$$RD_g = \sum_{d=1}^{m_g} EOC_{dg} \tag{2}$$

RD_g: Result of the domain "g"

The evaluation of each domain is calculated using the following expression:

$$ED_g = W_g \times RD_g \times 100 \tag{3}$$

ED_g: Evaluation of the domain "g"

W_g: Weight of the domain "g"

III. Determination of indicator I_{GTI}. Graphical representation of results

The indicator to evaluate the level of IT Governance (I_{GTI}) is calculated as shown:

$$I_{GTI} = \sum_{g=1}^{4} ED_g$$

(4)

We define the scale for assessment of IT Governance from Non-existent level to Optimized, as shown in table 1 considering the maturity levels proposed in COBIT. The determination of intervals was made using the simulation of results. We propose a graphical representation of results, using control radars and Cause-Effect graphics like shown in figure 4.

Table 1. Scale for assessment of IT Governance

Intervals I_{GTI} (%)	IT Governance Assessment
($95 \leq I_{GTI} \leq 100$)	Level 5: Optimized
($75 \leq I_{GTI} < 95$)	Level 4: Managed
($55 \leq I_{GTI} < 75$)	Level 3: Defined
($35 \leq I_{GTI} < 55$)	Level 2: Repeatable
($15 \leq I_{GTI} < 35$)	Level 1: Initial/Ad Hoc
($I_{GTI} < 15$)	Level 0: Non-existent

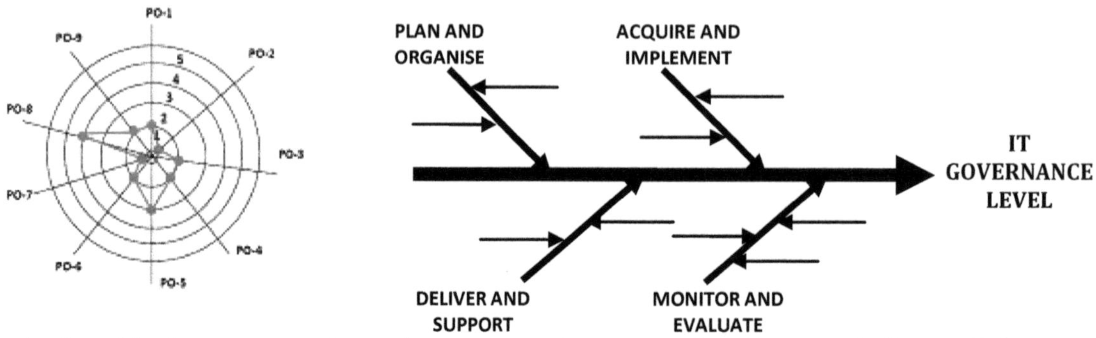

Fig. 4. Graphical representation of results, using control radars and Cause-Effect graphics

IV. Preparation of evaluation report

From the results obtained in the previous stages, this step is required to produce a report which includes assessing: the analysis of IT resources and alignment to business objectives, analysis of IT risk management, the analysis of the characterization of employee satisfaction, and a list of domains and control objectives that reflected greater difficulty. The main problems affecting IT governance in the organization should be noted.

Stage 8: Proposal for corrective, preventive and / or improvement actions

Once made, the IT governance diagnosis, the report prepared by the team may indicate the need for corrective, preventive and / or improvement actions, as applicable. At this stage we proceed to develop the proposal for such actions.

3.2 Phase 2: Design of the IT governance process

The design phase has been formed under the approach of Business Process Management (BPM). The analysis of the current state of IT governance in the organization was realized in the previous phase, so in case there is a defined IT process in the organization, phase 2 begins with As-Is process modeling, otherwise it goes to stage 10.

Stage 9: Modeling and analysis of As-Is process

At this stage we model the IT governance process that currently exists in the organization. We recommend using BPMN for business process modeling. The team should define the notation and the tool to use for modeling. The modeling of the current situation allows the identification of opportunities for process improvement. From the diagnosis made we could point the deficiencies that might exist in the structure of the current process. Also, we could point the need to incorporate new sub-processes or activities based in the COBIT framework.

Stages 10 and 11 correspond to the proposed improvements to the AS-IS process.

Stage 10: Determination of required sub-processes

At this stage the analysis includes: COBIT processes that are pertinent or not in the organization and what processes are required in correspondence with the characteristics of the organization, which are not covered in the COBIT framework.

Stage 11: Design or redesign of each sub-process

At this stage the processes based on COBIT should be redesigned according to the characteristics of the organization. The design of the new additional processes is required. The elements to consider are: overview of sub-process, description of sub-process activities, inputs and outputs of sub-process, RACI Chart (Responsibility, Accountable, Consulted, Informed), goals and metrics of the process.

Stage 12: Design of To-Be process

Once each sub-process is redefined, we design the To-Be process, showing how to relate those sub-processes connected by their inputs and outputs. The steps in this stage are: Modeling the To-Be process, Evaluation and approval of the designed process, Redesign based on the assessment and Document the To-Be process.

3.3 Phase 3: Implementation

Stage 13: Develop an implementation plan

To ensure the successful performance of the designed process, an implementation plan should be established. This plan includes the actions to be taken into consideration to ensure the transition from the As-Is process to the To-Be process. The plan also defines the priorities that order the implementation of sub-processes, based on its importance for the enterprise.

Stage 14: Gradual implementation of sub-processes

From the priorities identified in the implementation plan, at this stage, we proceed to gradually implement sub-processes. In the implementation, it is of utmost importance to ensure the commitment of top management to achieve successful results. This commitment must be tangible through active participation, willingness to change, resource allocation, internal communications, process monitoring and taking actions to achieve goals. The preparation and training of managers and staff of the organization through training programs focused on developing knowledge and skills in IT governance can be useful at this time.

3.4 Phase 4: Control

This phase focuses on evaluating and controlling the behavior of the IT governance in the organization, with the IT process implementation. This phase constitute the "motor" of continuous improvement for the procedure, which may involve a return to earlier stages in terms of results. IT process control does not require that this has been fully implemented; it can be carried out independently by each sub-process, allowing you to make decisions during the implementation phase and maintain a control and monitoring system to ensure the successful completion of the actions provided. To control the overall performance of IT governance in the organization, we also propose to determine the IT Governance Level indicator proposed in the first stage, analyzing its behavior with respect to the state it was before implementing the improvements in the organization. IT balanced scorecard has also been designed.

Stage15: Control of sub-processes

At this stage it is proposed to calculate the KPI (Key Performance Indicators) during the performance of a subprocess and KGI (Key Goals Indicators) after implemented, to determine if they achieve their objective. KPIs allow determining how well the IT process is performing to achieve the goal, indicating whether it is feasible to achieve a goal or not. KGIs define measurements to inform if an IT process reached its business requirements.

Stage 16: Management control Tool. IT BSC

As a tool for management control at this stage we proposed to design a balanced scorecard for IT. We propose a generic design based on IT BSC (W. Van Grembergen, 2000) . This design and the proposed indicators should be adapted by the organization in terms of the IT process designed, their interests and special characteristics.

Stage 17: IT Process Evaluation

17.1 Recalculation of the IT Governance Level indicator

The recalculation of the indicator allows a comparison of the behavior results of the current situation, once the IT process is implemented. This check allows to verify the effectiveness of the proposed process and establishes the relevant improvements if necessary.

17.2 Situation analysis

If the proposed process is suitable for IT governance in the organization and has led to tangible improvements, its performance will need to be reviewed periodically. The return to stage 2 could be necessary, depending on the characteristics of the organization and changes that might be generated internally or externally. If the organization's performance has not evolved positively, we must analyze the causes. The analysis might reveal problems in the implementation of the process or its design, in which case we will proceed to improve it. Also to be considered external events that, during the period considered for assessment, could have influenced these results.

3.17 Proposing improvements

After the situation analysis we proceed to the proposal of measures contributing to the continuous improvement. To achieve the necessary improvements, this analysis can include the return to phases 2 or 3 of the procedure for the redesign of the process, depending on the deficiencies identified in its initial design or its implementation. If the return is not necessary, we continue with the implementation and consolidation of IT process in the organization.

4   RESULTS

The application of the procedure in four case studies lets us verify their implementation feasibility as effective methodological instruments to, first of all, assess the IT governance in these enterprises focusing on the main problems, and in second place to determine improvement opportunities that contribute to IT-Business alignment and risk management.

We consider achieving a balance between the enterprise selected, including two software development enterprises and two commercial enterprises. In this article we presented a synthesis of the results in one software development enterprise and the global analysis for the rest. The application of the procedure in this enterprise allows the design and implementation of a new IT governance process according to their peculiarities. The IT governance improvement is evident in the elevation of the indicator to evaluate the level of IT Governance since 25.87% to 44.81%, resulting from a considerable improvement in all domains as shown in figure 5 (red color represent the early assess).

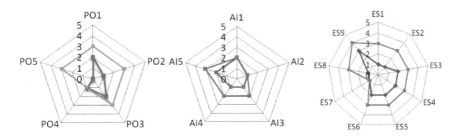

Fig. 5. Graphical representation of results, using control radars.

The IT BSC design includes four perspectives. It was selected a set of metrics balancing key performance indicators and key goals indicators, to guarantee the proactively in the monitoring of IT governance at the enterprise.

In the other enterprises the first stage was finalized, identifying the problems and the improvement actions recommended. These results are showed in (Pérez Lorences, 2010). The calculi of the indicator to evaluate the level of IT Governance showed all case studies´ results under the 40%, denoting a low level and the existence of several problems primarily in the Plan an Organize and Monitor and Evaluate domains. The analysis proves that a lack of adequate IT governance exists, based on business requirements.

The successful application of the procedure in the companies studied, both in software companies, trading companies, demonstrated its applicability to entities with different characteristics, being evidenced adequate operational flexibility. The ability to select the control objectives to be evaluated and to determine the relative importance they have on the company to obtain an assessment of their level of management, to ensure the flexibility of its application. This was demonstrated when methodological tools of the evaluation phase were applied to the software case studies. Similarly, it was found in the case of the other two companies under study, both traders. The flexibility of their instruments was demonstrated, making them desirable in principle, by other similar organizations, which support to a greater or lesser extent, their business on information technologies.

5 CONCLUSION

In this paper, we presented a new general procedure to analyze, evaluate, monitor and improve IT Governance in an organization. The procedure considers the alignment between business processes and IT resources, IT risk management, the approach of process maturity, the principles of Business Process Management and IT Balance Scorecard. All this is complemented by the COBIT framework, expression of best practices in the IT governance field. The structure and content of the phases proposed ensure the cycle of continuous improvement for IT governance. The evaluation phase integrates the best practices of the COBIT framework with tools of IT resources alignment and risk management, considering employee satisfaction, thus allowing a comprehensive assessment of IT governance in the organization. The design and implementation phases, based on the assessment and best practices, guide the construction of the IT governance process as a central proposal for improvement. The inclusion of a control phase is vital to ensure continuous improvement; this phase allows the monitoring, balancing goal and performance indicators that ensure proactive improvement actions.

REFERENCES

Bharadwaj, A. S. (2000). A resource-based perspective on information technology capability and firm performance. An empirical investigation. . *MIS Quarterly, 24*(1), 169-196.

Brito Viñas, B. (2000). *Modelo conceptual y procedimientos de apoyo a la toma de decisiones para potenciar la función de Gestión Tecnológica y de la Innovación en la empresa manufacturera cubana.*, UCLV, Villa Clara, Cuba.

Bulchand-Gidumal, J., & Melián-González, S. (2011). Maximizing the positive influence of IT for improving organizational performance. *The Journal of Strategic Information Systems, 20*(4), 461-478.

Commerce, O. o. G. (2011). ITIL v.3. Information Technology Infrastructure Library.

Dehning, B., Dow, K. E., & Stratopoulos, T. (2004). Information technology and organizational slack. *International Journal of Accounting Information Systems, 5*(1), 51-63.

Edwards, W., & Bytheway. (1991). *The Essence of Information Systems.* Hemel Hempstead: Prentice Hall International.

Huan, S.-M., Ou, C.-S., Chen, C.-M., & Lin, B. (2006). An empirical study of relationship between IT investment and firm performance: a resource-based perspective. *European Journal of Operational Research*, 984-999.

ISO. (2011). ISO 20000: Information technology -- Service management.

ISO. (2012). ISO/IEC 27000: Information technology -- Security techniques -- Information security management systems.

ITGI. (2007). COBIT 4.1 Control Objectives for Information and related Technology. : IT Governance Institute.

ITGI. (2009). *IT Governance Global Status Report 2008.*: IT Governance Institute.

ITGI. (2011). *Global Status Report on the Governance of EnterpriseIT*: IT Governance Institute.

Jiménez Quintana, C. (2002). *Indicadores de Alineamiento entre Procesos de Negocios y Sistemas Informáticos.*, Universidad de Concepción.

Kobelsky, K., Hunter, S., & Richardson, V. J. (2008). Information technology, contextual factors and the volatility of firm performance. *International Journal of Accounting Information Systems, 9*(3), 154-174.

Laurindo, F. J. B., Shimizu, T., Caravalho, M. M., & Rabechini Junior, R. (2001). O papel da tecnologia da informação (TI) na estrátegia das organizações. *Gestão e Produção, 8*(2), 160-179.

Little, A. D. (1981). *The Strategic Management of Technology*. Cambridge. Massachussets. U.S.A.

Luftman, J. (2004). Assessing Business-IT Alignment Maturity *Strategies for Information Technology Governance* (pp. 99-128). United States of America and United Kingdom: Idea Group Publishing.

Lunardi, G. L., Becker, J. L., & Macada, A. C. G. (2012). Um estudo empírico do impacto da governança de TI no desempenho organizacional. *Producao, 22*(3), 612-624.

MacFarlan, F. W., & macKenney, J. (1983). *Corporate Information Systems Management*. Homewood, Illinois: Richard D. Irwin Inc.

Masli, A., Richardson, V. J., Sanchez, J. M., & Smith, R. E. (2011). Returns to IT excellence: Evidence from financial performance around information technology excellence awards. *International Journal of Accounting Information Systems, 12*(3), 189-205.

Neirotti, P., & Paolucci, E. (2007). Assessing the strategic value of Information Technology: An analysis on the insurance sector. *Information & Management, 44*(6), 568-582.

Pérez Lorences, P. (2010). *Procedimiento para evaluar y mejorar la gestión de tecnologías de la información en empresas cubanas.* Universidad Central Marta Abreu de Las Villas, Villa Clara, Cuba.

Peter, W., & J, R. (2004). *IT governance: how top performers manage IT decision rights for superior results.* Boston, MA: Harvard Business School Press.

Peterson, R. R. (2004). Integration Strategies and Tactics for Information Technology Governance *Strategies for Information Technology Governance* (pp. 37-80). United States of America and United Kingdom: Idea Group Publishing.

Piñeiro Sánchez, C. (2006). Un estudio transversal sobre la contribución de las tecnologías de la información al éxito empresarial. *Revista Europea de Dirección y Economía de la Empresa, 15*(2), 61-78.

Prasad, A., & Heales, J. (2010). On IT and business value in developing countries: A complementarities-based approach. *International Journal of Accounting Information Systems, 11*(4), 314-335.

Prasad, A., Heales, J., & P, G. (2010). A capabilities-based approach to obtaining a deeper understanding of information technology governance effectiveness: evidence from IT steering committees. *International Journal of Accounting Information Systems, 11*(3), 214-332.

Roberto Giao, P., Mendes Borini, F., & Oliveira Júnior, M. d. M. (2010). The influence of technology on the performance of Brazilian call centers. *Journal of Information Systems and Technology Management, 7*(2), 335-352.

Standardization, I. O. f. (2008). ISO 38 500. Corporate Governance of Information Technology.

Van Bon, J. (2008). This is NOT IT Governance. *UPGRADE The European Journal for the Informatics Professional, 9*(1), 5-13.

Van Grembergen, W. (2000). The Balanced Scorecard and IT Governance. *Information Systems Control, 2*.

Van Grembergen, W., & De Haes, S. (2009). *Enterprise Governance of Information Technology. Achieving Strategic Alignment and Value*. New York: Springer Science + Business Media.

Van Grembergen, W., De Haes, S., & Guldentops, E. (2004). Structures, Processes and Relational Mechanisms for IT Governance *Strategies for Information Technology Governance* (pp. 1-36). United States of America and United Kingdom: Idea Group Publishing.

Yao, L. J., Liu, C., & Chan, S. H. (2010). The influence of firm specific context on realizing information technology business value in manufacturing industry. *International Journal of Accounting Information Systems, 11*(4), 353-362.

12

INFORMATION SYSTEMS AND ORGANIZATIONAL MEMORY: A LITERATURE REVIEW

Victor Freitas de Azeredo Barros
Centre ALGORITMI, University of Minho, Guimarães, Portugal

Isabel Ramos
Centre ALGORITMI, University of Minho, Guimarães, Portugal

Gilberto Perez
Universidade Presbiteriana Mackenzie, São Paulo/SP, Brazil

ABSTRACT

The advancement of technologies and Information Systems (IS) associated with the search for success in the competitive market leads organizations to seek strategies that assist in acquisition, retention, storage, and dissemination of knowledge in the organization in order to be reused in time, preserving its Organizational Memory (OM). Organizational Memory Information Systems (OMIS) emerge as an enhancer of the OM, providing effective support and resources for the organization, assisting in decision making, in the solution of problems, as well as in quality and development of products and services. This article is an analysis of some OMIS selected from a literature review about its features and functionality in order to understand how these information systems are seen by the organizations. With this research, we realized that the relationship between OM and IS is still inexpressive, even with the existence of some cases of success in the use of OMIS in the literature. The literature reveals that an individuals' knowledge is not integrated in information systems management process in most organizations; much of this knowledge is generated in the organization retained in an individual himself/herself. It is easy to see that there is a need for strategies and mechanisms in the organization to stimulate and provide better knowledge sharing between individuals which, when associated to IS, allows greater control and effective use of Organizational Memory.

Keywords: Strategy, Knowledge management, Competitiveness, Decision-making.

Address for correspondence / Endereço para correspondência

Victor F. A. Barros, Researcher at Centre ALGORITMI, University of Minho, Campus de Azurém, 4800-058 Guimarães, Portugal.

Isabel Ramos, PhD in Information Systems and Technology, Assistant Professor with Aggregation at the Department of Information Systems, University of Minho, Campus de Azurém, 4800-058 Guimarães, Portugal.

Gilberto Perez, Doutor em Administração pela Universidade de São Paulo (USP). Professor do Programa de Pós-Graduação em Administração (PPGA) da Universidade Presbiteriana Mackenzie. Rua da Consolação, 930 - 01302907 - São Paulo, SP - Brasil.

1. INTRODUCTION

In an increasingly competitive and globalized world, organizations are constantly changing in order to stay in the market. This constant competitiveness leads organizations to seek more and more quality not only in the products and services offered but also in their strategies, decisions and structures. However, these changes in the organization, whether strategic or structural, may result in a loss of the accumulated knowledge retained in an individual.

> "[...] factors such as global competition, changing organizational structures, massive layoffs of middle managers, and the emergence of 'virtual organizations' are causing organizations to lose valuable experiential knowledge that exists only in the memories of individual workers." (Morrison, 1997, p. 300).

Once the knowledge generated in the organization over time is one of the primary factors to remain competitive in the market, it is important that organizations are aware of and seek mechanisms and strategies that enable to keep this accumulated knowledge in the organization. This set of accumulated knowledge accumulated being preserved through time is called organizational memory (OM).

> "OM may be thought of as comprising stocks of data, information, and knowledge (the memories) that have been accumulated by an organization over its history. When an individual accesses OM, he performs an act of interpretation on the memory(ies) that is(are) accessed and may or may not act on it (them)." (Cegarra-Navarro & Sánchez-Polo, 2011, p. 1).

OM provides support both to the development of the individual and the organization. For the individual by aggregating knowledge and learning from the experiences, strategies and actions taken by the organization over time, and for the organization by using this range of accumulated knowledge that, when associated with the current knowledge of this individual, aids in actions and decisions to be taken in the organization as well as in the generation of new solutions, products and services.

In order for OM to be useful and effective for the organization, it is necessary that the organization guides its strategy to the creation of a favorable environment that fosters and encourages collaboration and the sharing of knowledge, ideas, experiences and relevant information among its members, in order to feed this OM consistently. It is also important to ensure that the Information System (IS) supporting its processes facilitates both acquisition and retention and the dissemination of this knowledge in the organization.

> "Since the Organizational Memory shows up as a fertile field of research while challenging, the purpose of this essay was to better understand its mechanisms of operation, associating them with the Information Systems, given the complexity and scope of such systems, which has as one of its main purposes, the preservation of organizational memory." (Perez & Ramos, 2013, p. 543)

Also known as organizational memory information systems (OMIS), these systems should be flexible to adapt to the changes as well as to support the demand of the information and knowledge submitted them over time, increasing the capacity and the speed of response of the organization.

> "[...] the impact of OMIS on knowledge receipt from the recipient side can be intervened by the firm's potential absorptive capacity. The internal systems of the recipient affect the extent to which a firm recognizes and evaluates the usefulness of knowledge transferred by the focal firm and the

extent to which a firm can internalize the knowledge." (Yu, Dong, Zuo, & Xu, 2012, p. 7).

The purpose of this article is to explore how information systems, more specifically OMIS, enhance and support the creation, storage, and dissemination of knowledge in the organization over time in order to ensure an effective management of OM.

To support this research, section 2 discusses the methodology adopted, followed by section 3 with a synthesis of some of the main theoretical concepts and definitions of organizational memory (OM) and organizational memory information systems (OMIS) addressed in this investigation. From this, section 4 shows an analysis of some selected OMIS in the literature regarding its structure, features and advantages for organizations. Finally, sections 5 and 6 are, respectively, a discussion of the results obtained and some final thoughts about this study.

2. MATERIALS AND METHODS

This research is characterized as exploratory, since it seeks to understand through content analysis (Bardin, 2000) the context in which this study is fitted and to provide greater familiarity with the subject of study (Cervo, Bervian, & Silva, 2007). For its accomplishment, a systematic review of the literature was carried out, making it possible to identify, evaluate and interpret relevant studies addressing the topics of the research, in particular, organizational memory (OM) and organizational memory information systems (OMIS). To achieve this, the following steps were followed: (i) planning the review; (ii) identification of the main sources of literature; (iii) selection of literature based on keywords, followed by criteria for inclusion and exclusion.

In the review planning step, the research was directed according to the purpose of the article, namely, to explore the approaches to OM and OMIS existing in the literature, with the aim of analyzing the described concepts, models, application, features and functionalities. The selected scientific sources of the research work were the Scopus, Web of Science, IEEEXplore and AIS Electronic Library (AISeL) because they are commonly considered the most representative scientific bases around the information systems (IS) area.

To find relevant articles, it was carried out a systematic search in the selected scientific bases articles including, either in the title, abstract or keywords, the two central themes of this study: information systems and organizational memory. Table 1 describes the number of publications over the last 20 years (1994-2013).

Table 1. Number of publications over the last 20 years (1994-2013) on scientific bases Scopus, Web of Science, IEE Xplore and AISeL and search code on information systems and organizational memory.

YEAR [1994-2013]	SCIENTIFIC BASIS			
	Scopus [137]	Web of Science [60]	IEEEXplore [09]	AISeL [09]
1994 [01]	-	-	-	1
1995 [08]	5	3	-	-
1996 [02]	2	-	-	-
1997 [12]	8	2	2	-
1998 [16]	11	4	1	-
1999 [22]	13	7	1	1
2000 [20]	12	8	-	-
2001 [09]	4	4	1	-
2002 [13]	7	6	-	-
2003[11]	6	4	1	-
2004 [13]	9	3	-	1
2005 [20]	13	5	1	1
2006 [15]	9	5	-	1
2007 [16]	14	1	1	-
2008 [12]	9	2	1	-
2009 [09]	5	3	-	1
2010 [05]	3	1	-	1
2011 [05]	4	1	-	-
2012 [02]	1	-	-	1
2013 [04]	2	1	-	1

From this search, it was obtained a set of 215 scientific articles that were read and analyzed, and are discussed in the remaining sections of this article. For the analysis of the gathered articles, a set of keywords related to the central themes of this research was selected to a further selection of articles for this literature review (Section 3) without compromising the quality of the obtained results; for the selection of the main OMIS described and discussed in this article (Section 4), a subset of the latter group of articles was chosen. Table 2 shows the related keywords that were used to refine the set of articles to analyze within the central topics of this study (OM and OMIS).

Table 2. List of the keywords related to OM and OMIS found in the literature review.

CENTRAL SUBJECTS	KEYWORDS
Organizational Memory (OM)	Organizational Memory; Corporate Memory; Cooperative Memory; Social Memory; Collective Mind; Group Memory; Corporate knowledge management; Knowledge Memory.
Organizational Memory Information Systems (OMIS)	Organizational Memory Systems; Organization Memory Information System; Knowledge Management System; Corporate Repository; Knowledge Repositories; Process Memory Systems; Shared knowledge Base.

Following the execution of these delimiters emphasizing the articles clearly related and relevant to the aims of the study being, 20 scientific articles were selected because they are clearly related to OMIS and quote one or more cases relevant to this study. Based on this set of scientific articles, 7 OMIS were selected. Table 3 shows the main OMIS found from this literature review, the description of the author and the year of publication, as well as the research method used by the author (s).

Table 3. Relation of Organizational Memory Information Systems (OMIS).

OMIS	AUTHOR(S)	YEAR	RESEARCH APPROACH
Answer Gardner	Mark S. Ackerman	(1994a)	Field Research
	Mark S. Ackerman	(1994b)	Field Research
Lotus Note	Kenneth Moore	(1995)	-
	Thomas H. Davenport	(1998)	Case Study
Project Memory System	Joline Morrison	(1997)	Literature Review
	Mark Weiser and Joline Morrison	(1998)	Laboratory Experimentation (Prototype)
KnowMore System	Andreas Abecker, Ansgar Bernardi, Knut Hinkelmann, Otto Kühn and Michael Sintek	(1998)	Laboratory Experimentation (Prototype)
	Andreas Abecker, Ansgar Bernardi, Knut Hinkelmann, Otto Kühn and Michael Sintek	(2000)	Laboratory Experimentation (Prototype)
Handbook	Thomas W. Malone, Kevin Crowston, Jintae Lee, Brian Pentland, Chrysanthos Dellarocas, George Wyner, John Quimby, Charles S. Osborn, Abraham Bernstein, George Herman, Mark Klein and Elissa O'Donnell	(1999)	Case Study
Thoughtflow	P. Balasubramanian, Kumar Nochur, John C. Henderson and M. Millie Kwan	(1999)	Case Study
KnowledgeScope	M. Millie Kwan and P. Balasubramanian	(2003)	Actual Experimentation (Implantation)

From this selection of OMIS existing in the literature, it was performed an analysis based on concepts, features and classifications, which allowed the classification of OMIS, considering as criteria the types of knowledge supported by these systems and the process of acquisition, retention, storage and dissemination of these knowledge through individuals.

3. LITERATURE REVIEW

3.1 Organizational Memory (OM)

Day after day, most organizations lose a great volume of their generated knowledge due to the lack of mechanisms that allow its retention for the organization, keeping great part of this knowledge retained only in an individual.

According to Walsh & Ungson (1991, p. 57), "to the extent that organizations exhibit characteristics of information processing, they should incorporate some sort of memory". In this sense, when the organization can obtain, retain and store the knowledge over time and make it available as necessary, it could be said that this organization can assure and feed consistently organizational memory (OM).

> "[...] with updated hard memories, individuals will have the advanced tools to increase efficiency through automated workflow features or enhance individual achievements through application of explicit knowledge. Therefore, providing the appropriate Hard-OM is critical in the future success of today's companies [...] is the streamlined, interconnected backbone of an entire company, into which all individuals will be able to connect and share information." (Cegarra-Navarro & Sánchez-Polo, 2011, p. 13).

In this scenario, Walsh & Ungson (1991) created a model of OM (Figure 1) providing a possible explanation for how an organization obtains, retains and retrieves the generated information, enabling this information to be used in actions and decisions that are taken by individuals in the organization and emphasizing that "the structure of organizational memory is composed of a number of storage bins: individuals, culture, transformations, structures, ecology, and external archives."

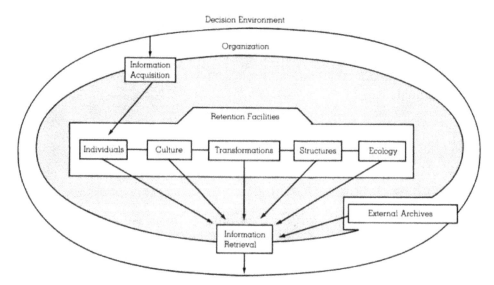

Figure 1. The structure of Organizational Memory (OM) proposed by Walsh & Ungson (1991, p. 64).

For the authors, maintaining a rich and functional OM, it is necessary to interlink all information repositories in the organization and, in particular, individuals who compose it. "The most important keys to understanding acquisition, retention, and retrieval processes is to understand the nature of the individuals that compose the organization." (Walsh & Ungson, 1991, p. 77).

As individual influences directly the OM, everything that involves an individual in the organization, i.e., the organizational setting in which this individual is, also influences the behavior of the individual. "[...] the acquisition, retention, and retrieval of knowledge and experience from retention repositories (i.e., memory) influence individual behavior by the company." (Walsh & Ungson, 1991, p. 58).

Therefore, all this accumulated knowledge, whether retained in the individual or in the environment, in both physical and organic structure, the transformations and changes in the organization, as well as the culture and policies adopted by the organization, are the main factors that feed the Walsh & Ungson model so that the organization may have an effective OM. "This knowledge integrates and coordinates all organizational activities even the transmission of new knowledge throughout the system. This facility, of course, is an organization's memory." (Walsh & Ungson, 1991, p. 72).

In addition to all this internal knowledge management for an effective OM, the authors also consider as part of OM the knowledge that can be acquired from the organization's social context, whether obtained from associations, partner companies, customers, suppliers, working groups, public institutions, among others. "Just as when an individual's memory fails, he or she can turn to others to help recall the particular event, an organization is surrounded by others who follow its actions." (Walsh & Ungson, 1991, p. 66).

For authors like Morrison (1997), Cegarra-Navarro & Sánchez-Polo (2011) and others, the organization's knowledge can be acquired and stored in OM both in the form of explicit knowledge (also called hard, concrete knowledge or "Hard-OM") and of tacit knowledge (also called abstract, episodic knowledge or "Soft-OM").

Tacit knowledge is that which cannot be expressed, such as the individual's experience, structures, myths, culture, contexts and actions; whereas explicit knowledge refers to any information that can be expressed in documents, numbers, processes and transactions (Cegarra-Navarro & Sánchez-Polo, 2011).

Table 4 summarises the "types of knowledge" that could compose the OM that were found in the selection of literature classified by levels of abstraction of knowledge, with the description of their origins and importance to the organization.

Table 4. Classification of types of knowledge that could compose the organizational memory according to the level of abstraction of knowledge, with the description of their origins and importance in the organization.

Abstration/Level	Type	Description	Importance
Concret/ Hard/ Explicit "Hard-OM"	Record of transactions and data bank	Documents of transactions in the organization from reports, data regarding to database archiving.	Contains trends, historical contexts and varying interpretations.
	Documentary record	Items of information dissemination such as summaries web pages, articles, news, among others; formal documents such as reports and versions; manuals, reports, digitalized documents.	
	Individual record	Informal documents related to creation of artifacts (e-mail, memos, letters, etc.)	
Abstract/ Episodic/ Tacit/ "Soft-OM"	Process e Rules	Interpretative, systematic and observable components; production process, work process, concepts.	Knowledge, experiences, events and standardized artifacts, remembrance, single interpretations and diagnosis of multiple point of views determining improvements in actions and decisions in the organization.
	Experiences and Transformations	Mind of the specialists, decision-makers, Project developers (individuals), practices, observations, organizational decisions. New projects, budgets, market, planning, procedures, among others	
	Structure, Myths, Policies and Culture	Acquisition, retention and knowledge share in the organizational structure; symbols, stories repeated in the set of information transmitted among the individuals in their organizational environment, physical structure and organizational policy	

Source: adapted from Blue, Andoh-Baidoo, & Osatuyi (2011); Cegarra-Navarro & Sánchez-Polo (2011); Morrison (1997); Walsh & Ungson (1991).

As a way to enhance this organizational memory (OM), information systems (IS) came to support the process of acquisition, retention, storage, and dissemination of knowledge in the organization, thus enabling new strategies for the sharing of knowledge, ideas, experiences and information thus making more effective the decision making, troubleshooting, innovation and quality of products and services. These systems are referred to in this study as organizational memory information systems (OMIS).

3.2. Organizational memory information systems (OMIS)

As a way to enhance, "feed" and support the organizational memory (OM) in organizations, information systems (IS) should make possible the acquisition and retention of knowledge, whether explicit or tacit, the storage and dissemination of this knowledge when needed. The supporting of an effective knowledge management process is the challenge of organizational memory information systems (OMIS).

Nevo et al., (2008) argue that the model by Walsh & Ungson (1991) is appropriate to support the research efforts in the field of information systems and technologies. The basic assumption is that information technology can be used to create a uniform, complete, consistent, updated and integrated set of knowledge that can be made available for the decision-making processes at all levels of the organization.

OMIS can be defined as any IS used in the organization that allows to enhance the process of acquisition, retention, storage, and distribution of knowledge over time, even involving those individuals who are not part of the organization, promoting (i) an effective knowledge management process and organizational memory; and (ii) optimizing the processes of decision-making, problem-solving, quality assurance and development of products and services in the Organization (Kwan & Balasubramanian, 2003; Stein & Zwass, 1995).

> "Broadening the repertoire of the information-systems support for organizational memory helps human actors cope with a possible information overload and supports their roles as information processors. [...] With its response repertoire constantly replenished from the arising cases, the system is a part of the company's organizational memory." (Stein & Zwass, 1995, p. 90).

Knowledge-based systems, document management systems, semantic networks, object-oriented and relational databases, decision support systems (DSS), expert systems, collaborative systems, social networks, intranets, simulation tools, distributed systems; document management; geographic information systems (GIS); contextual indexes; metadata; navigator; e-mail; search/retrieval of tools; information repositories; web server; agents/filters; external services server; videoconferencing; knowledge-based systems (KBS); data mining; information and communication technologies (ICTs); artificial intelligence (AI); database technology; modeling; among others are examples of systems and tools that support organizational memory (Alavi & Leidner, 2001; Dorasamy, Raman, & Kaliannan, 2013).

To support this concept, Stein & Zwass (1995) created a framework to represent OMIS based on theoretical criteria of organizational memory. This framework can be viewed in Figure 2.

Supporting Activities Leading to Organizational Effectiveness

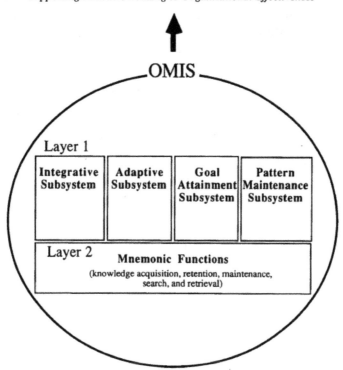

Figure 2. Framework for an organizational memory information systems (OMIS) proposed by Stein & Zwass (1995, p. 98).

According to Stein & Zwass (1995), OMIS consist of two layers; the first layer is subdivided into four sub-processes: (i) the integrative, that supports the organizational knowledge sharing through time at all levels of the organization; (ii) the adaptive, which recognizes, captures, organizes and distributes knowledge in the organizational environment adapting it to the changes of environment over time; (iii) the attainment, which seeks to achieve the performance goals of the organization not only the storage of knowledge goals; and (iv) the maintenance, which preserves the knowledge development in the organization throughout the time through attitudes, values, standards, routines and self-knowledge, contributing to the cohesion and morale of the organization.

The second layer corresponds to the process explored in the previous section (section 3.1) with regard to acquisition, retention and availability of knowledge. The authors have added the maintenance process and research that are directly linked to the process of acquisition, retention and availability of knowledge, respectively. The maintenance process represents the capacity of the system to assimilate the new knowledge that is being retained with the existing knowledge, and the search process refers to agility and reliability in the pursuit of that knowledge already stored in the system for their reliable recovery.

All this focus on what ensures the consistency of this model in order to perceive how knowledge can be acquired by the organization, the way it will be stored and maintained over time, as well as the agility and reliability of providing the representation of knowledge in information systems.

Some systems such as: Answer Garden, Project Memory System, Knowledge Scope, among others, are some examples of systems that present characteristics of an organizational memory information system (OMIS). These systems were chosen to be described in section 4.

4. ANALYSIS AND COMPARISON OF ORGANIZATIONAL MEMORY INFORMATION SYSTEMS

As already discussed in the previous sections, the effective management of the organizational memory (OM) supported by information systems (IS) improves the organization's capability to acquire, retain, store and disseminate the knowledge generated over time, not only the explicit, which is commonly stored and made available in organizations, but also the tacit, which is retained in the minds of individuals and that most often is not shared among the members of the organization.

In the literature, it was found some conceptual models and applications that have characteristics of an organizational memory information system (OMIS). In this section, some of these systems found in the literature will be described and related to the characteristics of the OMIS reference model proposed by Stein & Zwass (1995) and the type of organizational knowledge described in Table 3.

4.1. Answer Gardner

The Answer Garden provides an environment for questions and answers categorized by subject. It is composed not only of an extensive database, but also of a panel of experts who, if the user does not find the solution to her/his problem, the system itself selects a specialist according to the specific nature of the problem. These experts, in turn, provide such a solution if it had not been found before and update the database.

According to Ackerman (1994b), who examined six organizations which used the Answer Garden, only one organization actually makes constant use of this system. One of the problems is that it does not provide contextual information of the problems, which complicates the resolution of new problems and, in many cases, does not answer the questions of the users. Another difficulty is that individuals feel its use is very complex, reducing the motivation to access the system and to update the database.

For organizations that use information extensively, this system is very useful, since it is always changing, emerging from new questions and answers being fed into the system.

However, feeding the database and answering the questions of the users demand a lot of time and work, requiring that this system be integrated into the workflow of the individuals in the organization so that it does not cause a lack of interest both for the users and the experts.

4.2. Lotus Note

Companies like Price Waterhouse, HP and others used the Lotus Notes system arguing that this system played an integrating role in the organization (Davenport, 1998). At Price WaterHouse, for example, this system was used to integrate all the knowledge of its members located throughout the world; this extensive sharing of knowledge reduced costs and time to perform particular processes, in addition to optimizing decision making (Kawell Jr., Beckhardt, Halvorsen, Raymond, & Greif, 1988).

Another company that included that system in the organization was HP, which used the Lotus Note as a mechanism to assist the sharing of ideas, collaboration and learning between individuals in the organization, recognizing that this strategy was one of the factors of success and growth of the company (Davenport, 1998).

Lotus Notes is a software used by several organizations in the world and is based on a platform of mail flow. It has as tools the electronic mail integrated with discussion groups and allows individuals to create, index, alter and update various documents whenever necessary (Kawell Jr. et al., 1988). Thus, every individual can perform the necessary changes, making its use and supplementation more flexible, given that the Lotus Notes "empowers individuals and organizations to collaborate and share information." (Moore, 1995, p. 427).

Considering the concept of organizational memory information system, it might be said that the Lotus Notes fits perfectly in it, because it supports the storing of all the information of an organization and makes that information available so that all parts are connected.

4.3. Project Memory System

The system, Project Memory, uses approaches for managing data projects that can capture the processes, contexts, fundamentals, or artifacts in a way that allows members of new projects to familiarize themselves quickly with all the history of the project (Weiser & Morrison, 1998).

This system basically breaks down the information on a particular project into five distinct classes: projects, users, events, meetings and documents. In addition, the model describes the people, temporal events (such as meetings or items of an individual scheduling in a meeting) and archival documents that are created within a project or support some of its aspects (Morrison, 1997).

A positive point of this system is that information retrieval is based on any contextual information, such as the date on which the project was created or last revised, the keywords of the project, the one who created this project or even the relation of this project with others projects in the organization. A disadvantage of this system often mentioned in literature is that all individuals are represented as members of the project and do not take into account their roles, relationships and affiliations.

4.4. KnowMore System

The KnowMore system aims to provide a support for a large amount of tasks performed in an organization from a system able to retain knowledge and make it available taking into account the context (Abecker et al., 1998).

According to Abecker et al. (2000) the KnowMore Project has as its main feature the possibility of integrating the workflow of the organization so that the system becomes an assistant able to provide information as necessary. This is, in a particular task to be performed or in a particular process running in the organization, a query to the system's knowledge bases and the actions taken within a certain workflow performed automatically and presented to the individual during the performance of this activity/task/execution.

The advantage of this system functionality is that it assists the individual in performing various business activities and tasks by providing relevant information recovered from the organization's knowledge base.

From a technical point of view, the process and modeling are based on ontological knowledge, metadata and heuristics, thus ensuring the reliability of its execution. It provides a framework for easy handling, with boxes of tools that help create applications to support the user (Abecker et al., 2000). Thus, at any given time when the individual performs a certain task, the system leads him/her to relevant information providing suggestions and aiding in decision making.

The structure of the system is able to provide some support information, if the user has some difficulty handling or understanding the information provided. In addition, the system can direct the user to other individuals in the organization who hold relevant knowledge to achieve a successful decision.

As points for improvement for KnowMore Project, it is highlighted the way it deals with the data acquisition and retention from the ongoing activity. In the KnowMore system, all kinds of information are treated in a similar manner, whether they are formal and/or informal data. In addition, it is entirely focused on resources only for recovery of knowledge, not processing the knowledge of activity/task/thing in question.

4.5. Knowledge Scope

The KnowledgeScope is a system capable of capturing representations of knowledge generated in the organizational setting supporting the integration of processes and information in a workflow, organizing all acquired knowledge acquired to be used whenever necessary.

The Knowledge Scope, the process of acquisition and retention of knowledge is performed through the capture of documents, processes and strategies of the organization and the system provides a version control of these documents. What distinguishes it from the traditional systems is that this system supports an integrated workflow management, making available user strategies, projects, ideas, among other forms of knowledge already in use, which can be retrieved at any moment.

> KnowledgeScope organizes knowledge around the organizational processes in which the knowledge is created, captured, and used. [...] KnowledgeScope to (1) reduce the documentation burden by automatically capturing knowledge and its context as it is created, and (2) provide knowledge with contextual information to the right person at the right time in the right place." (Kwan & Balasubramanian, 2003, p. 483)

In addition, the system has a discussion forum and may have different standpoints on certain actions of the project. It also provides a guide of notes so that the user can make notes of any ideas that, then, are stored in the system. The system also provides a search system for an individual to find specific items of interest such as projects, customers and any other individual with characteristics necessary for executing her/his project.

4.6. Other OMIS

The PRISM system, described by Palvia, Perkins, & Zeltmann (1992), is one of the most extensive human resources information system, deployed to the Federal

Express Corporation. This system maintains the history of training, safety, benefits and structural changes of the entire organization.

The HandBook is a system that captures the knowledge of the process (Malone et al., 1999). As the processes contain descriptions of different types of processes from different organizations, the system classify them by using an approach that incorporates the concepts of guidelines to objects of inheritance and abstraction.

The gIBIS organizes the logic of a design process using a knowledge structure based on an argument that defines the interchange of knowledge in a discussion in three categories: issues, positions and arguments. The gIBIS captures only the contents, but not the context in which the discussion takes place, such as the roles of the participants and the tasks from which problems arise (Conklin & Begeman, 1988).

Other systems use this logic of structure and integrate all information of the documentation processes. One such system is Thoughtflow that organizes the logic of a process in a form of an audit trail of goals and decisions picking up the context of decisions, decision roles, resources, schedules, and so on (Balasubramanian et al., 1999).

4.7. OMIS Comparison

With the description of some of the existing organizational memory information systems (OMIS), it is possible to highlight that organizations are seeking effective ways of knowledge management and memorization because there is a prevalent notion that they are crucial for improving the organization's performance. Table 5 provides an overview of the systems presented in the previous section showing to which process of knowledge memorization they provide support.

The memorization processes that we used to create the table are knowledge acquisition, retention, storage, and dissemination as proposed by Morrison (1997). As for the process of acquisition and retention, it is considered the recovery and storing of information in databases (AR1); the user requests of information, namely: searches and information recovery performed by individuals (AR2); periodic queries to individuals in the form of satisfaction surveys and reports about usage (AR3); and information (external and/or internal) directed to the individual as memos, lists, forums, among others (AR4). For the dissemination process, two possibilities are considered: the active (ACT), for willful and conscious recovery; and the passive (PAS), for information retrieved in informal personal contacts or internal communications.

Table 5. Overview of types of knowledge supported by systems and strategies for acquisition, retention, and dissemination of this knowledge.

OMIS	Type of Knowledge						Acquisition/Retention				Dissemination	
	TDBR	DR	IR	PR	ET	SMPC	AR1	AR2	AR3	AR4	ACT	PAS
AnswerGardner				X	X		X	X	X		X	
LotusNote	X	X	X		X		X	X		X	X	X
Project Memory System	X	X	X	X	X		X	X				X
KnowMore System		X	X	X			X	X	X	X	X	X
KnowledgeScope		X	X	X	X		X	X		X	X	X
HANDBOOK				X			X				X	
Thoughtflow		X	X	X			X	X			X	

Legend:

TDBR = Transaction and Database Record

DR = Documental Record

IR = Individual Record

AR1 = Information put in database by individuals

AR2 = User requests data

ACT = Proposital and Aware of individual

PR = Processes and Rules

ET = Experiences and Transformations

SMPC = Structure, Myths, Policies and Culture

AR3 = Regular consultations to individuals

AR4 = external and/or internal information directed to individual

PAS = Informal contact or internal communication

From the table, it is possible to identify a wide variety of knowledge types that are handled by the systems, with an emphasis on individual records and processes. As for acquisition and retention strategies, it is clear that individuals use the systems to access necessary documents and some systems collect requests by users.

However, regarding the Structure, Myths, Policies and Culture, they are given no involvement and interaction by the systems, making it difficult for the users to use them at a time that is appropriate. For dissemination, in most of cases, the systems support its intentional search.

The Answer Garden, for example, while providing an environment for questions and answers that help individuals whenever they have any questions, with support from experts, does not provide information according to the context, making the interpretation of recovered information harder.

The KnowledgeScope, Project Memory System and KnowMore System systems can retain knowledge together with its context, allowing individuals to understand a particular process or task being performed, and use it in the current context as a support for solving a particular problem or for decision-making.

Moreover, the KnowledgeScope and the Lotus Note systems, in addition to retaining knowledge, assist in the exchange of experiences among individuals of this organization, allowing to add and/or modify any component of an existing project to a current reality without having to remake the whole process.

5. DISCUSSION

This research, in the form of a literature review on organizational memory (OM) and organizational memory information systems (OMIS) makes it possible to understand the extent and nature of the studies carried out within the field of organizational memory (OM) and information systems (SI), which includes the process of acquisition, retention, and dissemination of knowledge in the organization. From an extensive search in some of the major scientific bases it was possible to understand that, over the years, there are few authors who perform studies addressing OM. These authors have been demonstrating that organizational memory processes supported by information systems help to increase organizational performance and productivity, thereby becoming effective in supporting organizations in accomplishing their goals.

It is necessary to mention that, despite the focus on the need of retaining knowledge, few case studies analyzed how information systems are used in organizations to assist the process of knowledge construction.

The issue of terminology is also a factor that hinders the studies in this area. There are several terms used to refer to organizational memory information systems. This terminological inconsistency points to the need for a greater consensus about the term to use so that research on OMIS can be consolidated.

From the models selected and described in section 4, it can be highlighted that while OM research focus on how organizations memorize knowledge, the area of OMIS has been focusing on a particular kind of knowledge, explicit knowledge or information. Moreover, the literature also stresses clear difficulties in managing that information, so it can be reused in a different context from the one where it was produced. Thereafter, it is important to have more studies to develop a better understanding about which knowledge/information can be retained by OM and how this knowledge/information can be retained to ensure its effective reuse to support future decisions.

This is the case, for example, of the KnowledgeScope and the Lotus Note systems, which can promote the exchange of knowledge and experience between individuals, allowing to change, add and/or modify stored information as well as include new information readily available to all organizational members.
The performed literature review also confirms that it is not enough to have an organizational memory information system in place to ensure an effective OM. It is also necessary an organizational culture that fosters the use of this knowledge in a shared and collaborative manner so that it can generate more knowledge, more ideas, more creativity and innovation to the organization.

6. CONCLUSION

Organizational memory information systems (OMIS) can be used to retain organizational knowledge (explicit and tacit), therefore they are used to support the structuring of organizational activities, and the communication and knowledge sharing between individuals in the organization. Thus, these systems play an important role in OM, structuring and enhancing OM's role in decision making, in solving problems as well as in the innovation and quality control of products and services in the organization. OMIS also add knowledge management functions, creating an environment that encourages the collaboration and the sharing of ideas and experiences between individuals, aiming to enhance the acquisition, retention, storage, and distribution of organizational knowledge over time, which are major functions of OM.

Regarding the literature review, organizational studies applying empirical research, including case studies and/or action-research are necessary. This way developed theoretical models and frameworks can be applied and validated so that they can become effective tools for organizational interventions aimed at diagnosing and improving OM. Moreover, this applied research would enable a better understanding of factors underlying the success of OMIS in organizational settings.

As to the analysis of the selected OMIS, it was observed that organizations are aware of the importance of OM and invest in the preservation of relevant knowledge that can provide them with competitive advantage.

The challenge for organizations is, then, in identifying and implementing a system that adequately supports organizational memory, by assisting organizations in the decision-making process. An OMIS should provide a well-defined environment for the acquisition and retention of the semantically correct knowledge, allowing its reuse in a reliable and safe manner. It should also provide, facilitate and encourage collaboration and sharing functionalities.

It is expected that this literature review can provide the necessary basis for further analysis of the relationship between organizational memory (OM) and information systems (IS), whether in its theoretical context, with conceptual analysis of the relationship between OM and IS, and/or in its practical context, with analysis of the used information systems and their impact on OM; and they can ensure a safe competitive advantage in the market, since they represent key components for the effective management of the knowledge generated in the organization.

ACKNOWLEDGEMENTS

This work was supported by **CAPES Foundation**, Ministry of Education of Brazil and by **FCT** – Foundation for Science and Technology within the Project Scope UID/CEC/00319/2015.

REFERENCES

Abecker, A., Bernardi, A., Hinkelmann, K., Kühn, O., & Sintek, M. (1998). Toward a technology for organizational memories. IEEE Intelligent Systems, 40–48. Retrieved from http://ieeexplore.ieee.org/xpls/abs_all.jsp?arnumber=683209

Abecker, A., Bernardi, A., Hinkelmann, K., Kühn, O., & Sintek, M. (2000). Context-Aware , Proactive Delivery of Task-Specific Information : The KnowMore Project. Information Systems Frontiers, 2(3/4), 253–276.

Ackerman, M. S. (1994a). Augmenting organizational memory: a field study of answer garden. In Proceedings of the ACM Conference on Computer-Supported Cooperative

Work, CSCW-94 (pp. 243–252). Retrieved from http://dl.acm.org/citation.cfm?id=290159.290160

Ackerman, M. S. (1994b). Definitional and contextual issues in organizational and group memories. In Proceedings of the 27th Hawaii International Conference on System Sciences, HICSS-94 (pp. 191–200). IEEE Comput. Soc. Press. doi:10.1109/HICSS.1994.323444

Alavi, M., & Leidner, D. (2001). Review: Knowledge management and knowledge management systems: Conceptual foundations and research issues. MIS Quarterly, 25(1), 107–136. Retrieved from http://www.jstor.org/stable/10.2307/3250961

Balasubramanian, P., Nochur, K., Henderson, J. C., & Kwan, M. M. (1999). Managing process knowledge for decision support. Decision Support Systems, 27(1-2), 145–162. doi:10.1016/S0167-9236(99)00041-X

Bardin, L. (2000). Análise de conteúdo. Lisboa: Edições 70.

Blue, J., Andoh-Baidoo, F. K., & Osatuyi, B. (2011). An Organizational Memory and Knowledge System (OMKS): Building Modern Decision Support Systems. International Journal of Data Engineering, IJDE, 2(2), 27–41. Retrieved from http://www.cscjournals.org/csc/manuscript/Journals/IJDE/volume2/Issue2/IJDE-47.pdf

Cegarra-navarro, J.-G., & Sánchez-Polo, M. T. (2011). Influence of the open-mindedness culture on organizational memory: an empirical investigation of Spanish SMEs. The International Journal of Human Resource Management, 22(1), 1–18. doi:10.1080/09585192.2011.538963

Cervo, A. L., Bervian, P. A., & Silva, R. da. (2007). Metodologia Científica (6th ed.). São Paulo: Prentice Hall.

Conklin, J., & Begeman, M. L. (1988). gIBIS: A Hypertext Tool for Exploratory Policy Discussion. ACM Transactions on Office Information Systems, 6(4), 303–331.

Davenport, T. H. (1998). "If only HP knew what HP knows..." Perspective on Business Innovation, 1(1), 20–25.

Dorasamy, M., Raman, M., & Kaliannan, M. (2013). Knowledge management systems in support of disasters management: A two decade review. Technological Forecasting & Social Change, 20. doi:http://dx.doi.org/10.1016/j.techfore.2012.12.008

Kawell JR., L., Beckhardt, S., Halvorsen, T., Raymond, O., & Greif, I. (1988). Replicated document management in a group communication system. In Proceedings of the 1988 ACM conference on Computer-supported cooperative work. Retrieved from http://dl.acm.org/citation.cfm?id=1024798

Kwan, M. M., & Balasubramanian, P. (2003). KnowledgeScope: managing knowledge in context. Decision Support Systems, 35(4), 467–486. doi:10.1016/S0167-9236(02)00126-4

Malone, T. W., Crowston, K., Lee, J., Pentland, B., Dellarocas, C., Wyner, G., … O'Donnell, E. (1999). Tools for Inventing Organizations: Toward a Handbook of Organizational Processes. Management Science, 45, 425–443. Retrieved from http://mansci.journal.informs.org/content/45/3/425.short

Moore, K. (1995). The Lotus notes storage system. In ACM SIGMOD Record (pp. 427–428). Retrieved from http://dl.acm.org/citation.cfm?id=223859

Morrison, J. (1997). Organizational Memory Information Systems: Characteristics and Development Strategies. In Proceedings of HICSS- 97 (pp. 300–309). IEEE Computer Society Press.

Nevo, D., Furneaux, B., & Wand, Y. (2008). Towards an evolution framework for knowledge management systems. Information Technology Management, 9(4), 233–249.

Palvia, P. C., Perkins, J. A., & Zeltmann, S. M. (1992). The PRISM System: A Key to Organizational Effectiveness at Federal Express Corporation. Management Information Systems Research Center, 16(3), 277–292. Retrieved from http://www.jstor.org/stable/249529

Perez, G., & Ramos, I. (2013). Understanding Organizational Memory from the Integrated Management Systems (ERP). Journal of Information Systems and Technology Management, 10(3), 541–560. doi:10.4301/S1807-17752013000300005

Stein, E. W., & Zwass, V. (1995). Actualizing Organizational Memory with Information Systems. Information Systems Research, 6(2), 85–117.

Walsh, J. P., & Ungson, G. R. (1991). Organizational memory. Academy of Management Review, 16(1), 57–91. Retrieved from http://www.jstor.org/stable/10.2307/258607

Weiser, M., & Morrison, J. (1998). Project Memory: Information Management for Project Teams. Journal of Management Information Systems, 14(4), 149–166. Retrieved from http://www.jstor.org/discover/10.2307/40398295?uid=38169&uid=3738880&uid=2&uid=3&uid=67&uid=38165&uid=62&sid=21101569347643

Yu, Y., Dong, X., Zuo, M., & Xu, W. (2012). Constitutive Roles Of External And Internal Information Systems For Effective Interorganizational Knowledge Transfer: A Dyadic Approach. In Pacific Asia Conference on Information Systems, PACIS'12 (pp. 1–12). Retrieved from http://aisel.aisnet.org/pacis2012/45/

13

THE INFLUENCE OF SHARED MENTAL MODELS BETWEEN THE CIO AND THE TOP MANAGEMENT TEAM ON THE STRATEGIC ALIGNMENT OF INFORMATION SYSTEMS: A COMPARISON BETWEEN BRAZILIAN AND US COMPANIES

Nicolau Reinhard
José Ricardo Bigueti
University of São Paulo, São Paulo, São Paulo, Brazil

ABSTRACT

The gap in the understanding between the chief information officer (CIO) and the management team (TMT) has been cited as a contributing factor to their often troubled relationship. The objective of this study is to examine the development of shared mental models (SMMs) between the CIO and TMT about the role of information systems in the organization. An SMM is conceptualized as a multidimensional construct spanning the dimensions of shared language and shared understanding. The study posits that knowledge exchange mechanisms and relational similarity between the CIO and TMT are key antecedents to the development of SMMs. SMMs between the CIO and TMT are expected to guide the strategic orientation of the organization and may influence strategic alignment and organizational outcomes. The model was tested via a field survey of CIO – TMT pairs using structural equation modeling. Results show that relational similarity and formal mechanisms of knowledge exchange (e.g., formal CIO membership in the TMT, CIO hierarchical level, and formal educational mechanisms by the CIO) are important to the development of SMMs. Contrary to expectations, informal social mechanisms of knowledge exchange and physical proximity were not significantly related to SMMs.

Keywords: IS alignment, CIO, shared mental models, knowledge exchange, Brazilian companies

Address for correspondence / Endereço para correspondência

Nicolau Reinhard, Nicolau Reinhard is a professor of management at the School of Economics, Administration and Accounting of the University of São Paulo, Brasil. His research interests and publications are related to Management of the IT function, the use of IT in Public Administration and Information Systems Implementation. Prof. Reinhard has a degree in Engineering, a PhD in Management, and, besides his academic career, has held executive and consulting positions in IT management in private and public organizations. School of Economics, Administration and Accounting University of São Paulo Av. Prof. Luciano Gualberto, 908 05508-010 São Paulo – Brasil

José Ricardo Bigueti, has a bachelor degree in Computer Science, an MBA in Information Technology Management and an MSc in Administration from the University of São Paulo. He is presently a Senior I/S Security Manager for The Dow Chemical Co., in Midland, Michigan, USA. School of Economics, Administration and Accounting, University of São Paulo Av. Prof. Luciano Gualberto, 908 05508-010 São Paulo – Brasil

1.   INTRODUCTION

Strategic IS alignment has been reported as one of the major preoccupations of the Chief Information Officer (CIO) (Reich; Benbasat, 2000; Chan, 2002; Leonard Seddon, 2012), IS alignment being defined as the congruence between the business strategy, managed by the Top Management Team (TMT), and the IS strategy in the organization (Henderson; Venkatraman, 1999; Sabherwal, 2001).

Despite their heavy investments in IS, many organizations have not been able to reap significant business results. In fact, IS investments will not improve business performance unless they are made according to an IS strategy that is aligned with the organization's business strategy. This alignment has proved to be a hard to achieve goal (Weill, 1990).

Understanding the organizational factors that contribute to this goal has been a research objective for a long time (Chan, 2002; Ball *et al*, 2003), with communication between the CIO and the TMT, organizational characteristics and an understanding of the IS competencies (Reich; Benbasat, 2000; Chan, 2002) among them.

This paper focuses on the shared language and shared understanding between the CIO and the TMT that, collectively, constitute the Shared Mental Model (SMM), on the strategic IS alignment and the factors leading to the development of this shared language and understanding. CIOs are expected to be key contributors in this process and, therefore, this paper will focus on the CIOs and on their the importance achieving the sharing of language and understanding with the TMT. (Preston; Karahana, 2009; Preston, 2004).

The research questions are

1 What is the relationship between the SMM and the strategic IS alignment?

2. What are the antecedents to a SMM of the CIO and the TMT?

3. Is there a difference between Brazilian and US companies in this respect?

As a by-product, the study also aims at validating in a different context (the IT function in Brazilian business), the research model and instruments developed by Preston 2004, including the questionnaire and constructs for SMM.

This paper also aims at verifying the applicability of SMM concepts and in management principles developed in different cultural and business contexts Brazilian companies.

2 LITERATURE REVIEW AND RESEARCH MODEL CONSTRUCTS

Our research is based on a basic conceptual model, developed by Preston 2004. The components of this conceptual model are depicted in Figure 1.

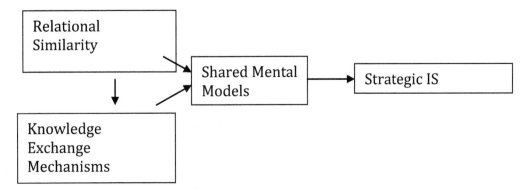

Figure 1 The basic conceptual model

Previous research has indicated Mechanisms for knowledge exchange and Relational similarity as antecedents to SMM. Knowledge exchange mechanisms comprise knowledge systems and mechanisms for educating the CIO and the TMT. This includes structure (for example, the CIO's position in the hierarchy and his/her participation in the TMT), physical systems (the CIO's office being located close to the TMT office) and social systems (such as, informal interaction between the CIO and the TMT), thus allowing the CIO to be proactive in facilitating the knowledge exchange by educating the TMT and therefore contributing to the development of a SMM. (PRESTON, 2004)

Relational similarity considers the demographic similarity and the similarity of past experiences of the CIO and the TMT. The Upper Echelon Theory is used to link these factors to the organization's strategies (for example, the IS alignment). (Hambrick; Mason, 1984). The principle of attraction by similarity provides a basis for linking relational similarity with knowledge exchange mechanisms, especially social knowledge systems. (Orpen, 1984; Byrne, 1971).

2.1 Strategic IS alignment

Strategic alignment is consistently ranked as a key issue for IS managers, due to its strategic benefits to the organization. This has led to a strong tradition in IS alignment research, with different developments in theory, addressing the changing issues faced by IS managers. (Leonard; Seddon, 2012)

For this research IS alignment is defined as the congruence between the business and IS strategy in the organization: the degree in which the mission, goals and plans for IT support and are supported by the mission, goals and plans for the business (Reich; Benbasat, 1996). Past research has indicated two benefits of this strategic alignment: IS effectiveness (Chan, 2002) and IS higher performance (Sabherwal; Chan, 2000; Sabherwal *et al*, 2001).

Strategic IS alignment, as opposed to structural IS alignment, focuses on the intellectual dimension (the content of the organization's plans) and social dimension (the actors in the organization, their values, communication and understanding of their domains). The intellectual dimension is a state or a result (with antecedents being the alignment, the communication among the actors, the business and IS plans), while the social dimension is the congruent understanding of the persons involved in the alignment (Reich; Benbasat, 2000).

Other antecedents for the strategic alignment of IS in the organization are: the Relationship between the CIO and the TMT (Rockart *et al*, 1996; Chan, 2002), shared knowledge and understanding between the CIO and the TMT (Armstrong; Sambamurthy, 1999; Reich; Benbasat, 2000), the organization's business strategy (Reich; Benbasat, 2000; Sabherwal), senior executives' planning process (Reich; Benbasat, 2000; Chan, 2000). Strategic IS alignment has also been shown to be linked to agility and firm performance (Tallon; Pinsonneault, 2011)

2.2 Mental Models and Shared Mental Models

There are multiple definitions of Mental Models (MM), such as set of beliefs, understandings, mental representations, cognitive constructs, cognitive systems, assumptions, habits and paradigms (Denzau; North, 1994), (Van den Bosch; Volberda, 1999), (Peterson et al, 2000).

The Shared Mental Model (SMM) has also multiple definitions in the literature. Examples are: values, myths, shared standard operational procedures and beliefs (KIM, 1993); an understanding of the organization or mental representation of the group's key elements, a frame of the structure, processes and tasks of a group, which its members have in common (Mohammed *et al*, 2000). In this paper, we will use Preston's (Preston 2004, p.18) definition: "Shared Mental Models are shared beliefs and understanding of the role of Information Systems in the organization, together with a common shared language that has its own vocabulary and nuances". This definition suggests two different dimensions in SMM: a shared language and a shared understanding.

According to Preston (2004), the strategic alignment of IS can be achieved through this multidimensional SMM between the CIO and the TMT. Previous research, although not using the same language, also supports this contention. (Madhavan; Grover, 1998) (Lederer; Mendelow, 1987)

The shared language dimension of SMM between the CIO and the TMT has clear implications for the CIO. His/her success will depend on how well this executive communicates with the other executives in the organization. Nelson and Cooprider (1996) argue that a shared language can create a positive social influence among the top managers; therefore the CIO should communicate using business terms comprehensible to the top manager, instead of a technical language full of acronyms (Feeney et al, 1992).

2.2.1 Shared understanding

SMM have been associated with shared understanding (Mohammed *et al*, 2000; Peterson *et al*, 2000), congruence of visions (Feeny *et al*, 1992; Kim, 1993). Other researchers have associated SMM with knowledge shared among individuals or groups: shared knowledge structures (Richards, 2001); shared social knowledge structures (Swaab *et al*, 2002); and shared previous knowledge (Madhavan; Groover, 1998).

Shared understanding is not the same as shared knowledge. In fact, shared understanding is facilitated by the mechanisms of knowledge exchange. Shared understanding can be obtained when the CIO and the TMT have respectively high levels of business knowledge and IS knowledge and exchange this knowledge (Armstrong; Sambamurthy, 1999). These exchange mechanisms will allow the CIO and the TMT understand how IS can be best used to improve the organization's performance.

Studies that have focused on the SMM antecedents have identified communication and feedback (Rasker; Post, 2000) and negotiation (Swaab, 2002) as key elements for the development of SMM among the parties. Preston (Preston, 2004) extends this list to include the following antecedents of SMM:knowledge exchange mechanisms and relational similarity.

There is evidence that the CIO and the TMT often do not have a shared language and understanding of the role of IS, due to a limited IS strategy of the TMT and a limited business knowledge of the CIO (Armstrong; Sambamurthy, 1999). Knowledge exchange mechanisms are therefore an important antecedent for the alignment of the IS strategy.

The literature presents two primary mechanisms for knowledge exchange that contribute to the development of a SMM between the CIO and the TMT: knowledge systems and the CIO's education mechanisms.

2.2.2 Knowledge systems

Organizations provide their members with multiple ways to interact and exchange knowledge. According to Nahapiet and Ghoshal (1998) organizational competencies to generate and share knowledge derive from factors, such as special means to create and transfer tacit knowledge; the organizational principles according to which individual and functional abilities are structured, coordinated and communicated and used by individuals to cooperate; the nature of organizations as social communities. For individuals to transfer knowledge, they have to have the ability to interact with one another. Systems in the organization that provide this ability are called knowledge systems.

According to Armstrong and Sambamurthy (1999) formal and informal interactions between top management allows stronger knowledge integration. Knowledge systems reflect the possibilities of CIO and TMT to access richer channels, develop more effective social relations and communication patterns (Armstrong; Sambamurthy, 1999)

Three dimensions can be identified in a knowledge system:

1 structural knowledge systems, comprising the formal interactions permitted by the established organizational structure,

2 physical knowledge systems, related to the interactions allowed by the proximity of the CIO and TMT's offices and

3 Social knowledge systems, related to the informal interactions among CIO and TMT.

Structural Knowledge Systems

Structural knowledge systems allow the CIO to interact with the TMT. In addition to the formal communication channels, these systems include the CIO's hierarchical level (Feeny et al, 1992; Watson, 1990) and his/her participation in the TMT itself (Watson, 1990).

The higher the CIO's hierarchical position, the higher his/her opportunity to understand the corporation and its strategy (Lederer; Mendelow, 1987), impact organizational decisions (Schrage, 1996), exercise power (Karimi; Gupta 1996; Rockart et al, 1996; Smaltz, 1999) and ultimately corporate effectiveness (Armstrong, 1995).

Participation in the TMT has been shown to be vital for the CIO's effectiveness (Rockart *et al*, 1996, Smaltz, 1999), allowing an effective information exchange information with the TMT. In fact, if the TMT does not fully accept the CIO and allow his/her participation, this will minimize his/her influence in the organization (Smaltz, 1999).

Physical Knowledge Systems

Organizational proximity is defined as persons occupying the same space, with the opportunity and psychological obligation to face-to-face communication (Monge *et al*, 1985). With an office located close to the TMT's, the CIO will increase his/her opportunity to engage in this face-to-face communication, allowing a more effective communication of complex messages and reaching a common perspective on ambiguous issues (Daft *et al*, 1987; Watson, 1990).

Social Knowledge Systems

Social knowledge systems focus on informal interactions contribute to communication and knowledge sharing (Alavi; Leidner, 2001), increase exchange of ideas and common understanding (Watson, 1990; Armstrong, 1995; Chan, 2002).

2.2.3 CIO education mechanisms

The literature indentifies the advantages of the CIO being allowed to formally educate the TMT about the IS competencies, in order to facilitate the common understanding between the CIO and the TMT. (Smaltz, 1999; Enns *et al*, 2003). Preston (2004) also indicates the importance of knowledge exchange facilitated by the CIO in educational activities.

As mentioned before, poor IS alignment is also caused due to the lack of the TMT's understanding of IS strategic competencies. The CIO's educational function can help bridging this gap. This knowledge exchange is not necessarily captured by the organization's knowledge system. The CIO can use every opportunity for interaction with the TMT, but also formal events to educate the TMT about IS competencies. According to Preston (2004) these mechanisms contribute to the development of sharing Mental Models between the CIO and the TMT.

2.2.4 Relational Similarity

Relational Similarity is defined as similarity between the CIO and the TMT in basic characteristics, such as demographic (age and gender), past experiences (knowledge of the organization, time in executive position in the organization, functional origin, educational level and personal interests)

Upper Echelon Theory provides support for relating the basic characteristics of the TMT and the strategic IS alignment and between SMM and IS strategic alignment. This theory states that organizational results can be predicted from the basic characteristics of top level executives (not just the CEO, but of the dominating coalition), such as gender, age, past experiences, education, etc and that these results reflect their values and perceptions (Hambrick; Mason, 1984). These results include performance and strategic decisions.

Hambrick and Mason (1984) have argued that basic characteristics reflect one's person cognitive map and therefore impact their capacity to interpret data and transform them into knowledge. Thus making strategic business and IS decisions should be influenced by the managers' basic characteristics: demographic and those related to past experiences.

Preston (2004), based on the Upper Echelon Theory, proposes SMM as a mediating variable to capture the cognitive map of the dominating coalition that can then be used to mediate the relationship of past experiences and demographic characteristics of the CIO and TMT and the organization's strategic choices, leading to the IS alignment.

Demographic Similarity

Demographic Similarity refers to comparable demographic characteristics of members of couples or groups that are in a position of involvement in regular interaction. The conceptual basis for relational demography is the paradigm of attraction by similiarity, which suggests that individuals tend to be attracted to those that are more similar to them.

Interpersonal attraction is based on the similarity of individuals on various dimensions, such as attitudes, age, gender, time in the organization, educational level, area of graduation, market experience, time in the team or company, functional or professional specialty (Allinson *et al*, 2001; Van der Vegt, 2002).

3. THE RESEARCH MODEL

The reference model and research method used in this research are based on Preston (2004), with adaptations to the Brazilian situation made by Bigueti in his MS dissertation (Bigueti, 2007). In this survey the term CIO is used in a rather loose form, referring to persons with different titles, as long as they are the principal or most influential IS/IT executives in the organization. (Grover *et al*, 1993; Armstrong, 1995).

TMT is defined as the CEO and the most senior and influential executives in the organization, reporting directly to the CEO. (Finkelstein; Hambrick, 1996).

Based on the previously discussed importance of the relationship between the CIO and the TMT, our research focuses on the couple CIO – TMT in the organization, positing the relationships depicted in Figure 2.

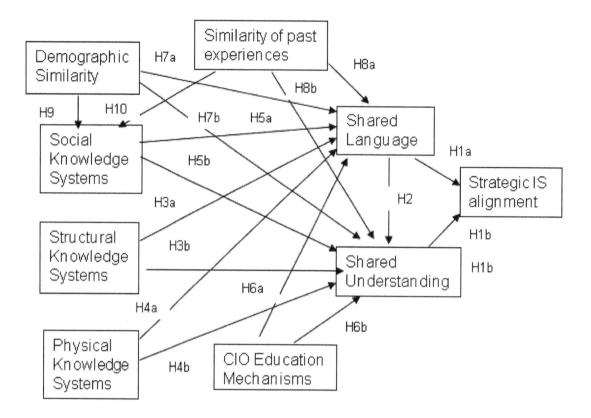

Figure 2 – Research model – constructs and hypothesized influence relationships

3.1 Research hypotheses and Operationalization of Constructs

There are two groups of hypotheses:

1. Related to the strategic IS alignment in the organization and

2. Related to the SMM between the CIO and the TMT.

3.1.1 SMM and Strategic IS Alignment

The literature provides evidence of the relationship between IS alignment and communication and common understanding between the CIO and the TMT. SMM should then contribute to provide a congruence of visions related to key IS issues and improve the alignment of business and IS decisions, providing the rationale for the following research hypotheses:

H1: high levels of SMM between the CIO and the TMT contribute to the alignment between IS and business strategies in the organization

H1a: high levels of shared language between the CIO and the TMT contribute to the alignment between IS and business strategies in the organization

H1b: high levels of shared understanding between the CIO and the TMT contribute to the alignment between IS and business strategies in the organization

3.1.2 Shared Language and Shared Understanding

Nahapiet and Ghoshal (1998) and Boynton *et al* (1992, p.32) have shown that the creation of a shared understanding is unlikely in the absence of a common shared language [between the CIO and the TMT], therefore justifying the hypothesis:

H2: a shared language between the CIO and the TMT contributes to a shared understanding between the CIO and the TMT on the role of IS in the organization

3.1.3 Shared Mental Model antecedents

Our research model considers three primary antecedents that contribute to the development of a SMM between the CIO and the TMT: knowledge systems (structural, physical and social), CIO education systems and relational similarity. All three are seen as influencing directly the SMM, while the relational similarity is also supposed to influence the organization's social knowledge system.

3.1.4 Knowledge Systems and SMM

Knowledge exchange, which is considered critical for the development of a SMM between the CIO and the TMT, can be achieved through structural knowledge systems, physical knowledge systems, social knowledge systems, according to authors (Armstrong; Sambmurthy, 1999). Two aspects of the structural knowledge systems are considered in the model, which, according to Feeny et AL (1992), are essential for the CIO's performance: direct reporting to the CIO and participation in the TMT. There is research indicating that these situations contribute to the development of SMM between the CIO and the TMT (Watson, 1990; Smaltz, 1999).

H3a: Structural knowledge systems contribute to the development of a shared language between the CIO and the TMT

H3b: Structural knowledge systems contribute to the development of shared understanding between the CIO and the TMT.

3.1.5 Physical Knowledge Systems and SMM

Physical proximity of the CIO and the TMT's offices influences communication and knowledge exchange, allowing the CIO a better perception of organizational objectives, of commonalities with the TMT and a more effective engagement in the management process. Therefore:

H4a: Physical knowledge systems contribute to the development a shared language between the CIO and the TMT.

H4b: Physical knowledge systems contribute to the development of a shared understanding between the CIO and the TMT on the role of IS in the organization.

3.1.6 Social Knowledge Systems and SMM

Frequent informal networking helps developing SMM among individuals, by developing shared language and understanding (Denzau; North, 1994). Successful CIOs value informal communication and socialize with the TMT, becoming able to evaluate their motivations, meanings and priorities and testing their business vision (Earl; Feeny, 1994). Therefore:

H5a: Social knowledge systems contribute to the development of a shared language between the CIO and the TMT.

H5b: Social knowledge systems contribute to the development of a shared understanding between the CIO and the TMT on the role of IS in the organization.

3.1.7 CIO education mechanisms and SMM

CIOs should use their specialized IS knowledge to continually educate the TMT on IS competencies and help them interpreting new external ideas, experiences and success stories and manage expectations and thus maintaining their SMMs. (Lederer; Mendelow, 1987). Therefore:

H6a: The CIO's educational mechanisms contribute to the development of a shared language between the CIO and the TMT.

H6b: The CIO's educational mechanisms contribute to the development of a shared understanding between the CIO and the TMT on the role of IS in the organization.

3.1.8 Relational Similarity and SMM

Individuals with a similarity of demographic characteristics and past experiences tend to develop common language, attitudes, perceptions, understanding, values and beliefs and a convergent mental model (Denzau; North, 1994; Hodgkinson; JOHNSON, 1994). Therefore:

H7a: Demographic similarity contributes to the development of a shared language between the CIO and the TMT.

H7b: Demographic similarity contributes to the development of a shared understanding between the CIO and the TMT on the role of IS in the organization.

H8a: similarity of past experiences contributes to the development of a shared language between the CIO and the TMT.

H8b: similarity of past experiences contributes to the development of a shared understanding between the CIO and the TMT on the role of IS in the organization.

3.1.9 Relational Similarity and Social Knowledge Systems

Relational similarity should also contribute to the informal interaction among individuals.

Relational similarity of the CIO and the TMT should benefit their interaction, since individuals with similar demographics and past experiences tend to communicate, act favorably and value their association more than dissimilar groups. Therefore:

H9: Demographic similarity between the CIO and the TMT contributes to the development of social knowledge systems (i.e. the increase of informal interaction between the CIO and the TMT)

H10: similarity of past experiences between the CIO and the TMT contributes to the development of social knowledge systems (i.e. the increase of informal interaction between the CIO and the TMT)

3.2 Operationalization of the constructs

The operationalization of the constructs and survey questionnaire was adapted from Preston (2004) with the translation of the survey questions. The questionnaire was validated by a sample of local CIOs and TMT in order to assure the adequate understanding of the questions.

4 RESEARCH METHODOLOGY

This survey is based on a convenience sample of large Brazilian companies, using a structured questionnaire to be answered by pairs of CIOs and TMT members of the same company.

4.1 Operationalization and measurement of the variables

Demographic Similarity and Similarity of Past Experiences: This construct includes the questions about age, gender, education background, time in the organization and the present position and experience in other functions. These dimensions, measured for the CIO and the TMT, are the input to a similarity measure, obtained from an adapted Euclidian distance function between the CIO and the TMT (Wagner *et al*, 1984; Young; Buchholtz, 2002). The operationalization of the variables, presented in Figure 2, follows the Preston 2004 study, in order to allow the comparison of results of the US and Brazilian cases.

4.2 Target Population and Survey Sample

Since the research focuses on the development of SMM between the CIO and the TMT, only organizations that have an IS manager in executive position are considered in the sample.

The requirement that the survey be responded by pairs of CIOs and CEOs (or TMT members), required special motivation of otherwise overloaded individuals, for which the influence provided by national industry and professional associations, as well as the researcher's networks was instrumental in obtaining the survey sample and the needed follow-up mechanisms.

The questionnaire was first distributed over the Internet (by e-mail addressed to potential respondents with a link to the questionnaire web page), thus also ensuring the respondents' anonymity, with the already mentioned follow-up, resulting in respondents from multiple segments: private companies of varied sizes, in the industry and service segments, with national and multinational capital.

4.3 Data collection

The survey consisted of two questionnaires, one for the CIO and the other for the TMT member. For a questionnaire to be considered valid it had to be responded in pairs for each company.

Several organizations provided contacts and encouraged their member to answer: GUI, a group of 16 CIOs of large companies, GETI, another association of IT executives of various industries, ABIQUIM, the Brazilian Association of Chemical Industries, AMCHAM, the American-Brazilian Chamber of Commerce, USP-MBA alumni, the association of MBA alumni of the University of São Paulo. The data were collected between January and April 2007.

The e-mail referring to the questionnaires, with letters of recommendation from the Associations Leadership, was sent initially to the companies' CIOs, asking them to provide a respondent from their TMT.

5 RESULTS ANALYSIS

5.1 Descriptive statistics

Response rates for surveys requiring CIO CEO paired responses are usually low, with reported 7 to 20% response rates. In our research 180 companies were contacted, resulting in 62 reponses , with 35 usable response pairs, a 32.2% valid response rate.

The breakdown of responses by control variable is presented in Table 5

One of our basic goals was to identify differences of SMM development and IS alignment between Brazilian companies and multinational companies (the other being the comparison with the US-based Preston 2004 study).

However, an ANOVA variance analysis on the national/multinational variable and also the service/industry classification showed no significant difference among the groups. Therefore the hypotheses were tested for the responses as a single group.

The data collection process led to a sample that contains large companies only, with a breakdown by segment and capital origin presented in Table 1

Segment	National	Multinational
Services	4	6
Industry		
Chemical-Petrochemical	3	10
Cosmetics	2	1
Food	1	0
Mechanical	1	3
Consumer goods/electronics	1	3
Total	12	23

Table 1: Distribution of responses by industry and capital ownership

5.2 Factor Analysis and Hypotheses testing

Construct validation: The structuring of the constructs from the basic variables (questionnaire items) was validated through a confirmatory Factor Analysis, demonstrating the validity of all constructs in terms of factor loads, internal consistency and discriminant validity.

5.2.1 Hypotheses Testing

In order to maintain the compatibility with the Preston 2004 study, the test of hypotheses will be made using PLS Partial Least Squares, a technique sufficiently robust for small samples.

Table 2 presents the results of the Hypotheses test and the comparison with the results of the Preston 2004 study, highlighting the differences in findings.

Hypotheses	Brazil	PRESTON
H1a: Shared language → Strategic IS alignment	NS	NS
H1b: Shared understanding → Strategic IS alignment	S (*)	S (**)
H2: Shared language → Shared understanding	S (*)	S (**)
H3a: Structural knowledge system → Shared language	NS	NS
H3b: Structural knowledge system → Shared understanding	S (*)	S (**)
H4a: Physical knowledge system → Shared language	NS	S (**)
H4b: Physical knowledge system → Shared understanding	NS	NS
H5a: Social knowledge system → Shared language	NS	NS
H5b: Social knowledge system → Shared understanding	NS	NS
H6a: CIO education mechanisms → Shared language	NS	NS
H6b: CIO education mechanisms → Shared understanding	S (*)	S (**)
H7a: Demographic similarity → Shared language	NS	NSt
H7b: Demographic similarity → Shared understanding	NS	NS
H8a: Past experiences similarity → Shared language	NS	S (**)
H8b: Past experiences similarity → Shared understanding	NS	NS
H9: Demographic similarity → Social knowledge system	S (*)	S (**)
H10: Past experiences similarity → Social knowledge system	S (*)	S (**)
S (*) Supported at 5% significance level, N=35		
S (**)Supported at 5% significance level, N=125		
NS: not significant		

Table 2: Comparison of results of the Brazilian and US studies (Preston 2004)

Figure 3 illustrates the research model with the hypotheses supported by the analysis

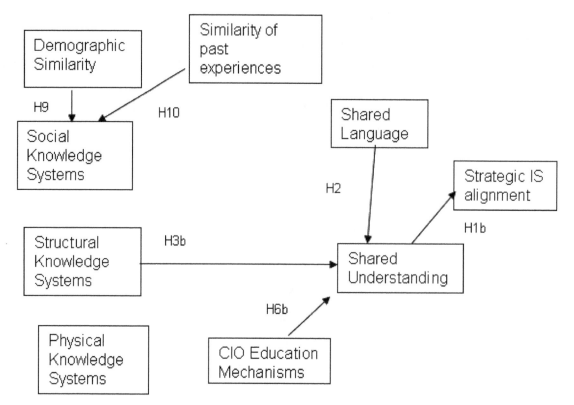

Figure 3: Constructs and significant relationships

Table 3 presents the variance of the dependent variables explained by the model.

Dependent Variable	Explained Variance %	Antecedents and significant paths
IS strategic alignment de SI	35,8%	Shared Understanding (*)
Shared Understanding	64,3%	Shared Language (*) Structural Knowledge Systems (*) CIO Education Mechanisms (*)
Social Knowledge Systems	22,1%	Demographic Similarity (*) Similarity of Past Experiences (*)
(*) significant at 5% level		

Table 3: Dependent Variables' variance explained by the model

5.2.2 Comparison between the Brazilian and the US (Preston 2004) study results

Table 2 demonstrates the consistency of the results of both studies. The absence of a significant influence of the social dimension (and even the demographic and past experiences in the Brazilian study) on the development of SMM and IS alignment can be interpreted as the result of a high degree of formality of the CIO function and its relation to the TMT.

Organizational proximity and similarity of past experiences, identified in the Preston 2004 study (Preston 2004) as influencing the development of a shared language between the CIO and the TMT, were not confirmed in our study, a result that can also be interpreted as a sign of the weakening of the strategic role of IS and the CIO. These results run against the general belief of the importance of informal relations in the Brazilian national and managerial culture and deserve further research.

6 CONCLUSIONS

The first result of the study was a new statistical validation of the constructs proposed by Preston 2004 using the Brazilian sample. The relationships among the constructs that resulted from the analysis are almost identical with the Preston 2004 findings, confirming the robustness of the model.

Strategic IS alignment is, according to our study, influenced by shared understanding, with the latter being influenced by the structural knowledge system and the CIO education mechanisms. In addition, shared understanding is also influenced by the shared language construct.

These findings show that mainly formal aspects determine the CIO/TMT relationship. The social dimensions of the relationship that have been evidenced in other authors' previous research did not show up as significant in our study. In this respect our results differs from the Preston 2004 study which had found also a significant influence of similarity of past experiences and physical knowledge system (organizational proximity) on the shared language construct, and therefore indirectly on the strategic IS alignment.

The answers to the proposed research questions

1. What is the relationship between the SMM and the strategic IS alignment?

The study validated an influence path: structural knowledge system on shared language on the shared understanding between the CIO and the TMT on the strategic IS alignment, with an additional influence of CIO education mechanisms on shared understanding. This path explained 35.8% of the variance of the strategic IS alignment construct.

Demographic characteristics and shared past experiences were also shown to influence the social knowledge system, but without significant influence on the shared mental model constructs and strategic IS alignment.

2. What are the antecedents to a SMM of the CIO and the TMT?

This study analyzed the influence of two primary antecedents on shared mental models: mechanisms of knowledge exchange and relational similarity. The results support only the influence of structural knowledge systems and CIO education mechanisms as antecedents to Shared Mental Models. These constructs explain a significant 64.3% of the variance of the shared understanding construct.

As for relational similarity, the constructs were shown to influence only the social knowledge system and explaining only a small percentage of its variation (22.1%).

3. Is there a difference between Brazilian and US companies in this respect?

Our study provided additional support to the Preston 2004 model, by validating again the questionnaire and constructs and high consistency with the results of that research, providing additional evidence to the robustness of the model.

Further research would be required for the analysis of the model in other segments, like public administration, smaller companies, also taking into account the continuously changing of the IT organization and its management.

REFERENCES

Alavi, M; Leidner, D. (2001) *Review: Knowledge management and knowledge management systems: Conceptual foundations and research issues.* MIS Quarterly v.25(1):107-133

Allinson, C *et al.* (2001) *The effects of cognitive style on leader-member exchange: A study of manager-subordinate dyads.* Journal of Occupational & Organizational Psychology v.74 (2):201-221.

Armstrong, C. (1995) *Creating business value through information technology: The effects of the chief information office and top management team characteristics.* College of Business. Tallahassee, Florida, Florida State University.

Armstrong, C. Sambamurthy, V. (1999) *Information Technology assimilation in firms: The influence of senior leadership and IT infrastructures.* Information Systems Research v.10(4):304-328.

Boynton, Andrew *et al.* (1992) *Whose responsibility is IT management.* Sloan Management Review v.33(4):32-39.

Byrne, D. (1971) *The attraction paradigm.* New York, Academic Press.

Chan, Y. (2002) *Why Haven't We Mastered Alignment? The Importance of the Informal Organization Structure.* MIS Quarterly Executive v.1(2):97-112.

Daft, R (1987) *et al. Message equivocality, media selection and manager performance.* MIS Quarterly v.11(3):355-366.

Denzau, A; North, D. (1994) *Shared mental models: Ideologies and institutions.* Kyklos v.47(1):3-32.

Earl, M; Feeny, D. (1994) *Is your CIO adding value?* Sloan Management Review v.35(3):11-21.

Enns, H *et al.* (2003) *CIO lateral influence behaviors: Gaining peer's commitment to strategic information systems.* MIS Quarterly v.27(1):155-176.

Feeny, D *et al.* (1992) *Understanding the CEO/CIO relationship.* MIS Quarterly v.16(4):435-449.

Finkelstein, S; Hambrick, D. (1996) *Strategic Leadership: Top Executives and Their Effects on Organizations.* Minneapolis, MN, West Publishing Company.

Finneran, M. (2003) *The end of hubris: IT doesn't matter.* Business Communications Review v.33(7):2-3.

Grover, V *et al.* (1993) *The chief information officer: A study of managerial roles.* Journal of Management Information Systems v.10(2):107-131.

Hambrick, D. (1994) *Top management groups: A conceptual integration and reconsideration of the team label.* Research in Organizational Behavior v.16:171-215.

Hambrick, D; Mason, P. (1984) *Upper echelons: The organization as a reflection of its top managers.* Academy of Management Review v.9(1):193-206.

Henderson, J; Venkatraman, N. (1999) *Strategic alignment: leveraging information technology for transforming organizations.* IBM Systems Journal v.38(2/3):472-485.

Hodgkinson, G; Johnson, G. (1994) *Exploring the mental models of competitive strategists: The case for a processual approach.* Journal of Management Studies v.31(4):525-552.

Karimi, J; Gupta, Y. (1996) *The congruence between a firm's competitive strategy and information technology leader's rank and role.* Journal of Management Information Systems 13(1):63-89.

Kim, D. (1993) *The link between individual and organizational learning.* Sloan Management Review v.35(1):37-51.

Lederer, A; Burky, L. (1988) *Understanding top management's objectives: A management information systems concern.* Journal of Information Systems v.3(1):50-67.

Lederer, Albert; Mendelow, Aubrey.(1987) *Information resource planning: Overcoming difficulties in identifying top management's objectives.* MIS Quarterly v.11(3):388-400,

Leonard, J; Seddon, P. (2012) *A Meta-model of Alignment*, Communications of the Association for Information Systems: v 31, Article 11.

Madhavan, R; Grover, R. (1998) *From embedded knowledge to embodied knowledge: New product development as knowledge management.* Journal of Marketing v.62(4):1-13.

Mohammed, S *et al.* (2000) *The measurement of team mental models: We have no shared schema.* Organizational Research Methods v.3(2):123-166

Monge, P *et al.* (1985) *The dynamics of organizational proximity.* Management Science v.31(9):1129-1142.

Nahapiet, J; Ghoshal, S. (1998) *Social capital, intellectual capital, and the organizational advantage.* Academy of Management Review v.23(2):242-266

Nelson, K; Cooprider, J. (1996) *The contribution of shared knowledge to is group performance.* MIS Quarterly v.20(4):409-433.

Orpen, C. (1984) *Attitude similarity, attraction, and decision-making in the employment interview.* Journal of Psychology v.117(1):111-121.

Peterson, E *et al.* (2000) *Collective efficacy and aspects of shared mental models as predictors of performance over time in work groups.* Group Processes & Intergroup Relations v.3(3):296-317.

Preston, D. (2004) *Shared Mental Models between the Chief Information Officer and Top Management Team: Towards Information Systems Strategic Alignment*, Unpublished PhD Thesis, The University of Georgia, Athens.

Preston, D; Karahana, E. (2009)*How to Develop a Shared Vision: The Key to IS Strategic Alignment.* MIS Quarterly Executive 8(1)

Rasker, P.; Post, W. (2000) *Effects of two types of intra-team feedback on developing a shared mental model in command and control teams.* Ergonomics v.43(8):1167-1190.

Reich, B; Benbasat, I. (1996) *Measuring the linkage between business and information technology objectives.* MIS Quarterly v.20(1):55-62.

Reich, B; Benbasat, I. (2000) *Factors that influence the social dimensions of alignment between business and information technology objectives.* MIS Quarterly v.24(1):81-114.

Richards, D. (2001) *Coordination and shared mental models.* American Journal of Political Science v.45(2):259-267.

Rockart, J *et al.* (1996) *Eight imperatives for the new IT organization.* Sloan Management Review v.38(1):43-56.

Sabherwal, R; Chan, Y. (2001) *Alignment between business and IS strategies: A study of prospectors, analyzers, and defenders.* Information Systems Research v.12(1):11-34.

Sabherwal, R *et al.* (2001) *The Dynamics of Alignment: Insights from a Punctuated Equilibrium Model.* Organization Science v.12(1):179-197.

Schrage, M. (1996) *Organizational charts really do matter.* Computerworld v.30:33-34.

Smaltz, D. (1999) *Antecedents of CIO effectiveness: A role-based perspective.* College of Business. Tallahassee, Florida, Florida State University.

Stephens, C *et al.* (1992) *Executive or functional manager? The nature of the CIO's job.* MIS Quarterly v.16(4):449-468.

Swaab, R *et al.* (2002) *Multiparty negotiation support: The role of visualization's influence on the development of shared mental models.* Journal of Management Information Systems v.19(1):129-150.

Tallon, P; Pinsonneault, A, (2011) *Competing Perspectives on the Link between Strategic Information Technology and Organizational Agility; Insight from a Mediation Model*, MIS Quarterly, v35(2): 463-486

Van den Bosch, F; Volberda, H. (1999) *Coevolution of firm absorptive capacity and knowledge environment: Organizational forms and combinative capabilities.* Organization Science v.10(5):551-569.

Van der Vegt, G. (2002) *Effects of attitude dissimilarity and time on social integration: A longitudinal panel study.* Journal of Occupational & Organizational Psychology v.75(4):439-453.

Wagner, W. G *et al.* (1984) *Organizational demography and turnover in top management groups.* Administrative Science Quarterly v.29:74-92.

Watson, R. (1990) *Influences on the IS manager's perceptions of key issues:Information scanning and the relationship with the CEO.* MIS Quarterly v.14(2):217-232

Weill, P. (1990) *Strategic investment in information technology: An empirical study.* Information Age v.12(3):141-148.

Young, M; Buchholtz, A. (2002) *Firm performance and CEO pay: Relational demography as a moderator.* Journal of Managerial Issues v.14(3):296-314.

Permissions

List of Contributors

Ademir Antonio Ferreira
University of São Paulo, São Paulo, SP, Brazil

Márcio Shoiti Kuniyoshi
University of São Paulo, São Paulo, SP, Brazil

Adriano Weber Scheeren
Getulio Vargas Foundation, Rio de Janeiro/RJ, Brazil

Joaquim Rubens Fontes-Filho
Getulio Vargas Foundation, Rio de Janeiro/RJ, Brazil

Elaine Tavares
Coppead, Federal University of Rio de Janeiro, Rio de Janeiro/RJ, Brazil

Jose Marcelo Almeida Prado Cestari
Pontifical Catholic University of Parana, Curitiba, Parana, Brazil

Arthur Maria do Valle
Pontifical Catholic University of Parana, Curitiba, Parana, Brazil

Edson Pinheiro de Lima
Pontifical Catholic University of Parana, Curitiba, Parana, Brazil

Eduardo Alves Portela Santos
Pontifical Catholic University of Parana, Curitiba, Parana, Brazil

Jayr Figueiredo de Oliveira
Getúlio Vargas Foundation, São Paulo, São Paulo, Brazil

Marcelo Eloy Fernandes
Nove de Julho University, São Paulo, São Paulo, Brazil

Carlos Roberto Camello Lima
Methodist University of Piracicaba, Santa Bárbara d'Oeste, São Paulo, Brazil

Gelson Heindrickson
Tribunal de Contas da União, Brasilia, DF, Brazil

Carlos D. Santos Jr.
University of Brasilia, Brasilia, DF, Brazil

Ernesto Galvis-Lista
Universidad del Magdalena, Santa Marta, Colombia

Jenny Marcela Sánchez-Torres
Universidad Nacional de Colombia, Bogotá, Colombia

Lúcio Melre da Silva
Catholic University of Brasilia, Brasília, Distrito Federal, Brazil

João Souza Neto
Catholic University of Brasilia, Brasília, Distrito Federal, Brazil

José Rogério Poggio Moreira
Universidade Salvador (UNIFACS) – Salvador, Bahia, Brazil

Paulo Caetano da Silva
Universidade Salvador (UNIFACS) - Salvador, Bahia, Brazil

Angel Cobo
University of Cantabria, Santander, Spain

Adolfo Alberto Vanti
Universidade do Vale do Rio dos Sinos, Brasil

Rocío Rocha
University of Cantabria, Santander, Spain

William Allassani
University of Professional Studies, Legon-Accra, Ghana

Patricia Pérez Lorences
Central University "Marta Abreu" from Las Villas, Santa Clara, Cuba

Lourdes Francisca García Ávila
Central University "Marta Abreu" from Las Villas, Santa Clara, Cuba

Victor Freitas de Azeredo Barros Centre ALGORITMI
University of Minho, Guimarães, Portugal

Isabel Ramos
Centre ALGORITMI, University of Minho, Guimarães, Portugal

Gilberto Perez
Universidade Presbiteriana Mackenzie, São Paulo/SP, Brazil

Nicolau Reinhard
University of São Paulo, São Paulo, São Paulo, Brazil

José Ricardo Bigueti
University of São Paulo, São Paulo, São Paulo, Brazil

Printed in the USA
CPSIA information can be obtained
at www.ICGtesting.com
JSHW051430221024
72173JS00006B/1420